W. Todd (William Todd) Martin

The Evolution Hypothesis

A Criticism of the new cosmic Philosophy

W. Todd (William Todd) Martin

The Evolution Hypothesis
A Criticism of the new cosmic Philosophy

ISBN/EAN: 9783337071424

Printed in Europe, USA, Canada, Australia, Japan

Cover: Foto ©ninafisch / pixelio.de

More available books at **www.hansebooks.com**

THE

EVOLUTION HYPOTHESIS:

A CRITICISM

OF THE

NEW COSMIC PHILOSOPHY.

BY

W. TODD MARTIN, M.A., D.Lɪᴛ.,

MINISTER OF THE PRESBYTERIAN CHURCH IN IRELAND.

EDINBURGH:
JAMES GEMMELL, GEORGE IV. BRIDGE.
1887.

TABLE OF CONTENTS.

CHAPTER I.

INTRODUCTORY.

CHAPTER II.

THE COMPLETE UNIFICATION OF KNOWLEDGE IMPOSSIBLE.

CHAPTER VIII.

THE PERSISTENCE OF FORCE.

CHAPTER IX.

POSTULATES OF EVOLUTION.

CHAPTER X.

THE FORMULA OF EVOLUTION.

CHAPTER XIII.

THE PHYSIOLOGICAL UNIT.

CHAPTER XIV.

THE ORIGIN OF SENTIENT LIFE.

CHAPTER XV.

THE ORIGIN OF ORGANIC FORMS.

Vast multiformity in organized matter—Evolution bound to show that all forms *must* have sprung from one primordial mode of living matter, and to show how—Only on these conditions can a philosophy of evolution be established— Facts divided into two classes, organisms as at present known and those found in the geological record—No direct evidence of transition from lower to higher species— Gradual advancement from lower to higher forms throughout the geological periods inevitable—Science looks in

CHAPTER XVII.

THE EVOLUTION OF MORALS.

Life directed towards an end voluntarily chosen—Moral life everything to man—Aim of Mr. Spencer's philosophy to find scientific basis for right and wrong in conduct— His ethics must be outcome of his system—Apologists do not disparage moral lessons drawn from nature—Revealed moral teaching could not be accepted as true if antagonistic to the first principles of morals—Religion has been the most important source of moral impulse— 1. Moral law can only be obeyed in conscious freedom— Moral obedience willing obedience—Evolution determines action by physical law—The Calvinist contends for liberty —He rejects an imaginary liberty—Evolution ethics sheer dynamic determinism—2. The evolutionist account of sense of obligation—Race-needs enforce the sacrifice of present to future pleasures—Moral self-restraint, how originated—Two elements in the "notion of obligation" —(a) surrender of present pleasure for sake of future

CHAPTER XVIII.

CREATION.

Contents.

CHAPTER XIX.

SUMMARY AND CONCLUSION.

The Evolution Hypothesis looks outward to find one dominant principle—All mental and moral phenomena regarded as modes of experience determined by physical

THE EVOLUTION HYPOTHESIS.

CHAPTER I.

INTRODUCTORY.

THE Evolution Hypothesis has stamped its impress on the thought of our time. It claims to dominate the whole field of experience, and to direct all inquiry. As a theory of universal truth, it lies open to the criticism of every student of philosophy. How far in certain groups of physical phenomena it expresses justly the law of change, I do not discuss. Examination in detail, over the whole extent of the knowable, can be effectively conducted only by division of labour among many workers, each handling some part of the question, which he has made the subject of special study. In this way the measure of truth contained in the hypothesis must ultimately be defined. My purpose is to deal with the theory as it undertakes to formulate the entire cosmic movement within the knowable—as it aims at the unification of all knowledge.

The following criticism takes the form of an ex-

A

amination of the system elaborated by Mr. Herbert Spencer. Choosing the ablest expositor of the hypo-thesis, and testing it as shaped by him, the critic escapes the necessity of settling amid minor varieties of opinion the exact statement of the point in debate. We may be confident that we shall find all that is essential to evolutionism, * carefully reasoned out in Mr. Spencer's works. The theory, as he states it, may be discussed with the assurance that we are not beating the air. If the doctrine fail in the hands of the master, it will not triumph in the hands of his disciples.

Mr. Spencer's System of Philosophy is a life-work, remarkable as well for the high order of intellectual power displayed in it, as for the vast and varied stores of exact knowledge by which it is enriched. The whole is worked out with rare analytical and constructive skill. The apt instances and illustrations, gathered from the entire range of physical science, give apparent breadth and solidity, and are introduced with such nice adjustment, that want of coherence is not readily de-tected. I propose to test at vital points the soundness of the structure. To follow Mr. Spencer step by step, through volumes that contain the results of the scien-tific and literary labours of a busy life, would be im-possible, and, if possible, for my purpose needless. It is enough to examine the essential and distinctive

---

* I use the term Evolutionism to express the Evolution Hypo-thesis as a theory co-extensive with the knowable.

features of his philosophy, so as to judge of the worth of evolutionism as an all-comprehending hypothesis.

The question is not one lying in some remote and barren region of metaphysical debate : it touches vitally the present and real interests of men. "The matter," Mr. Spencer tells us, "is one which concerns each and all of us more than any other matter whatever. Though it affects us little in a direct way, the view we arrive at must indirectly affect us in all our relations—must determine our conception of the universe, of life, of human nature—must influence our ideas of right and wrong, and so modify our conduct." * This estimate of the results that would ensue on the acceptance of evolutionism, as the true philosophy, is not an exaggeration. Before it old things would pass away, and all things become new. Under its universal sway Christianity must wither : religion in any real sense would be impossible. Morality must find another basis, or disappear with faith. The matter does, indeed, concern each and all of us "more than any other matter whatever." An hypothesis claiming to be the true interpretation of all the knowable, and deeply affecting the interests of mankind, challenges the keenest criticism. We shall need to be fully persuaded of its truth, before we discard the old beliefs, and begin to repeat the new *credo*.

Every age has its fashionable philosophy. "We

---

* *First Principles*, Part I., § 8.

are constituted not merely to know, but also to imagine and construct; and though with more or less mistrust of the definite validity of what the understanding and the senses have to offer us, yet mankind will ever hail with joy the man who understands how, by the force of his genius, and by employing all the constructive impulses of his era, to create that unity in the world and in our intellectual life, which is denied to our knowledge. This creation will, indeed, be only the expression of the yearning of the age after unity and perfection; yet even this is no small thing, for the maintenance and nourishment of our intellectual life is as important as science itself, although not so lasting as this is: since the investigation of the details of positive knowledge, and of the relations which are the exclusive objects of our knowledge, is absolute, owing to its method, while the speculative apprehension of the absolute can only claim a relative importance as the expression of the views of an epoch." *

The yearning of this age after "unity in the world and in our intellectual life" finds expression in evolutionism. But evolutionism is not content to rest in "relative importance as the expression of the views of an epoch;" it advances a claim to absolute importance "owing to its method," as being the unification of all truth. It is a characteristic of the intellectual

---

* Lange's *History of Materialism,* Book I., Chap. III.

temper of our time to be dissatisfied with less than
unity. Science, looking on nature as continuous, accounts it her task to disclose how phenomenon is linked
to phenomenon throughout the entire cosmos. The
evolution doctrine satisfies this craving after manifested continuity. It proposes to reveal the universe
as one in co-existence and succession throughout all
space and all time. It is the embodiment of the
modern scientific spirit. The man of science recog-
nises in it the articulate expression of his mental
attitude towards the universe. His faith in the hypothesis stands not in the conclusiveness of the proofs
adduced in its support, but in his sense of its fitness
to harmonize the separate parts of his knowledge,
and to answer his intellectual yearning after organized completeness of thought. In that inner scientific
sense—analogous to the spiritual feeling that responds
to religious truth—there is a strong persuasion in
favour of the doctrine. To the inquirer who knows
his mind at rest; who, if we might venture to borrow
the expression, "has found peace" in the new mode
of conceiving the order of the universe, the conviction
of its truth seems irresistible. He discovers confirma-
tion where the doubter finds contradiction. He becomes impatient as a zealot with those who cannot
see with his eyes and receive his teaching. Every
soul that will not accept his gospel is under condemnation, and in danger of being left in the outer
darkness. No article of religion has been maintained

by the most bigoted ecclesiastic with greater arrogance, or in a narrower spirit. Mr. Spencer, for his part, follows out his conclusions with the confidence of one assured of their validity, yet without disparagement of those who interpret nature from a different standpoint; but the disciples outrun the master, and one who boldly questions the popular creed may look for rough handling as a heretic.

It does not lie in my way, in the following discussion, to engage in the well-worn controversy as to the relations of science and religion. Mr. Spencer has devoted a chapter to the exposition of his view that the knowable is the realm of science and the unknowable the home of religion. Into this question I do not enter. The harmony of these contrasted departments of knowledge, too often placed in apparent conflict, will be most effectively established by a careful examination of their distinctive principles and methods, and a clear recognition of the just claims of each in its own province. Religion, in so far as it touches science, is only concerned in securing veracity in searching for and dealing with facts, so as to arrive at a truthful elucidation of the complex world in which man lives and serves. Faith is not directly concerned in the acceptance or rejection of any theory lying clearly within the domain belonging of right to science. No interpretation of the order of nature within the limits of actual or possible discovery conflicts, or can conflict, with any distinctively religious truth. Whether the earth revolves round the sun, or the sun round the earth; whether the visible universe has been shaped by gradual solidification from a gaseous mass or had its origin in solid orbs; whether the divisions of animal and vegetable life arose as perfect and distinct species or have been differentiated through processes of change—questions like these do not in the least impinge on man's belief in the existence of a personal God, the Maker of heaven and earth, or on the assurance with which faith receives the testimony of Scripture as to the person and mission of Jesus Christ. It is when generalizations are lifted out of their place in the realm of experimental knowledge, and are invested with the authority of universal truths, that the teaching of science conflicts with the doctrines of the Church. The progress of truth is slow. The discussion of the order of the cosmos is not closed. Science has as yet advanced but a little way in deciphering the vast records. Faith can afford to wait: *nullum tempus ecclesiae.* The Church of God will be dealing with the great questions of life and duty when the thunders of these conflicts shall have been long silenced, and the smoke of the battlefield shall have cleared away, revealing the brightness of an unclouded heaven encompassing the little world of human thought.

The dominance of the new system of philosophy would prove as great a peril to scientific as to spiritual truth. If every fact is to be studied in the light of evolution, if dynamical law is to be recognized as ruling all processes and events, the growth of intelligence will be distorted and the advancement of knowledge impeded. The Scholastic Philosophy, through its formal completeness, became an intolerable bondage. System strangled truth. It left no room for the free pursuit of inquiry, and stood a barrier in the way of the forward movement of thought. A like danger threatens in the present stage of progress. The evolutionist is the schoolman of our day. He will have his hypothesis prevail everywhere. He constitutes it the criterion of truth. Observations are recorded, and experience read in the light of it. Everything that will not fall into position under it, he condemns. These are not conditions favourable to the right exercise of intelligence. Intellectual freedom is overborne; well-springs of knowledge are sealed up; a one-sided and iron system rules. It is imperative, in the interests of progressive thought, that this yoke be broken, that the mind may be free in the pursuit of truth.

The following discussion, directed to the disproof of the Evolution Hypothesis as a system co-extensive with knowledge, is not constructive, but critical. The inquiry is not, What is the truth? but, Is Evolutionism true? The final answer is a decided negative. The argument is cumulative; to find it inconclusive at some points will not invalidate its effectiveness in others. It deals only with questions that seem to be of vital importance to the doctrine under examination. Whatever may be the worth of the argument, no one can doubt the gravity of the issues involved. The highest interests are at stake. Evolutionism, if accepted, must eventually crush the liberty of the spirit in man; and the liberty of the spirit is indispensable to the progress of humanity.

CHAPTER II.

THE COMPLETE UNIFICATION OF KNOWLEDGE
IMPOSSIBLE.

MR. SPENCER defines philosophy as "completely-unified knowledge."* Before proceeding to the examination of his system, which claims to answer this definition, a previous question must be determined, Is the complete unification of knowledge possible? In other words, Is philosophy, in Mr. Spencer's meaning of the term, possible?

I answer in the negative. It is a fundamental error to assume that thought is competent to embrace all the knowable in one organic whole in a comprehensible unity. A necessary condition of scientific progress is to accept the limits of intelligence. From the Eleatic to the Evolutionist an overweening desire for systematized unity has perverted science. The system-builder has been one of the chief hindrances in the way of advancing knowledge. Intellectual progress cannot proceed with steady step along the whole line of the knowable, until it is clearly seen and frankly acknowledged that complete unification transcends

---

* *First Principles*, Part II., § 37.

the limits of intelligence, and that every system pro-
fessing to have reached such completeness is thereby
self-convicted as being necessarily false.

In discussing the unification of knowledge, it is to
be kept in view that we are not dealing with the
question of method. We are not inquiring as to the
criterion of truth or the form of correct reasoning.
The unity aimed at is not the coherence and congruity
of our thinking; not the unity of the mental process,
but the unity of knowledge as knowledge of objects,
as conversant about things and their relations: it is
the unity of knowledge dealing with all knowable
modes of existence. "If philosophy," says Mr. Spencer,
"is completely unified knowledge—if the unification
of knowledge is to be effected only by showing that
some ultimate proposition includes and consolidates
all the results of experience; then, clearly, this ultimate proposition which has to be proved congruous
with all others must express a *piece of knowledge,* and
not the *validity of an act of knowing."* * "Philosophy, as we understand it, must not unify separate
concrete phenomena only; and must not stop with
unifying separate classes of concrete phenomena; but
must unify all concrete phenomena."†

The task which philosophy undertakes in attempting this complete unification of all concrete phenomena is one the magnitude of which it is not easy at

---

* *First Principles,* § 42.   † *Ibid.,* § 186.

first sight to apprehend. It is nothing less than
an attempt to present, in the unity of thought, the
unity of all real existence and all relations of real
existence, in co-existence and succession throughout
all time. All orders of persons and things, and all
processes of change, must find their due place in the
reproduction in thought of that organic whole which
is assumed to embrace all things in its totality. The
vastness of such an undertaking might well impart
a feeling of mistrust to the boldest and most self-
confident. Man buried, according to the doctrine of
the evolutionist, in the depth of this incomprehensible
universe of concrete being, tossed like a particle of
dust in the whirl of its incalculable eddies, stretching
hopelessly towards its infinite bounds, groping blindly
after its origin and end—man, in his felt insignificance
over against the unsearchable actuality, might well
enter with hesitancy on the task of framing, in the
shape of organized knowledge, a true representation
of the whole range of being from God to inanimate
nature, and of the law of the activities, inter-relations, and changes of the whole and every part. Yet
this is the achievement which a philosophy, successful
in the task of unifying all knowledge, must accomplish. For "it is not enough to unify different classes
of phenomena; philosophy must unify all concrete
phenomena."

The goal of unity has been sought along various
lines.

(1.) The Calvinist finds that unity in God. All, things have been ordered according to His will; they are the manifestation of His power, and have their harmony in His decree. This is unification; but it is the attainment of that aim through faith, not through knowledge. The co-ordination of all departments of knowledge in one organic and comprehensible whole is not reached by this method.

(2.) The unification of knowledge may be approached by positing the unity of the object of knowledge. But our knowledge is not of One Thing; it is of many things. To know individual things as individual things, is to difference them; and the knowledge is diverse as the objects. Knowledge is at first of individual things; to reach unity of knowledge through the unity of the thing known, the Eleatic removed the many, affirming reality only of the One. We need hardly pause to show that the knowledge of the One as thus attained is not real knowledge. There is no knowledge without judgment, and no judgment without comparison, and no comparison without likeness or difference; nor these without plurality. So that in the removal of the multiple and the positing of the One the conditions of knowledge have vanished. Like Samson, who at one stroke overthrew his enemies and sacrificed himself, knowledge, in sweeping away plurality, is self-destroyed. So soon as the unification is complete, thought is extinguished. If, then, the existence of the object as one be essential to the unity aimed at, unification is impossible; for knowledge itself is impossible. Again, to know the object of knowledge as one is incompetent owing to the fundamental contrast between the *ego* and the *non-ego :* unity is not complete until the subject and object are reduced to identity. In the pursuit of the unity of knowledge along the line of the unity of the object known, we are driven to look for it in an ultimate real oneness of the *ego* and *non-ego :* but the identification is unthinkable; it cannot arise in expe- rience. The contrast between subject and object is essential to thought. If I am no longer able to say, I myself exist, I am no longer capable of conscious in- tellection. Knowledge itself is impossible.

(3.) Unity may be sought, not in the One eternal and unchanged—the absolute in being—but in the One eternally self-revealing, that is, in an absolute process. In every attempt to reach unification of the phenomenal through the absolute, whether in being or in process, there is involved the implication that the absolute is known. That a philosophy based on knowledge of the absolute is impossible, has been, once for all, demonstrated by Sir William Hamilton, in his "Philosophy of the Unconditioned." Unifica- tion based on such assumed knowledge is clearly invalid. All search for unity by the way of the absolute must fail; for it involves acts of intelligence that transcend the limits of thought.

Driven back from the attempt to reach unity from the side of the absolute, are we left without any hope of combining the different elements and separate parts of truth in one consistent and organic whole ? Must we abandon in despair all endeavour after the unification of knowledge ? From Heraclitus to Mr Herbert Spencer there has been a succession of philosophers who have looked for the unifying principle, not in oneness of being, or in the self-revelation of the absolute, but in the process of ceaseless change. The present state of knowledge is especially favourable to such a doctrine. Knowledge proceeding from the cognition of individual things, strives towards unification by combining the many in one through unity of law. The rapid development of experimental science, revealing order everywhere, has impressed all minds with a sense of the universality of law, and prepared the way for a philosophy claiming to have discovered, in a law governing all change, the principle of that complete unification of knowledge which has been sought so ardently.

The problem then is, to find one unifying principle actually operative over the whole extent of being and of mutation. The principle sought must embrace the immeasurable spaces of the material world, and govern every thrill of each atom, and every movement of the entire mass : it must be seen in operation at the first moment, when the universe emerges into the field of thought, and must regulate the entire course of change

onward to the end of time: it must bring to light the
beginning of life, and disclose the origin and growth
of every individual and every species: it must show
how organic sensibility came to be, and elucidate the
complex and wonderful adaptations by which, even in
the case of microscopic forms, the living creature is
fitted to its habitat, and enabled to maintain itself in
life during its brief day, and perpetuate the existence
of its kind: it must account for the human consciousness, and explain how it has arisen: it must determine
how the faculties of mind have come to be, and reveal
the origin of conscience: it must unveil the source of
religious feeling, and furnish the key to the indestructible · belief in God: it must afford explanation of the
marvellous achievements of intelligence in unravelling
the complexities of things, and making known their
order and law; in accomplishing astounding feats of
power and skill, by the combination of resources
through political and social organizations; in producing works of art, whose beauty rivals the perfection
of nature; in attaining moral ends through the sense
of personal freedom voluntarily submitting to the
law of duty; in reaching spiritual results through
knowledge that pierces the encompassing veil, and
through devotion that freely sacrifices self. It must
thus account for man, the most wonderful of all the
phenomena of the universe; it must, above all, account
for the appearance in this world of the man Christ
Jesus, for the power of His teaching and life, and for

the transforming influence of that most notable of all phenomena—the Christian Faith.

And this gigantic task is to be accomplished, not in the region of ideas, but in the realm of fact. The principle that unifies is to be known as a principle operative throughout the entire range of knowable existence, as the bond which unites in one organic and indivisible whole all objects, from the molecule that vibrates at the centre of the universe to the Almighty Source of all things, as the law that regulates all events throughout the entire succession of change from everlasting to everlasting.

The facts, which are to be brought together in one, lie in clearly marked departments or kingdoms, each distinguished from the others by a well-defined line of discrimination, which science, as it advances, does nothing to obliterate; on the contrary, the clearer the light of science, the deeper and the more marked the distinction is seen to be. These objects of knowledge are :—

(1.) Supreme over all—GOD.

(2.) The self-conscious intelligence of man.

(3.) Objects endowed with life and sensibility.

(4.) Objects endowed with vegetal life.

(5.) Inorganic matter.

Throughout the entire series of created existence, there are common characteristics that reveal a certain sort of oneness. But that unity is far different from the oneness of an organic whole, the same in substance

B

throughout, moulded and moved in every part by the same active principle. It is community of the sort we recognize when we observe in different works traces of the same intelligence, touches of the same hand.

Consider these fields of knowledge, and it will be evident how fruitless is the attempt to find in them one operative principle by which they may be reduced to unity.

(1.) God exists in the view of thought: it is impossible, if we would, to rid ourselves of that Presence. Mr. Spencer bears convincing testimony to this fact. Under the veil of what he calls the Unknowable, a something—the Absolute Reality—lies present to thought in every process of reasoning. Granted that our consciousness of it is vague, undefined, still the inscrutable actuality is there. This element—being a real and necessary element of consciousness—brings into view, though it may be indefinitely, a real existence. To unify all objects of whose existence we have proof is manifestly impossible, until we shall have brought this Reality into organic relation with all other concrete existences known to us. But no principle can be discovered which will effect such unification. There is here a manifest and insuperable breach of continuity in our knowledge. Till continuity is established at this point, it is clear that the totality of existences—not imaginary but concrete existences, existences of which we have indubitable evidence— cannot be brought together in one. Much more, if we follow the Christian doctrine of the Divine Personality,¹ is it impossible to institute an organic oneness between God and His creatures.* However imperative it may be, that we should recognise the presence and power of the Divine Being as manifested in all things, religious faith refuses to confound the Creator with His works: it sees a line of distinction which cannot be obliterated or transcended, differencing all created beings from the eternal source from which they have sprung. The continuity of knowledge is broken. God and the universe cannot be brought together in one. Philosophy cannot "unify all concrete phenomena."

(2). Man is conscious of himself. In every act of intelligence he knows himself as differenced from the surrounding world. The line that separates the *ego* from the *non-ego*, runs throughout all conscious intellection. No unifying principle can obliterate it. The knowledge which the mind has of its own operations is primary. No other source of knowledge can assert superior authority. What consciousness attests in its primary exercise, cannot be set aside by secondary evidence. All knowledge ultimately rests on its veracity. Even if there were a principle adequate to the unification of consciousness and the object of consciousness, it would be impossible that that prin-

---

* The incarnation does not lie within the scientific field : its significance is spiritual. It is an unwarrantable use of the doctrine to constitute it a link in a cosmic theory.

ciple should be realized in thought; for to apprehend
the unity of itself and its objects, consciousness must
transcend itself, and contemplate the relation from
without. But such an achievement is manifestly
impossible : it would be fatal; for consciousness must
perish in the act. The law of continuity is violated
in every exercise of conscious intelligence. Self-consciousness is an insuperable barrier in the way of the
complete unification of knowledge.

(3). Life manifested in organisms endowed with
sensibility presents another wide and distinct department of phenomena, which has hitherto defeated all'
attempts at reducing it to knowable unity with other
modes of concrete existence. The animal kingdom is
divided by an impassable separation from that of
vegetable life. It may be alleged that the lowest
forms in both are hardly distinguishable from each
other. But even though these lowest forms should
be to us indistinguishable, it does not follow that they
are not distinct. The higher organisms are not distinguishable in their earliest stage; yet these germs,
whose differences are indiscernible, pursue, with un-
erring and infallible certainty, paths of development
which result in clearly differenced structures. The
germs out of which animals of different species are
developed, must have, though not discernible by us,
characteristics by which they are discriminated. Even
in the same species the germs, though altogether indistinguishable, are of quite distinct varieties. That

the lowest forms cannot be, with certainty, classified, does not prove that they are not separated by any real difference into animal or vegetal, but only that science is not able to bring the difference to light, and that our classification is no more than a rough approximation to reality. To affirm that there are no discriminating marks, because we cannot discover them, is to assume, against all experience, that science succeeds in tracing the lines of demarcation in nature wherever such lines exist. Every living germ is a witness to the contrary. The primal forms of the higher species cannot be sorted by science.

(4). The vegetal kingdom forms another vast group of organisms, separated on the one side from inorganic matter, and on the other, from organisms endowed with sensibility. The differences on either side must be accounted for before unification is complete. The origin of organization lies—and seems as if it would for ever lie—a mystery to science. No attempt to trace the process of change from the inorganic to the organic has succeeded, or has come near success. It still remains an unsolved problem to find an operative principle adequate to the task of bringing organic and inorganic processes together in a real oneness. We shall have to look more closely at this point in another part of the discussion.

(5). Nor is it possible to unify knowledge even within the compass of inorganic matter. The laws of the inorganic world cannot be unified. No one dynamic principle will account for the play of forces in nature, or reduce all their operations to unity. To explain the action of inorganic matter there is more needed than the persistence of force. "The antecedent forces must be adequate in their quantities, kinds, and distribution." * When the imagination has pushed back the conception of matter and force to the utmost limit, to derive the universe that is, the evolutionist must assume a certain position of the atoms, certain orderly relations among the atoms, certain activities and their laws—a conception as complex and as far from being resolved into unity as the visible cosmos. The world that now is lay, by hypothesis, wrapped up in that original collocation of matter and force. Systems on systems of atoms rising through systems on systems of molecules, according to Mr. Spencer, constitute the imperceptible out of which the visible has been shaped. This infinitely complicated and inexplicable series of systems is necessary, even in one field of observation, to the conception of that unity which science seeks. How inconceivable the complexity, when we survey the whole world of thought!

As the stream of created being flows forth from the unseen, obedient to the Divine word, like the Edenic river, it is "parted into four heads":—inor-

---

* Spencer's *Principles of Biology,* Vol. I., Appendix.

ganic matter, organisms endowed with vegetal life, organisms endowed with animal life, and man endowed with self-conscious intelligence and a moral nature.

These great fountain-heads of created being are distinct throughout all the cosmic history in so far as we can know it, and they seem destined to continue distinct departments of knowledge until the existing framework of things shall be dissolved. No principle has been discovered, nor is, as we believe, discoverable, which will unite all these orders of existences in one coherent organic body. No principle can be found—and if it could be found its applicabilty must be for ever undiscoverable—through which it can be shown how consciousness may rise out of and sink again into the unintelligent world. No principle has heretofore been brought to light, nor can be, which, operative in all forms of being and furnishing an explanation of their distinctive characteristics, is adequate to bring existences subject only to dynamic laws, and those which are subject to the higher laws of life, sensation, and mind, together in one.

The unification of knowledge is not complete; nor, is completeness of unification possible. The pretence of completeness can only be attained by hiding the difficulties from view. But to do so is to be false to scientific progress. Knowledge advances towards perfection by clearing, not blurring, the lines of discrimination. If there are distinctions in nature, these must

have their counterpart in a corresponding demarcation in thought. The great departments of inquiry
are mutually helpful, and throw light one upon the
other. They have much in common; but they can
never be brought together in a complete unity of
knowledge. Each must in the main pursue its own aim
by'its own appropriate methods. The results reached
along this way will be solid additions to science and
valuable contributions to human well-being; when, on
the other hand, research is set to the task of filling up
the empty outline of a universal system of organised
knowledge, it ceases to be the devotee of truth, and is
transformed into the advocate whose business is to
compel every fact to fit his theory, and every witness
to give such evidence as suits his case.

The interests of science and of faith alike require
that thought should recognize the bounds set to it, and,
accepting its appointed conditions, work out patiently,
and with veracity, its task of deciphering such pages
of the book of the universe as are open to the view
of man. He is a false prophet of the natural who
will profess to write out the whole, or even to furnish
a complete table of contents. One of the greatest of the
prophets of the spiritual has laid down a principle as
entirely applicable to scientific as to religious thought:
" We know in part and we prophesy in part." *   The
complete unification of knowledge is impossible.

---

* *1 Corinthians* xiii. 9.

CHAPTER III.

THE LIMITS OF PHYSICAL SCIENCE.

THE Physical Sciences have advanced with such rapidity, and have succeeded in so large a number of instances in unifying what appeared to be altogether separate classes of facts by the discovery of their law, that at first sight it seems reasonable to hope for a still wider unification embracing all departments of truth.

"The truths of philosophy bear the same relation to the highest scientific truths, that each of these bears to lower scientific truths. As each widest generalization of science comprehends and consolidates the narrower generalization of its own division; so the generalizations of philosophy comprehend and consolidate the widest generalizations of Science. It is therefore a knowledge the extreme opposite in kind to that which experience first accumulates. It is the final product of that process which begins with a mere colligation of crude observations, goes on establishing propositions that are broader and more separated from particular cases, and ends in universal propositions. Or, to bring the definition to its simplest and clearest form:—Knowledge of the lowest kind is *un-unified* knowledge; Science is *partially - unified* knowledge; Philosophy is *completely-unified* knowledge." *

Mr. Spencer's system is framed of such "universal propositions" derived from generalizations of science beginning "with a mere colligation of crude observations." Do these generalizations furnish truths which may be turned into universals holding good over the whole universe of being, and dominating all thought? They do not. The truths of experiential science cannot be so used legitimately : and the philosophy founded on such a basis is demonstrably false.

To make this position clear it is necessary to inquire into the limits of physical science. The physicist may not add anything to nature : it is his business to see what is, and nothing but what is. His science is strictly bounded by observation, and can speak only in the name of known facts, and of such facts as are, in the points of comparison, precisely similar. Physical science is imperatively enclosed within the actually known. Where it deals with that which is not actually known, it must invariably carry forward into the unknown that which is known, and with the assumption that the conditions, so far as affects the matter dealt with, are identical. Given other conditions, and the result will be different. Science may

---

* *First Principles,* § 37.

not invent a conjectural state of things, and profess,
by setting out the operation of known laws in such
supposed circumstances, to extend the bounds of real
knowledge. All scientific work of that kind—and it
forms a considerable part of popular science — is
merely imaginative; it lies in the department of
romance.

There are bounds which ought not to be passed in
framing hypotheses to account for phenomena that
remain unexplained. It is not allowable to set up any
hypothesis which lies outside the possibility of being
established by evidence. Every legitimate conjecture
lies within the possibility of actual proof. It is fatal
to any hypothesis to show that it is incapable of being
proved. Its author is bound to point out a possible
line of adequate evidence, or his conjecture must be
rejected as illegitimate. The doctrine of universal
evolution belongs to this class of illegitimate hypotheses; if it were true, it could not be proved true.
The requirements of satisfactory proof transcend the
limits of human thought.

Every attempt to formulate truths derived from
experiential science that shall be held to be good over
the whole past, present, and future of concrete being,
encounters insuperable difficulties.

Man is not omniscient: he must gather his facts
from experience, and must interpret them by comparison and inference. At every step he comes in contact
with the inscrutable; and his intelligence is in every

process liable to error. Even if we grant that the mind is a quite perfect reasoning instrument, the physicist is beset with liabilities to misconceptions and mistakes. These sources of error may be grouped under five heads,—duration, extent, minuteness, complexity, and imperfection of the organs of sense.

(1.) Duration. The stretch of time which may be called the period of observation is as nothing compared with the supposed duration of the universe; and the period of skilled and reliable observation is still less. All scientific conclusions are based on observations made at one point in a boundless reach of movement and ceaselessly flowing change. Two sources of doubt lie in every instance;—(*a*) whether the whole thing, or all that is essential to the right understanding of it for the purpose in hand, has been seen on the side within the field of observation; and (*b*) whether the facts observed adequately represent the whole series, which is conceived as extending backward to a measureless distance in time. Observation, to yield a valid result, must conform fully to both conditions. If there be room for questioning the exactness or sufficiency of the facts observed, we are bound to refuse acceptance to any doctrine built thereon, when it transcends the immediate bounds of experience and formulates a law for all time. The divergence from reality may be infinitesimal at the outset, and within the range of experience of no practical account, but carried over the entire sweep of cosmic history, backward and forward to infinity, the result will be wholly false.

When the order of the universe, as at the beginning of its history it emerges out of and at the close of its history it passes again into the imperceptible, is deduced from present knowledge of phenomena, this liability to error is always present. Unless our knowledge of fact be precise and adequate—if aught be misread or omitted—all reasonings based on it, and extending before and after over unimaginable stretches of time, are fatally tainted with uncertainty. The result is wholly unreliable. The amount of reality with which the physicist set out remains a fixed quantity, while the margin of error has increased at every step. That which, within experience, was an imperceptible divergence from fact has widened to infinity.

(2.) The bounds of things as existing in space at any given point in time are practically infinite. However far scientific vision may reach, the cosmos extends beyond. The sphere of observation is but a speck in the limitless expanse. Now, to infer from the little portion observed to the vastly wider regions remaining for ever inscrutable, is fraught with peril. We must be assured not only of the similarity, but identity, of concrete existences within experience and beyond it, before we can venture to draw any conclusion with an approach to certainty.

In every case we are met by the initial difficulty of

assuring ourselves that the whole fact has been — for our purpose—discovered. If all nature form one cosmos, as the scientist assumes, the whole is joined together in a real unity, so that no one part is separable from any other part. Each instance is in effect the entire universe. Every object of inquiry thus extends immeasurably beyond the limits of possible experience; and that vast unknown is as essential to the instance before us as that in it which may be brought within the field of vision. We may sufficiently understand the phenomenon, and its relations within the visible, to reach conclusions that will be valid within experience; but we should need to exhaust every relation in which the object stands to every other mode of existence in the cosmos, before we could reason with confidence from the instance and its law to the limitless totality of things. Such completeness of knowledge is not given to man. The scientific inquirer must always remain in the attitude of expectance, willing to modify his doctrine should any new phase of the phenomena under investigation be presented. There are laws, within their proper limits, well-established and sure: but when the physicist carries them beyond the bounds of experience he is always beset by doubt; he cannot reason with the full assurance of one who deals with universal and necessary truth.

When, therefore, an hypothesis is framed to cover the whole extent of knowable existence, and is based

on professed observation, it must be always open to
the objection, and its certainty qualified by the consideration, that the vastly greater part of the contem-
poraneous fact was beyond the ken of the observer.

This source of error will appear the more formidable,
if we keep in view that the concrete existence forming
the matter of investigation is united with other existences not in our plane only, but in an infinite number
of planes intersecting at the point of observation.
We are not situated at a point in a level surface
over which the eye may range to the utmost stretch
of vision; we are enclosed within a sphere whose
centre is in relation to us everywhere, and its circum-
ference nowhere. The instances examined by the
scientist, and on the precise and complete knowledge
of which our cosmic theories are built, are assumed
to be one organically with every part of that unbounded whole, which in every direction passes beyond
the range of our experience into infinity.

We are not warranted, then, in concluding with
assured certainty, from the limits of our narrow and
imperfect experience, over the whole universe of concrete being. For whatever doubt attaches to the
completeness of our interpretation of nature, as seen,
expands and grows with every step outward, increasing as the sphere widens in every direction towards
illimitable space. A scientific truth, as close to reality
as any induction of physical science can be, and valid
within the range of experience, becomes, when carried

from the central point of observation over the whole
extent of co-existent things, so doubtful as to be value-
less. The error has enlarged at every step, while the
truth has remained a fixed quantity.

(3.) A further source of error presents itself when
we bring into view the fact, that as nature stretches
out of view beyond us in time and space, so it passes
out of view beneath us in indiscernible minuteness.
The instrumental aid by which the physicist brings
within the range of observation a vast extent of phenomena, imperceptible to unaided sense, has revealed
at the same time regions still more minute, forming a
part of the concrete whole, whose law science undertakes to expound. These infinitesimal forms of existence are beyond the reach of observation—" monads,
compared with which a grain of sand is an earth."*
But they are an integral part of the world we know.
It is made up of them. They are factors, it may be
the most important factors, in the processes of change.
Our rude manipulation leaves them in every experiment untouched. Too subtile to be apprehended, they
are none the less potent. What part they have played,
or may play, in the drama whose movement philosophy would formulate, we can never learn. They
may have been the leading actors in former scenes.
In omitting them when we write out the plot, we
may be leaving out the Hamlet of the play. This, at

---

* Spencer : *Psych.* Vol. II., Part VII., Chap. II.

any rate, we may boldly affirm, that the hypothesis which formulates the law of concrete being and explains the whole series of cosmic and individual change while it is confessedly ignorant of the law of that ever present and ceaselessly active world of real existence lying around us, and touching us at every instant, must have in it a large imaginative element.

(4.) The inexactness of all observation and experiment is further illustrated, when we bring into view the endless complexity of all causes and effects. Every experiment is complicated by the co-existence of a countless number of co-operating forces, each of which is correlated with all the rest, and contributes its part to the combined result. The scientific principle of the correlation of physical forces brings this aspect of the intricateness of nature very emphatically into view. The relations of forces, whether in masses or in molecules, are for man limitless. Every new discovery of correlation among the special sciences is fresh evidence of the boundless complexity of causes, and additional ground for questioning the perfect exactness of any experimental truth. Every correlation on which attention is fixed shows, with greater clearness, the exhaustless inter-relations of things. As we become more fully alive to the inconceivably complex whole which constitutes the totality of the universe, we shall advance with less assurance to universal truths from generalizations of science, valid so long as the scientist continues on the solid ground of experience, but which are not safer than the wings of Icarus when he attempts a flight towards the boundless distances of the cosmos, or poises himself above the ever-rolling ocean stream of change.

(5.) When we turn from the objects of knowledge to test the instruments of observation, the grounds of mistrust are multiplied. The field is narrowed by the limitations of the organs of sense. On the evolution theory the trustworthiness of the organs of sense is extremely limited. They are products of evolution, shaped in the gradual adaptation of man to his surroundings. They are in number and range determined by their utility in adjusting his organism to his environment. What is useful for this purpose, and nothing further, has been evolved. But the elaboration of a true system of philosophy is not a condition of the continuance of the human species. The race has persisted for a long period with, as the advocates of evolution believe, a very incorrect conception of the universe. It is not clear, then, how sense organs evolved for a quite different end can be relied on to give such a full and complete knowledge of the phenomena as will furnish a basis for a perfect cosmic theory. There may be, probably there are, many modes of activity continually operating throughout the universe, affecting the relations of its parts, and directing its movement, which are not in relation to our sensibility, and which we have no means of apprehending. The senses with which we are endowed are, on the hypothesis of evolution, defective in their adaptation to any purpose except the practical end of adjustment to environment, and so to the maintenance of man's life on the earth. Admirably fitted to serve the purpose for which they have been evolved, they fail us when applied to any other use. They cannot, therefore, be depended on as instruments of exact knowledge. The power of sight, for example, is extremely restricted in its compass. Our perception of colour is limited to a narrow range, and within that range is very imperfect. The lower animals are in many instances endowed with more perfect organs than man. Defective sense-perception is corrected by comparison, but even then the means are not furnished for attaining absolute precision. "The mind of man, as Francis Bacon said, is like an uneven mirror, and does not reflect the events of nature without distortion."* The most skilful observer cannot adjust his intellectual compensations with perfect success to defects of nerve and organ. The gift of exact observation is extremely rare. We tend to see that for which we look. "It is exceedingly rare," says Professor Jevons, "to find persons who can, with perfect fairness, estimate and register facts for and against their own peculiar views and theories."† The mind brings with it an anticipation which colours the event. Those parts of the concrete whole which favour the conclu-

---

* Jevon's *Principles of Science,* Vol. II., Book IV., Chap. XVIII.
† *Ibid.*

sion we wish to establish stand clearly out in view, while that which conflicts with the desired conclusion falls into the background. According to the common adage, "seeing is believing;" but it as often happens that "believing is seeing." What man is there, glowing and ardent in the pursuit of knowledge, and at the same time altogether unprejudiced and impartial, having no favourite view to support, nor any obnoxious opinion to impugn? What observer possesses an eye and mind perfectly achromatic? Human frailty scarcely warrants the supposition that such an one is to be found. Individual aberrations from exact truth are no doubt counteracted by the multiplication of observations and the ceaseless conflict of opinion. These compensations in the end work a truer balance of doctrine, and bring theories nearer to reality. But approximations to truth, however close the approach may be, are not sufficient when the philosopher is laying foundations on which his theory of all things is to be based. When he undertakes to unify all knowledge—to include in one formula the law of all processes throughout the universe during all time, approximations will not serve. We must build on reality the world of thought, if it is to correspond with the world that is. A slight want of precision, of no account when the target is at fifty paces, will prove fatal to accuracy of aim when the distance is a thousand yards; a trifling inaccuracy in measurement, not worth noticing in calculatiug the dimensions of a field, will involve disastrous consequences if it should occur in fixing a base line for the survey of a kingdom.

Taking together in one view these five sources of error, to each of which the observer is in every instance liable, no one can accept as secure and well-founded any world-embracing hypothesis based on the sciences of observation. Everyone will recognize the wisdom of the caution—" We can seldom trust our best established theories and most careful inferences far from their data." *

---

* Jevon's *Principles of Science,* Book VI., Chap. XXVI.

CHAPTER IV.

THERE is a suggestion of definiteness and certainty in the word *Law*, which imparts an air of solidity to the loftiest theories. Granted, it may be argued, that mutation is the order of the cosmos, granted that the greater part of every fact eludes the observer, still there is something invariable and constant within the bounds of knowledge. By the discovery of their law, the shifting mass of seemingly incoherent experiences may be knit into a compact and orderly system. A firm foundation can be thus laid for hypotheses that tower to heaven. We shall examine this ground of certainty.

(1). Natural law is not something existing apart from or outside phenomena. It is simply their order. When we speak of the laws of nature, we mean no more than the ascertained mode of behaviour of things. "A law of nature, as I regard the meaning of the expression, is not a uniformity which must be obeyed by all objects, but merely a uniformity which is, as a matter of fact, obeyed by those objects that have come beneath our observation."* Law has no

---

* Jevon's *Principles of Science*, Book VI., Chap. XXXI.

existence in itself: take away the things, and the mode of their action is taken away. If matter ceased to exist in ponderable form, the law of gravity would cease to have any real existence; if it remained it would exist, not as a law of things, but as a conception shaped by intelligence.

If, then, we build on the universality and necessity of any given physical law, if we found our theory on the certainty of its continuance throughout all time, and its dominance over the whole breadth of concrete existence, we put into the law a content to which it has no claim.

Wherever there are like things in like conditions, we necessarily find the same mode of action; for like things are things that behave alike: the truth in fact amounts to an identical proposition. But where the law is assumed to be constant, there is always, and must be presupposed, the existence of like things and like conditions. The law does not create the concrete realities that conform to it, nor does it subdue to its sway things lying outside its dominion. It is not a self-existent something exercising an independent authority: it is the mode of behaviour of objects. No law of nature has validity beyond the class of phenomena whose mode of action it expresses. If it be affirmed that any given law has existed at other periods of time, or exists in undiscoverable distances of space, the existence of like phenomena is invariably presupposed. If we are not entitled to assume the existence of phenomena, in all respects that are essential to the point of view in question, identical with those lying within experience, we are not entitled to assume the applicability of the law beyond the region in which its operation has been observed. No experiential law carries with it the authority of a universal truth.

(2). Every law of nature, being a generalization from experience, is more or less inexact. The degree of inexactness varies from rough approximations to formulæ which may be made the basis of calculations that are justified by the foretold event; yet it will not be claimed for any generalized experience that it is characterized by absolute precision. The laws of number and form dealing with purely abstract relations are absolutely true; but the laws of nature have to do with concrete things—not with abstractions. They express the mode of action of complex realities. No experiential law can be established by demonstration. Its truth lies in the exactness with which it interprets the mode of action of classes of concrete existences, and is not in any case absolute. It might, indeed, be questioned if any object whatever has been known to act with perfect precision according to any known law or combination of known laws. Law, as generalized from observation, is not in any instance obeyed perfectly. Law is abstract: objects are concrete. The formula which expresses a law of nature cannot include the conditions which are an inseparable part of the instance. "All laws and explanations are in a certain sense hypothetical, and apply exactly to nothing which we can know to exist." *

Throughout all nature there is not found a straight line, or a perfect circle, or an exact ellipse: these are abstract notions, not real things. Nor does nature furnish an example of motion in a straight line, or in a perfect circle or ellipse, or in a curve whose law may be mathematically expressed. The earth does not in its orbit round the sun move in an ellipse whose form is mathematically exact, nor does it trace the same line in each succeeding year. No two plants are exactly alike; nor in inanimate nature are there ever found two instances of absolute sameness.

Did we know the totality of laws and know each and the whole perfectly, we should then, no doubt, see the entire concrete fact and comprehend it : but such knowledge implies omniscience. So far as discernible by us, the action of every concrete object is more or less erratic, and is not perfectly conformable to any one law or to all known laws. "Only a mind which stood at the centre of this real world, not outside individual things, but penetrating them with its presence, could command such a view of reality as left nothing to look for, and was therefore the perfect image of it in its own being and activity. But the

---

* Jevon's *Principles of Science*, Book IV., Chap. XXI.

human mind does not thus stand at the centre of things, but has a modest position somewhere in the extensive ramifications of reality."*

(3.) The inconceivable complexity of relations in the universe involves inter-relations of laws of like complexity. It is impossible to ascertain with anything approaching certainty in how far any given uniformity is the resultant of the combined action of conflicting laws, and how far such uniformity will be found to recur in conditions but slightly modified. A law may be subsumed under a higher law, or counteracted by forces lying outside or beneath the ken of science, or modified by altered relations arising out of the movement of cosmic change. Taking into view the immeasurable field of existence, and the infinite complexity of the inter-relations of things, it is wholly impossible to affirm with certainty the applicabilty of any law generalized from experience, outside the bounds of circumstances identified with the experiences from which it has been derived. To carry a law over the whole length and breadth and height and depth of being, back to the first beginning of things and forward to the end, is to multiply at every step occasions of doubt, and to end in removing every ground of certainty.

(4.) One other source of uncertainty may be noticed. Science cannot in any instance determine with com-

* Lotze, *Logic*, Introduction, § IX.

plete confidence whether a law derived from observation represents a permanent or a variable and transient condition ; whether it sets out a mode of action essential in the constitution of things, or but a passing interaction of forces as they sweep onward in vast curves of change. We cannot follow with certainty the path of any great cosmic movement. We see too minute a portion of the line to assert with confidence whether it be straight or curved. What is true of the physical sciences is true, *mutatis mutandis*, of all the sciences which proceed on the experiential method. So far as they formulate the results of experience they are reliable; when they extend their formulæ into other departments or make them rules for all forms of being they are delusive. The experiential laws of mind will not elucidate the problems of matter; nor the dynamic laws of matter solve the problems of intelligence. Experience, good in its own channel, is an unsafe pilot in strange waters. Assurance of the permanence and universality of any law, supposed to cover the whole field of knowledge, cannot be based on experience.

It is a delusion to suppose, if the evolution hypothesis be true, that experience gives us knowledge of stability. Stability is, according to the evolution doctrine, the seeming, mutability the real in experience. Not stability but mutability is the condition which evolution teaches us to recognize as the mode of concrete being. Evolution discloses to us the homogeneous becoming heterogeneous, through the integration of matter and dissipation of motion, and so onward to dissolution. " Apparently the universally-co-existent forces of attraction and repulsion, which, as we have seen, necessitate rhythm in all minor changes throughout the universe, also necessitate rhythm in the totality of its changes—produce now an immeasurable period during which the attractive forces predominating, cause universal concentration, and then an immeasurable period during which the repulsive forces predominating, cause universal diffusion—alternate eras of Evolution and Dissolution."* There is then no stability: all is everlasting flux. No mode of force is fixed : forces are being constantly transformed. No law is stable; for laws are but the relations of forces. Fixedness based on law is as fleeting as the forces whose mode of action the law expresses.

Among the generalizations from experience, the law of gravitation may be taken as established beyond cavil ; it is accepted not only as holding good throughout all actual experience, but as forming a solid basis for deductions that are valid beyond the reach of observation. Yet we are not thoroughly imbued with the evolution doctrine if we regard it so. Bodies, as we know them, tend towards one another according to this law. But it is not demonstrable that gravity is a property of matter universally.

Spencer, *First Principles*, § 183.

Body—matter in the aggregate—is a temporary mode of force. We cannot reason from matter in mass to matter in all its forms. All modes of force, ponderable and imponderable, come under the universal principle of the transference and equivalence of forces. The ponderable may then become imponderable, and the imponderable ponderable; in which case gravity must be accepted as no more than a temporary quality attaching to certain changeable modes of force. Assuming gravity to be an attribute universally of the form of force we call matter, it is far from proved that its law is constant. There is, according to Mr. Spencer, a rhythm of motion in all moving force, from the vibrations of a tuning-fork to the oscillations of the earth in its orbit.. We cannot fix the range or determine the limits of rhythmic movements. That manifestation of force called gravity, instead of being fixed, may be constant only in changing. It is not unreasonable to suppose that the law of gravitation, as we now express it, is true only for the present; it may be a mode of force at the moment of the return of a curve of oscillation, and be true but for a brief period of time. Carried into the past and future, it may lead only to error. We are ephemera at best, and the age of scientific knowledge is but a span. In the line of the limitless sweep of cosmic forces we cannot measure so much as an handbreadth; and our instruments are rude and clumsy, forbidding us to hope for absolute exactness, even within our narrow horizon. How can we then judge with certainty the direction or calculate the law of universal mutation? According to the principles of the evolutionist, we are driven to hold that conclusions regarding the past or future of the universe arrived at on the faith of the validity throughout all time of any physical law may—very probably do—rest on a mistake. Taking the position of the evolutionist, we must feel that to be slippery ground on which we stand, if stand it can be called, when we are submerged in a stream of constant change. That we have traced with precision the law of cosmic movement while we ourselves are drifting in the ceaseless flux, is surely open to the gravest doubt. One law after another which seemed well-founded having slipped away from us, we poise ourselves, as on the ultimate certainty, on a principle supposed to govern repeatedly recurring eras of evolution and dissolution,—" ever the same in principle, but never the same in concrete results."

But it is folly to speak of man as if he were the spectator of this eternal stream of change; he is himself an integral part of it: *nos mutamur in illis.* Reason, an evolved product, cannot stand apart and survey the ceaseless flow from the security of a self-conscious intelligence, which has derived its being from a super-sensual source. Mind is a phase of the mutation — an insignificant eddy in the vast — the unfathomable whirl. Reason has been evolved and passes towards dissolution. The play of the cosmic

forces has moulded it in forms of thought; but these
are mutable as the interactions of the forces which
have shaped them. The laws of thought are but the
reflection in consciousness of a temporary phase of
the illimitable stream. The stores of knowledge—
our boasted treasures of scientific discovery—are no
more than ever-shifting ripples thrown for a moment
into view in the never-ending flow of the absolute
and unknowable energy. Instability of the homogeneous is a principle frequently recurring in Mr.
Spencer's exposition. It is not the homogeneous alone
that is unstable. Instability is the only universal—
the summation of all we know. The one thing
fixed is that nothing is fixed; the one thing, certain
is that all is uncertain. To attempt to mark out the
law of the universe throughout the past and future
is an undertaking which, on evolution principles,
reaches the climax of absurdity. We who pretend
to determine what has been and what shall be, are
ourselves momentary manifestations shaped in that
swift-moving current whose ceaseless mutations form
the essence of the thinker and of his thought. Mr.
Spencer's philosophy overturns all law and destroys
all certainty: it dissolves in universal scepticism.

A survey of the possibilities of physical science
and of the limits of natural law, brings us back
to the point from which we set out, strengthening
the position that the complete unification of knowledge is impossible. An all-embracing philosophy,

based on experiential knowledge, falls to pieces. It will not stand the test of critical examination. If unity of thought be attainable, it must be sought elsewhere. This mistrust of intelligence, passing beyond its bounds, has characterised all the most illustrious of those who have spoken as prophets of the spiritual. They have, with Job, heard a voice from the whirlwind, challenging man's ability to reach a complete knowledge even of that which lies close around him.* Like Solomon, they are persuaded that "A man cannot find out the work that is done under the sun: because though a man labour to seek it out, yet he shall not find it; yea farther, though a wise man think to know it, yet shall he not be able to find it."† They willingly accept with Paul the limits of intelligence, "we know in part."‡ With the last of the great succession, they let fall on the intellectual impotence of man an immortal hope in God: "It doth not yet appear what we shall be, but we know that when He shall appear we shall be like Him, for we shall see Him as He is." ¶

---

* *Job*, Chap. XXXVIII.   † *Ecclesiastes*, Chap. VIII, 17.
‡ *1 Corinthians*, Chap. XIII. 9.   ¶ *1 John*, Chap. III. 2.

CHAPTER V.

A PHILOSOPHY undertaking to deal with all possible knowledge must determine the relation of thought to that which lies beyond experience: it must take account of the absolute. Experience has a beginning and bounds: it is conditioned. Is knowledge of that by which it is conditioned possible? We cannot estimate justly the Evolution Hypothesis, as formulated by Mr. Spencer, without first ascertaining, and carrying with us in our examination, his doctrine on this point. His theory of the Unknowable is a characteristic feature of his philosophy, and affects it in every part.

Can we have a real knowledge of that which transcends experience? The two great schools of thinkers —those who derive all knowledge from sensation, and those who hold the human intelligence to be itself a source of knowledge—are fundamentally opposed in their answers. The sensationalist cannot accept as valid any conception not ultimately resolvable into what he holds to be the primal constituent of all thought — sensation. The absolute cannot be so reached. It is, therefore, rejected as a pseud-idea,

D

and all knowledge limited to the phenomenal. The *a priori* school is not at one on the question. For the purpose in hand we may note three main divisions of opinion. (*a*) It is maintained that knowledge of the Unconditioned is possible: that the absolute may be positively construed to the mind. (*b*) All positive knowledge of the absolute is denied; the concept of the unconditioned is held to be a pure negation; but while the absolute is removed from the domain of knowledge, its certainty is regained through an act of faith. (*c*) The assumption that all knowledge is of the relative is rejected, and it is contended that knowledge of the infinite is attainable, that it may be thought under the form of a concept, which, though inadequate, is positive.

Mr. Spencer's position is distinct from all three. As in his account of intuitive or innate principles, he attempts to combine the *a priori* and experiential theories by his doctrine of the creation of forms of thought through the hereditary organization of experiences; so in this instance he introduces elements from both sides. He grounds his system on the relativity of all knowledge, but, at the same time, holds that we have a positive, though indefinite, consciousness of the absolute.

In discussing the question of the Unknowable, Mr. Spencer examines at great length the various modes under which the unconditioned has been supposed to be thought, and aims at showing that they are each impossible, as transcending the necessary limits of intelligence. Availing himself of the argument of Sir William Hamilton in his "Philosophy of the Unconditioned," he proceeds to show that no definite conception of the infinite is possible, that every attempt to think it lands us in contradictions. He supports his position by quoting the most telling parts of Mansel's "Limits of Religious Thought;" and by a criticism of the process and the product of thought, he endeavours to establish the principle that no concept of the absolute can be formed; all knowledge is, therefore, relative.

"Ultimate scientific ideas, then, are all representative of realities that cannot be comprehended. After no matter how great a progress in the colligation of facts, in the establishment of generalizations ever wider and wider—after the merging of limited and derivative truths in truths that are larger and deeper has been carried no matter how far; the fundamental truth remains as much beyond reach as ever. . . . . In all directions the investigations of the man of science eventually bring him face to face with an insoluble enigma; and he ever more clearly perceives it to be an insoluble enigma. He learns at once the greatness and the littleness of the human intellect —its power in dealing with all that comes within the range of experience; its impotence in dealing with all that transcends experience. He realizes with a special vividness the utter incomprehensibleness of the simplest fact considered in itself.   He, more than any other, truly *knows* that in its ultimate essence nothing can be known." *

But while Mr. Spencer goes fully with Sir William Hamilton in denying any definite conception of the absolute, and upholding the doctrine of the relativity of knowledge, he rejects the position that there is no positive content in our consciousness of the unconditioned.   He falls back on the fact that, notwithstanding the confutation of every definite concept which may be formed of it, the absolute still persists in consciousness ; and that it survives as a positive consciousness, and not merely as a negation of the conditioned.   Hence he concludes that " besides that *definite* consciousness of which logic formulates the laws, there is also an *indefinite* consciousness which cannot be formulated."†
" To say that we cannot know the Absolute is, by implication, to affirm that there *is* an Absolute.   In the very denial of our power to learn *what* the Absolute is, there lies hidden the assumption *that* it is ; and the making of this assumption proves that the Absolute has been present to the mind, not as a nothing but as a something.   The Noumenon, everywhere named as the antithesis of the Phenomenon, is throughout necessarily thought of as an actuality.   It is rigorously impossible to conceive that our knowledge is a knowledge of Appearances only, without at the same

---

* *First Principles,* § 21.   † *First Principles,* § 26.

time conceiving a Reality of which they are appearances. . . . Clearly, then, the very demonstration that
a *definite* consciousness of the Absolute is impossible to
us pre-supposes an *indefinite* consciousness of it. . . .
Impossible though it is to give this consciousness any
qualitative or quantitative expression whatever, it is
not the less certain that it remains with us as a
positive and indestructible element of thought. . . . .
It is impossible to get rid of the consciousness of an
actuality lying behind appearances."*

There is here a clear and important advance on the
teaching of the school of Comte. Mr. Spencer carries
us from phenomenon to noumenon. To admit the
existence of a consciousness of the absolute is fatal to
the positivist doctrine. The leading disciples of Comte
are, consequently, very wroth with Mr. Spencer for
giving so firm a foothold to those who believe in the
supernatural. Mr. Spencer has done good service in
emphasizing this element of consciousness and illus-
trating its existence as a fundamental fact. He has
at the same time put into the hands of his critics a
very effective instrument in the examination of his
own system. The co-existence with the knowable,
both in thought and in reality, of an Infinite Power
remaining for ever inscrutable renders, as we shall see,
every interpretation of observed facts doubtful outside the bounds of the facts observed: it eviscerates

---

* *First Principles*, § 26.

generalizations of all content as forming part of a doctrine of universal truth; it consequently reduces to a mere unprovable guess the Evolution Hypothesis.

Let us, with a view to the criticism of the evolution doctrine as Mr. Spencer expounds it, inquire what is, on his theory, the relation subsisting between that of which we are vaguely conscious, that is, the unknowable, and that of which we are definitely conscious, that is, the knowable.

The unknowable is not wholly unknown. Mr. Spencer predicates of it, in the most assured and positive manner, in several modes.

(1.) He affirms the consciousness of the unknowable to be an essential part of the exercise of thought. "By the necessary conditions of thought we are obliged to form a positive, though vague consciousness of this which transcends distinct consciousness."* The consciousness of the absolute lies, then, in every act of knowledge, as an essential part of it, determined by "the necessary conditions of thought." The mind carries with it always and everywhere as essential to its operations, a positive, though undefined, consciousness of the absolute.

(2.) By the use of a great variety of phrases, Mr. Spencer affirms the objective reality of that which is thus present to consciousness. He speaks of it as present to the mind "not as nothing but as a some-

---

First Principles, Part I., § 26.

thing." He describes it as "an actuality," "a reality," "the real existence," "reality which is behind the veil of appearance," "the ultimate existence." It is power, energy, force; "the absolute power," "the absolute force."

It is the "source of power," "the absolute cause," "the first cause," "the power which works in us certain effects," "that through which all things exist," "an absolute reality by which the relative reality is immediately produced," "the energy from which all things proceed;" "an infinite and eternal energy by which all things are created and sustained."*

(3.) The unknowable stands related to the cosmos as noumenon to phenomenon, power and the manifestation of power, cause and effect, reality and appearance. The cosmos, on the other hand, is "the totality of the manifestations of the unknowable," and spirit and matter are represented as "signs of the unknown reality which underlies both."

(4.) This absolute reality lies for ever beyond the reach of human thought. It is the "unknown reality,' "the unknown cause," "the inscrutable power," "the unknowable," "utterly inscrutable," "absolutely incomprehensible," "for ever inconceivable."

We have, in these affirmations, a very considerable amount of knowledge. It is evident that in the unknowable we are dealing with the largest part of the

* Mr. Spencer in 19*th Century*, No. 93, Nov. 1884, and *First Principles, passim.*

raw material given in consciousness. The circle of definite knowledge may extend ever more widely; yet still the wider circle of real, though incomprehensible, existence, is seen to enclose it.

But there underlies the entire doctrine of Mr. Spencer, a postulate into the validity of which we must inquire at some length. He assumes that the absolute, while co-existing with the conditioned in every experience, everywhere and at every moment, stands so related to the knowable that it adds nothing to it, nor takes aught from it, nor in any particular modifies the series of manifestations. The totality of matter remains fixed; the totality of motion is unchanged; the law of the redistribution of matter and motion proceeds uninterruptedly; the unsearchable actuality has not revealed itself throughout the entire course of mutation in any mode not implicily included in its primal manifestation. This postulate is so 'vitally important to the Evolution Hypothesis that we shall devote a separate chapter to a consideration of the relation of the Unknowable to the Knowable.

CHAPTER VI.

THE RELATION OF THE UNKNOWABLE TO
THE KNOWABLE.

WHAT we know is, on Mr. Spencer's theory, bound in an essential union, both in thought and reality, with that which transcends knowledge. The union is such that to take away the unknowable is to remove the knowable also. The unknowable is as necessary to thought as the knowable. "The connection, between the two being absolutely persistent in our consciousness, is real in the same sense as the terms it unites are real."* They co-exist in thought and co-exist in reality. In every affirmation as to the knowable there lies the implication that it stands in a real relation to the unknowable. In every affirmation as to the persistence of the knowable there is involved the implication that it persists as related to the unknowable; in other words, that its relation to the unknowable remains unaltered. The persistence of the absolute in sameness of relation to the conditioned is assumed. This regulative principle must, on Mr. Spencer's hypothesis, be taken for granted at every

---

* First Principles, § 46.

step in scientific inquiry. Wherever the mind turns in the investigation of cosmic phenomena, it is face to face with the absolute as, not only a part of the reality, but the reality itself. If, then, the inductions of science are to hold good beyond the immediate limits of observation, it must be constantly assumed that the absolute is fixed in a permanent and unchanging relation to the known. We have here a principle all-embracing in its application—a law for all time, reaching to the bounds of concrete existence, and penetrating to the unsearchable depths of actuality. Its validity is vital to all scientific generalizations, and, above all, is essential to the evolution doctrine, as claiming to interpret the entire compass of that which is, or may be, known.

At the risk of seeming tedious, we must examine this principle still more closely.

The underlying Unknowable Power stands related, according to Mr. Spencer's teaching, to the knowable as reality to appearance; it is the cause of the universe, that by which the knowable is "immediately produced."* At every instant in time and at every point in immensity this inscrutable Energy is present, forming a part of the object of thought, itself the real thing. The universe is the "conditioned effect of the absolute reality" and stands in "indissoluble relation with its Unconditioned Cause."†

---

* *First Principles*, § 50.   † *Ibid.*, § 46.

If then, discarding the idea of a Supreme Intelligence, we are to have a knowledge of the universe that shall be aught more than the cognition of individual instances, if we proceed from particular propositions to general truths, we need to be assured that the known is not at any point altered in its relations to the unknowable. If it shall be warrantable for us to group phenomena, to ascertain their law, to carry forward our generalizations beyond immediate observation; much more if we shall aspire to a complete unification of knowledge, we must have granted to us the postulate, that over the whole field traversed by thought the relation of the conditioned and unconditioned has remained fixed. We must assume that the underlying actuality is established in an unchanging relation to its phenomena, the absolute cause to manifested effects. If the inscrutable cause has not always revealed itself in the same manner; if the manifestations of the absolute power have been increased or diminished in amount, or modified in mode, at any point in the series of change, the Evolution Hypothesis is false.

But how may this uniformity of relation be established? Not by observation; for observation has not surveyed the whole extent of phenomena, or traversed the entire succession of the manifiestations of the infinite: not by knowledge of the absolute power; for that is, by hypothesis, for ever inscrutable. But there are open to us only these two methods of deter-

mining the relations of the known and the unknowable. We must either claim a complete knowledge of
all the manifestations of the absolute; in which case
we shall be able to affirm from observation that these
have not been either modified in kind or altered in
amount; or we must assume an exact knowledge of
the law of the manifestation of the incomprehensible
actuality—that is, we must . know the unknowable.
Either supposition is on the face of it absurd.

The absurdity of a postulate which affirms the persistence of the knowable as an unmodified revelation
of the unknowable, will be still more apparent, if we
fix our thought on the cosmos as effect and the
absolute as cause.

The absolute reality is the First Cause, the cosmos
is its effect. Now the inscrutable power manifested
in the cosmos is either exactly equal to the effect, so
that the whole cause passes into the effect, or it is
greater. Assuming the cause and effect to be equal
the effect is the measure of the cause, the cause is
fully manifested in the effect. To know the effect,
then, is to know the cause: if the effect, being exactly
equal to the cause, is completely known, the cause is
completely known ; there is nothing left to know.
Now the cosmos is known or knowable, and being
equal to its cause, the cause is alike known or knowable. But this Mr. Spencer denies; for he affirms
the first cause to be "utterly inscrutable," "absolutely
incomprehensible." We must conclude, then, that the

absolute cause is not measured by its cosmic effects. It is, therefore, greater than the cosmos.

Let us assume it to be greater. A cause can only exist as cause in relation to effects. Either, then, there are effects of the unknowable power which do not come within the domain of possible knowledge, or the causal energy of the first cause did not exhaust itself in the effects produced by it as first cause, and this portion of its causal energy remains. Take either supposition. If there are effects of the first cause which are not revealed in the universe we know, a relation subsists .between the knowable cosmos and other manifestations of the absolute lying outside it; in which case another disturbing element impinges upon the field of experience. In the new conditions, the law of the cosmos has to be determined over against a second unknowable, and scientific hypotheses reaching beyond observation are rendered doubly doubtful.

Let the other side of the alternative be taken; let it be supposed that the unexhausted energy of the first cause has not gone forth in effects beyond the knowable universe. On this supposition a new element of incertitude emerges. The causal energy of the absolute cause has not been at any moment fully manifested; there is something still in reserve at every point in cosmic history. There can be no certainty, then, that the inscrutable energy has not at various points in time, or continuously along the

whole stream of change, manifested itself in modes
not antecedently existent, in their entirety, within
precedent cosmic phenomena. It is, indeed, more
than possible, it is probable, that a cause which did
not in its primal passing into effect exhaust its causal
efficiency may have, in the processes of change
throughout the unimaginable cycles of time, revealed
itself in ways not implicitly included in antecedent
manifestations. But, however this may be, to affirm
positively, on the other side, that the absolute cause,
though its causal energy was not exhausted, did not
operate as cause in any new mode along the entire
course of cosmic history, and shall not in the future,
is either to assume definite knowledge of the incomprehensible, or to assert that experience yields a complete knowledge of past and future events.

That this criticism is not strained is evident, if it be
borne in mind that Mr. Spencer asserts the continuity
of the absolute reality with its phenomenal manifestation at all times everywhere. When we think of
the absolute cause, we are apt to think of it as that
to which the first link in the chain of causation is
attached ; we conceive of it as lying behind the stream
of causation at that point where its effects first rise
into view. When so conceived, the first cause can
be easily thought of as ceasing to act when secondary
causes come into operation, and as being thus excluded
from any real causal efficiency onward throughout all
succeeding phases of change. But the absolute cause

is not, on Mr. Spencer's theory, the initial link in a chain of successive causes and effects. It is the inscrutable power, the actuality revealed in that which is seen. At each instant of time it is the present reality, the something ever in process of manifestation, the underlying energy of which what we know is the effect.

To quantify these manifestations, and lay it down as an axiom that their sum total has never been greater or less,—a supposition necessary to the Evolution Hypothesis,—to fix the law of the production of its effects by the absolute power; to take it as a fundamental principle on which to found a system of philosophy that the mode of manifestation has been and shall be for ever the same; in other words, to determine the law of the unconditioned, and to regard it as necessarily operating thus and not otherwise, is most evidently to transcend the capabilities of intelligence : since on the one hand the conditions of thought are taken to necessitate the acceptance of the ultimate cause as wholly and for ever incomprehensible; and on the other, the totality of phenomenal effects cannot be brought within the field of experience, whether in co-existence or in succession.

Yet this postulate is vital to Mr. Spencer's philosophy. For if it be so that in the course of change, from the first moment at which the knowable passes into the view of thought onward, there has been any modification of the relation subsisting between the

unknowable power and the knowable in which it is
revealed ; if any new force has emerged out of, or any
manifestation of force has sunk again into, the inscrutable ; if there has arisen any new mode of
activity which did not exist implicitly in the primal
totality of the conditioned ; if any form of being or
forth-going of energy has welled up out of the depths
of the incomprehensible, the system which Mr. Spencer
has constructed with so much learning and labour is
disintegrated and dissolved—his evolution has ended in
dissolution ; for it is essential to his philosophy that
the relation between the unknowable actuality and
knowable appearance remain for ever fixed and constant—that the same quantity of the absolute energy
be emergent from age to age, ever equal in its sum,
neither less nor more. Doubt of this postulate is
doubt of the Evolution Philosophy; to doubt a
critical examination leads us, and through doubt to
denial.

CHAPTER VII.

THE EVOLUTION HYPOTHESIS A DYNAMIC THEORY.

"A PHILOSOPHY rightly so called" can, on Mr. Spencer's theory, only come into existence by finding a principle, operative throughout the whole range of the knowable, to which every line of research ultimately leads and from which the entire course of change may, with adequate enlargement of knowledge, be deductively demonstrated. "A philosophy stands self-convicted of inadequacy, if it does not formulate the whole series of changes passed through by every existence in its passage from the imperceptible to the perceptible and again from the perceptible to the imperceptible. If it begins its explanations with existences that already have concrete forms, or leaves off while they still retain concrete forms; then, manifestly, they had preceeding histories, or will have succeeding histories, or both, of which no account is given. . . . . The formula sought, equally applicable to existences taken singly in and their totality, must be applicable to the whole histories of each and to the whole history of all." * It is clear that unless

---

* *First Principles,* § 186.

such a formula be discoverable evolution cannot be raised to the dignity of an all-embracing hypothesis, or successfully maintained as a sufficient explanation of any individual thing. It has, in that case, no claim to rank as a cosmic philosophy.

A unifying principle is indispensable, if evolution is to be accepted as a rational theory. Under that principle every knowable law must be subsumed. There may not be any law discoverable in any department of thought that cannot be brought under it, as the lower under the higher generalization.

The weight of Socrates was determined by the dynamic law of gravity, and when his disciples covered his face after death his body was still subject to that law; but governing his action while alive were other laws—laws of the true Socrates. If among these there were any—the laws of thought and conscience, for example—not reducible to unity with the physical universe, it would be but trifling with the question to affirm that knowledge is unified, simply because the body of Socrates is known to have been included under physical law while the real Socrates, who passed out of reach of his disciples, is left out of account. The principle that is to unify all knowledge must account for all the known phases. of all known phenomena, and especially those characteristics by which they are differenced. It is not enough that it should deal with a part of concrete being, it must deal with all concrete being: it must face the task of accounting for all we know or can know.

Mr. Spencer thinks he has discovered the key which unlocks all knowable secrets—the law which brings together in one all possible knowledge—the principle whose sovereignty is wide as the bounds of being. It is a "dynamic principle."

"The law we seek must be," he says, "the law of the continuous redistribution of matter and motion. Absolute rest and permanence do not exist. Every object, no less than the aggregate of all objects, undergoes from instant to instant some alteration of state. Gradually or quickly it is receiving or losing motion, while some or all of its parts are simultaneously changing their relation to one another. And the question to be answered is—What dynamic principle true of the metamorphosis as a whole and in its details expresses these ever-changing relations. . . . A philosophy rightly so-called can come into existence only by solving the problem." *

The universality of this principle is stated more fully in another passage:—

"Setting out from an established ultimate principle, it has been shown that the cause of transformation among all kinds of existences cannot but be that which we have seen it to be. It has been shown that the redistribution of matter and motion must everywhere

---

* *First Principles*, § 92.

take place in those ways, and produce those traits
which celestial bodies, organisms, societies, alike display.   And it has been shown that this universality of
process, results from the same necessity which determines each simplest movement around us, down to
the accelerated fall of a stone, or the recurrent beat
of a harp-string.   In other words, the phenomena of
evolution have to be deduced from the Persistence of
Force.   As before, said—'to this an ultimate analysis
brings us down ; and on this a rational synthesis must
build up.'   This being the ultimate truth which
transcends experience by underlying it, so furnishing
a common basis on which the widest generalizations
stand, these widest generalizations are to be unified by
referring them to this common basis."*   " The detailed
phenomena of life and mind and society are to be
interpreted in terms of matter, motion, and force."†

As Mr. Spencer states the problem, in the solution
of which alone philosophy comes into existence, he
states it as a problem in dynamics.   The principle
which is to express the ever-changing relations of
concrete existences is " a dynamic principle "—the law
" must be the law of the continuous redistribution of
matter and motion."   It is indisputable that in choosing a dynamic principle he has, as an evolutionist,
chosen wisely.   Indeed it is with him a case of
Hobson's choice: no other principle is available.

---

* *First Principles,* § 147.   † *Ibid.* § 194.

Dynamic laws exist as an important part of experience. The evolution theory cannot furnish any higher principle under which these might be included. Either dynamic law is supreme, or it constitutes a separate kingdom: it must be enthroned as supreme, if knowledge be unified; for a separate kingdom is not admissible. Every fact capable of explanation, every thing that comes within the field of knowledge, is to be brought under " the law of the continuous redistribution of matter and motion." This law is made to account for the present form and order of the heavens and the earth ; the whole universe of inanimate matter is interpreted by its aid. Subtile molecular motions in complex systems, too minute to be discoverable by the most powerful microscope, emerge into the field of knowledge in the shape of living organisms, vegetal and animal. Like subtile combinations of moving molecules, built up into systems of inconceivable complexity, and with adjustments, the nice precision of which cannot be realized by the keenest scientific imagination, create those higher organisms, having their consummation and crown in man. His mental nature is not excepted from the all-pervading and all-govering dynamic principle. Thought and emotion, conscience and will take their place in the continuity of the correlation of physical forces. The rhythmic thrill of the atom, combined and recombined in relations whose complexity exceed immeasurably the utmost power of thought, is the ultimate conceivable

beginning of all concrete forms. The law of the
knowable universe is the law of the atoms and their
vibrations. They are aggregated into masses; their
movements are gathered together into the vast sweep
of celestial motions; their pulsations are the outer face
of the thrill of pleasure and the throb of pain; their
waves of molecular action, passing through the nerve
centres, are the shocks which, repeatedly recurring,
combined and recombined, call into being and mould
the self-knowing intelligence and world-embracing
thoughts of man. Such is the evolutionist theory
of concrete existence. Dynamic law rules. The oscil-
lating atom—matter and motion—the law of their
continuous redistribution — all knowable concrete
being is there. If there be any mode of existence
or of activity not included, of it we can have no definite knowledge: it is for ever hidden from man.
Evolution covers the knowable; and evolution is " an
integration of matter and concomitant dissipation of
motion."

This theory we are not allowed to speak of as
materialistic: Mr. Spencer repudiates the charge of
materialism. No one can have any desire to affix the
offensive word to his name or doctrine. He is on the
point an agnostic. He cannot tell what may be the
nature of the Ultimate Power, whether matter or
spirit, or both, or neither. He refuses to predicate of
it in any definite mode. But we are not in the least
concerned about the ultimate reality, whether it is

matter or something other than matter, if it is to remain for ever absolutely unknown. We want to
know what we are to think about that actuality as
conditioned in the knowable universe—as we see it
manifested within the compass of experience. In the
region of the visible, within the view of science, the
evolutionist doctrine is clear and unmistakable. Over
the whole field of scientific knowledge, over the whole
range traversed by intelligence, there is no law known,
or that can be known, that is not included under the
one regulative principle—that of the redistribution of
matter and motion; and there is no power operative
within the cosmos, as open to the view of science, that
does not operate in accordance with that supreme law.
The law of the continuous redistribution of matter and
motion rules all change : wherever the eye pierces, it is
there; wherever science illumines the depths of existence with the collected rays of organized knowledge, it
is there; thought can never pass beyond its domain or
escape from its grasp; it commands all the knowable.
Dynamic law is the one universal. Evolutionism is a
thorough-going dynamic theory.

Let us look at the breadth of the application of this
dynamic principle. We have already, in outline,
sketched the realm of knowledge as embracing the
Supreme Source of all things; and as including four
great streams flowing from that Source—the knowledge of the world of inorganic matter, the knowledge
of organisms endowed with vegetal life, of organisms

endowed with life and sensation, and of man possessed of self-conscious intelligence and a moral nature. The knowledge of God stands apart: it is the answer of mind to the Supreme Mind as His thought touches ours in the intelligible in the universe, or speaks to us in immediate revelation. The other departments of knowledge are at once combined and separate—combined in the operation of certain laws common to the whole; and separate in having each a system of laws peculiar to itself alone. The laws that run throughout the whole field are the mechanical laws of inorganic matter. Wherever we are able to subject matter to the scrutiny of science, we discover similar modes of action. The same kind of matter is the same in behaviour everywhere; our language implies this fact when we speak of it as of the same kind. If matter is ponderable, it will be found so whether in Saturn or in the brain.

Dynamic law is universal so far as the universe of material forces reaches. In so far as matter, however widely separated by distance in space, is the same kind of matter, its behaviour will be the same; it will be found subject to the same dynamic law. That matter should be continuous—that is, that matter should in all its visible forms, and in its modes that lie deeper than observations can reach, be essentially one in kind, and that it should pervade all cosmic space—though wholly unprovable—seems a probable hypothesis. Over all that reach its law will be the same ; for its mode of action, unless some Power intervene, will be uniform. In so far as the acceptance of dynamic law in its applicability wherever moving matter exists may be regarded as a unification of knowledge, no one will think it worth disputing that there has been a step—though a very short step, in the direction of unity. We are still, however, a long way from the great central questions. We have not so much as touched the extreme verge of the real problems of philosophy. If "divine philosophy" be narrowed to questions of dynamics—to the mechanical relations of matter, in whatever form matter is found— however subtile these relations may be, the greater part of knowledge is left out of view; knowledge is unified by being mutilated. A neighbour of mine has, by working out his idea year after year, succeeded in evolving out of a growing thorn-bush a figure having some resemblance to a peacock. The ingenuity and labour of the artist have been considerable, yet the result is a very ill-shaped thorn-bush, and a very poor representation of a peacock. The greatest skill and the most persistent toil expended in endeavouring to mould all kinds of knowledge into the hard outline of dynamic law is not likely to reach a more satisfactory issue.

For the distinctive features of each department are sacrificed to a pretence of oneness. That which constitutes the vegetal kingdom a distinct division of concrete existence is overlooked. The force that counteracts the law of gravity, and builds up the complex structure of the plant is not accounted for. Why the vegetal kingdom is what it is, as differenced from all other known things, is just what the dynamic principle fails to explain. It can tell us why the branches laden with fruit bend towards the ground, or why their curve is such as it is, and can tell us much more of substantially the same kind, gathered from mechanical or chemical science; but philosophy aims at interpreting that which is distinctive, and strives after a system of truth in which the separate departments of knowledge shall have each its due place.

Mr. Spencer applies his dynamic principle to the phenomena of animal life. Here also there is a large scope for the application of chemical and mechanical law. But the characteristic part of the phenomena— that which constitutes the animal organism a distinctive class of concrete existence—is the very thing the dynamic principle will not cover. Yet everything in the instance that will not come under the law of the redistribution of matter and motion is to be removed from the field of knowledge and relegated to the region of the unknowable.

The thinker is himself the great exception. To reduce himself in his self-knowledge, in his intellection, in his moral being, to an instance of dynamic law— to constitute himself a part of the redistribution of matter and motion—is the crucial test of the thoroughness with which the evolutionist carries out his theory.

Mr. Spencer does not shrink from this test. He not only asserts in general terms the universal applicability of his principle, but applies it in detail, with what success we shall subsequently inquire, to the phenomena of mind, and morals, and society. What we have here to keep steadily in view is the fact that Mr. Spencer's philosophy is a system dynamic throughout. It is thorough-going. He never falters in adhesion to his fundamental principle.

He takes exception to the term "mechanical" as applied to his hypothesis, though he himself characterises his biological doctrine as "the mechanical hypothesis" and speaks of proceeding "on mechanical principles." * "The common uses of the words 'mechanical' and 'mechanist' are," he says, "such as inevitably call up in all minds the notion of visible masses of matter acting on one another by measurable forces, and producing sensible motions. In the absence of explanations or illustrations serving to enlarge the conception thus suggested, so as to bring within it the oscillations of the molecules of matter and the undulations of the molecules of ether pervading all space, even the cultivated reader must carry with him an extremely crude and narrow idea of the 'mechanist theory,' and cannot fail to be struck with the seeming absurdity of interpreting vital phenomena in mechanical terms." †

* *Biology*, vol. I., § 5.
† *Biology*, vol. I. Appendix p. 490.

Now, however recondite what Mr. Spencer describes as the "developed ideas of matter and motion"
may be, it is matter and motion with which we are
still dealing, and nothing but matter and motion. The
play of atoms internal to the most minute molecule,
is as truly an instance of matter and motion as the
revolution of the earth round the sun. Differences in
size do not constitute differences of kind. "The play
of forces is essentially the same in principle throughout the whole region explored by our intelligence"; *
whether it be the movement of masses or "the oscillations of the molecules of either" the principle is the
same; and it matters little whether we call the
doctrine "dynamic" or "mechanical." Let the evolutionist extend as widely as he will the conception of
dynamic law, by imagining a series of systems reaching
towards infinity in their minuteness, subtilty, and
complexity; let him give freest play in the invention
of composition of causes adequate to the production of
any conceivable result; yet, however far the fancy
travels from the visible, however marvellous that
other world revealed in its worders to the scientific
imagination, the materials of which it is built up are
still the same—force manifested in the atom and its
vibrations, matter and motion, and the law of their
continuous redistribution shaping and ruling all

---

† *First Principles*, § 91.

things. Within the knowable evolution finds no other exercise of real power.

Are we again among the keen-eyed thinkers of ancient Greece? Are we sitting at the feet of Democritus or Epicurus, or listening to their teaching set in the vigorous verse of Lucretius? We see, as we have seen with their eyes, the fathomless immensity filled far as imagination reaches with the whirling atoms; we see matter and motion and ceaseless physical change occupying the whole field of vision. In the depths of this ocean-stream we seem to live, and move, and have our being. Above us, around us, within us, one supreme, all-ruling, and all prevading law — the dynamic principle of the continuous redistribution of matter and motion.

Into this abyss Evolutionism carries its disciples.

CHAPTER VIII.

THE PERSISTENCE OF FORCE

"THE sole truth which transcends experience by underlying it is the persistence of Force. This being the basis of experience, must be the basis of any scientific organization of experiences. To this an ultimate analysis brings us down ; and on this a rational synthesis must build up."* This "alone makes possible each concrete interpretation and at last unifies all concrete interpretations."† It is "the deepest of all truths."‡ It is "that primordial truth which underlies our intelligence,"|| "the truth by derivation from which all other truths are to be proved."§

The persistence of force is Mr. Spencer's ultimate principle. It is the measure of his system. His philosophy covers only what the persistence of force covers. If the persistence of force be too narrow include all knowledge, the evolution doctrine canno include all knowledge. If there be any truth, not

---

* *First Principles*, § 62.   † *Ibid.* § 191.   ‡ *Ibid.* § 162.
|| *Ibid.* § 155.   § *Ibid.* § 185.

derivable from the persistence of force, evolutionism falls short of its pretension as a philosophy embracing all truth. If, in the course of change in organisms or in the universe, there is aught that is not deducible from the persistence of force, the Evolution Hypothesis fails as a rational doctrine : science is left to describe, without explaining, phenomenal processes that are still unaccounted for. It is vital to Mr. Spencer's theory that the persistence of force should be accepted as a principle co-extensive with the field of knowledge; for it is the foundation on which the new cosmic philosophy is built. We must subject it to the closest examination.

Mr. Spencer claims for it the authority of an ultimate datum of consciousness. "If it can be shown," he says, "that the persistence of force is not a datum of consciousness, ... then indeed it will be shown that the theory of evolution has not the high warrant here claimed for it."* Let us test this claim.

It is at once granted that the cognition of force is a primary datum of consciousness. In every experience of material objects there lies the cognition of force. We know force in matter as resisting; we have a sense of active force in the effects produced on the organism and felt as sensations; we have also experience of force in the exertion of bodily strength in response to volition. The experience of something

* *First Principles,* § 192.

resisting, affecting, operating, is co-extensive with our
knowledge of the external world. That something
we know as independent of our consciousness of it.
Its existence is not commensurate with our cognition :
our thinking does not create it, nor does the cessation
of our thought annihilate it. It exists at the instant
when we cognize it; it remains in existence at the
moment when our cognition of it ceases. This is the
whole content of consciousness so far as it bears
primary testimony to the existence of external things.
In subsequent acts of cognition we add to this experience : we are again conscious of the same object; we
re-cognize it as the same. Hence we form a secondary judgment as to its perpetuity. It has been: it
is. But consciousness has no knowledge—it can have
none—as to the antecedent existence of the object
before our cognition of it, or its continuance in the
future. It has been: it is. But if we ask, How long
has it been ? How long shall it continue to be ?'
Consciousness cannot answer, for it has no means of
knowing. Its primary deliverance is limited to an
affirmation of the existence of an external object, or if
the word be preferred, the existence of force, as something independent of the mental act,—not originated
by the act of perceiving, nor ceasing with the cessation of that act. Further than this consciousness
cannot go.

But Mr. Spencer argues that "the assertion of an
existence beyond consciousness is itself an assertion

that there is something beyond consciousness that persists; for persistence is nothing more than continued existence, and existence cannot be thought of as other than continued."* That is, if the reasoning be sound, all existence is eternal. To assert "an existence beyond consciousness" is to assert its persistence, that is, its "continued existence;" in other words, its existence without beginning or end; for "existence cannot be thought of" otherwise. This doctrine is so astounding, whether viewed in relation to the nature of things or to the knowledge of things, that one is curious to obtain some fuller explanation of the terms. Turning to Mr. Spencer's Psychology, we find a fuller statement. In examining Hume's theory of impressions and ideas, he says : "To *be* is 'to remain,' 'to be fixed.' *Existence* is defined as 'continued being,' 'duration,' 'continuation.' Persistence is the root-notion running through all the meanings. So long as a pain persists we say it *is* still there. . . The flash of lightning, not having persisted, is regarded as having ceased to be. . . . . Above all, it is this continuity, or endurance, or fixity, or persistence, which we specially mean when we assert the existence of what may be called objects; among which, too, we draw the distinction between existing or ceasing to exist according as we do or do not find persistence."*

Mr. Spencer does not gain anything by this iden-

---

* *First Principles*, § 65. •   † *Psych.* Vol. II. § 394.

F

tification of *being* and *persistence;* for in the very
language he uses he contradicts himself. The lightning
flash "*ceases to be;*" but it must have *been* before it
could *cease* to be. Was there no "continuity, or
endurance, or fixity, or persistence," during the time—
and it matters not whether that time was a fraction
of a second or a cycle of years—precedent to this
ceasing? Is it an illegitimate use of words to speak of
something as *existing* when we know that it will cease
to exist? How are we to express the mode of being
of all the ever-changing manifestations of the absolute
force? They are; they cease to be: in the very recognition of their ceasing to be there is an affirmation
that they have been. It would close a great number
of debated questions, if it were received as the law of
our intelligence and of being, that all existence of
which we have consciousness is continued existence
without origin or end. But we are not here concerned
with questions of ontology; our business, meanwhile,
is but to interrogate consciousness and to ascertain
what this—the only available witness—has to testify.
The deliverance of consciousness is, as we have seen,
simply attestation of the existence of something outside itself, not dependent on the percipient mind for
its beginning or its continuance. The lightning flash,
of which there has been momentary cognition, may,
for all consciousness can attest, have originated at that
instant and have at that instant ceased to be. Our
consciousness of it is the act of perception, and nothing

more. The comet that is visible for a few successive nights may have come into existence with its first and ceased with its last appearance, in so far as consciousness can bear witness. The period of duration of existence is a question of fact, and — especially on a purely experiential theory — there can be no immediate knowledge of fact beyond the present, or that knowledge which results from a past cognition and a present re-cognition of the same. Consciousness testifies that force exists here and now; the testimony goes no farther and can go no farther.

The absurdity of assuming to have on the side of the persistence of force, as Mr. Spencer uses the phrase, a primary deliverance of consciousness is still more evident when we discover what it is that consciousness is supposed to attest. "What," he asks, "is the force of which we predicate persistence? It is not the force we are immediately conscious of in our muscular efforts; for this does not persist. As soon as an outstretched limb is relaxed the sense of tension disappears. True, we assert that in the stone thrown, or the weight lifted, is exhibited the effect of this muscular tension; and that the force which has ceased to be present in consciousness, exists elsewhere. But it does not exist elsewhere under any form cognizable by us."

Where then, we may ask, is the testimony of consciousness to its persistence? It has ceased to be "present in consciousness" and is no longer cognizable.

" Hence," Mr. Spencer adds, " the force of which we
assert persistence is the *absolute force of which we are
indefinitely conscious* as the necessary correlate of the
force we know." *   " The one thing permanent is the
Unknowable reality hidden under all these changing
shapes." †

This is a curious specimen of metaphysical theoriz-
ing. " The force we know " is the very thing—the
only thing about which we are concerned ; with it
science has to do, and with it alone. Does that known
force persist ?   No ; that of which we have definite
consciousness—that which furnishes the whole matter
of science—that does not persist.   We are not permitted to assert persistence of any existence in the
realm of knowledge, of any concrete thing with which
science is conversant.   The persistent force is the
absolute force ; but of it we are only " indefinitely
conscious."   What we know does not persist ; what
persists we can never know.   This is Mr. Spencer's
fundamental principle ; a doubtful foundation, surely,
on which to erect a temple of universal truth.

To bring his first principle within the primary data
of consciousness, Mr. Spencer falls back upon an impotence of thought.   He argues the validity of his axiom
from our inability to think matter either as coming
into being or as ceasing to exist.   " It is impossible,"
he says, " to think of something becoming nothing,

---

* *First principles,* § 62.   † *Psychology,* Vol. II., § 475.

for the same reason that it is impossible to think of
nothing becoming something — the reason, namely,
that nothing cannot become an object of consciousness." * The possibility of thinking the creation of
something out of nothing will come up for discussion
subsequently. It may be easily shown that pictur-
ability is not the measure of legitimate thought. But
suppose we grant that it is impossible to think of something becoming nothing, and suppose we are driven
to accept the persistence of force, because we cannot
represent to the mind any force ceasing to be, evolutionism has gained no solid advantage. If our inability to think force as becoming non-existent is
"immediately consequent on the nature of thought;"
if, therefore, it is through this mental impotence that
we are compelled to accept the principle of the persistence of force, the foundation of the evolution
doctrine as a system of positive truth is taken away.
For our inability to think cannot form the basis of
real knowledge. A system of positive philosophy
cannot be established on the warrant of an impotence
of intelligence. If Mr. Spencer were engaged only
with the coherence and conclusiveness of abstract
reasoning; if his system were a system of thought
and not of things; if his aim were to show us what
concepts are permissible to human intelligence and
what are not; if he were constructing an ideal

* *First Principles,* § 53.

universe instead of interpreting the universe that is, it would form an important part of his task to take account of the impotence as well as the potences of thought; or if his aim were to remove from the cosmos constructed by science imaginative additions for which no counterpart could be found in the cosmos as actually existent, it might be competent for him to base his reasoning on what the mind cannot do, and require science to keep within the limits of intelligence. But he has undertaken to construct a system of positive truth; he is dealing with concrete existences; he is interpreting a universe not created by our thought, but having a real existence outside our consciousness; to rest the foundation principle of this Philosophy, which is to unify all knowledge, on what the mind is unable to do, is to base science on nescience —to unify knowledge by ignorance.

Mr. Spencer calls consciousness as a witness bearing primary testimony to the persistence of force. The reader may interrogate the witness for himself. What is that of which consciousness attests the existence in the cognition of an external object? Is it not the existence of an external something here and now? It is this and nothing more. The fundamental principle of evolutionism has not the warrant of a primary deliverance of consciousness.

SECTION II.
WHAT IS INCLUDED IN THE TERM FORCE?

That there is no warrant for the acceptance of the persistence of force as a regulative principle authoritative over the whole range traversed by human intelligence will the more evidently appear from an examination of its terms.

First, let us inquire, What is included in the term force? We are familiar with force in its material modes. We cognize it under the form of matter; we see it manifested in the movement of bodies; we have experience of it in affections of the organism; we know it in the effect produced in obedience to the will. These experiences furnish us with the concept of force. To these and the like instances the word is in its original and proper signification limited.* In a secondary or metaphorical sense, we apply the term to express experiences of a wholly different nature. We speak of intellectual force, of force of character, of moral force, of the force of public opinion, including in such usage a meaning altogether different from that conveyed when we speak of the force of a blow.

---

* Force is defined by Thomson and Tait as being "any cause which tends to alter a body's natural state of rest or of uniform motion in a straight line." *Elements of Natural Philosophy*, Part I., § 183.

"Force in point of fact is a direct object of sense; probably of all our senses, and certainly of the muscular sense." *Ibid.* § 173.

In an exact use of terms there must be a clear recognition of this distinction. There is no more
fruitful source of error in philosophizing than the
confounding of metaphor and fact. It is unworthy
of scientific thinking to group under one term, as the
same, things that are only metaphorically alike.

Does the persisting force include Spirit? There
is an underlying something manifested in conscious
thought, does the persistence of force guarantee the
persistence of that unknown existence? If force persists, then the force manifested in mind persists. But
it is hard to comprehend how, on evolution principles,
this can be; for there was a time when all manifested
force was included in matter and motion. Mind sub-
sequenty arose. The cosmos is represented at two
points in time by the following equation:

$$\text{Matter} + \text{motion} = \text{matter} + \text{motion} + \text{mind.}$$

Mind is either a mode of matter and motion or it is
not. If it be taken as a mode of matter and motion,
we are landed in materialism, which Mr. Spencer repudiates. If we choose the other alternative, we are
compelled to maintain that a new manifestation of
force, not included in the primal manifestations, has
emerged, in which case fixedness of the relation between the knowable and the unknowable is rejected.
But if one new manifestation has emerged, there is no
limit to the modification of the knowable, and the
whole fabric of evolution is overturned. Besides, the
persistence of force is itself proved to be false, for one

of the corollaries necessarily following from it is that the relations among forces persist; but the persistence of relations is impossible, if new manifestations of unknown forces may from time to time intervene.

When we ask, Does the force manifested in mind persist? we receive no satisfactory answer. We know that the force manifested in matter and that manifested in motion persist; for matter is held to be indestructible and motion continuous. The force manifested in mind—not being matter—cannot pass into the force manifested in matter and motion. It exists for ever distinct. But in what mode has it existed? Where during all the ages did it lie hidden? How did it stand related to the other forces of the cosmos? The evolutionist has no intelligible answer. The force has not persisted so far as intelligence can discover. Within the knowable, the persistence of force as a universal principle is at a fault. If Mr. Spencer save his axiom, by carrying it out of the realm of knowledge into the incomprehensible, we do not care to follow him.

> " Vivida vis animi pervicit, et extra
> Processit flammantia mœnia mundi."

Section III.

The Force Persisting the Absolute Force.

Mr. Spencer's doctrine as to the relation of the knowable to that which transcends knowledge leads

in the analysis of his ultimate principle to inextric-
able ambiguities. In conformity with his ontological
theory, he employs the word force to denote two
things which are profoundly different—force as it is
the object of consciousness and within the limits of
definite knowledge, and force as it lies beyond the
ken of knowledge and is for ever inscrutable. The
necessities of scientific reasoning demand the persistence of a force that is within the reach of knowledge;
the validity of the axiom as a universal and necessary truth requires that we should take, not the
knowable, but the absolute force as that of which
persistence is predicated. Hence an ambiguous use
of the term which runs through Mr. Spencer's entire
system. His ordinary usage is to employ the word
in the sense of force as manifested and knowable.
For example, in dealing with the correlation of forces,
he says, "a certain amount of each is the constant
equivalent of certain amounts of others. Everywhere
throughout the cosmos this truth must invariably
hold. . . . . We must recognize the amounts of these
forces as determinate—as necessarily producing such
and such quantities of results, and as necessarily
limited to those quantities. . . . . Forces, unceasingly
metamorphosed are nowhere increased or decreased." *

   Elsewhere he affirms that this truth of the correlation of forces "is a necessary corollary from the

* *First Principles,* §§ 66, 67.

persistence of force. Setting out with the proposition that force can neither come into existence nor
cease to exist," it necessarily follows.* This reasoning is totally void of meaning, unless on the assumption that the persisting force is force within the range
of possible science, force as knowable and measurable.
We cannot quantify the unlimited. In like manner, he
has in view force which may be measured, when he
argues that "every antecedent mode of the unknowable must have an invariable connection quantitative
and qualitative with that mode of the unknowable
which we call its consequent. For to say otherwise
is to deny the persistence of force." † His synthetic
philosophy is the application of this principle to concrete phenomena. His reasoning would be altogether
inconclusive, if the force persisting is to be assumed
unthinkable. His philosophy proceeds throughout on
the supposition that the persistence of force holds
good over the entire domain of knowledge. Reasoning from this assumption, as his fundamental principle, he proposes to demonstrate the law of evolution
deductively, and show it to be the necessary law of
cosmic change. His whole system is founded on
the persistence of manifested force, in sameness of
quantity from everlasting to everlasting—on the recognition of a persisting force "ever changing its
manifestations, but unchanged in quantity throughout

---

* *First Principles*, §73.   † *Ibid.* § 63.

all past time and all future time." *   His reasoning is
wholly delusive, unless it be held true that the force
of which he predicates persistence is force as manifested, that is, force existing within the knowable.

But does force, as existing within the knowable,
persist ?   The individual manifestations of force are
continually changing, no mode of manifestation continues constant.   What we see is not persistence, but
change.   Is it, then, that amount of the Absolute
Force which is manifested in the individual instance
that persists ?   To affirm so is to frame an impossible
proposition ; for the absolute is unthinkable and inscrutable, and we cannot cut out of it a portion,
which may be supposed to be continually changing
its mode of manifestation while still retaining its
identity.

The peristence of force as known or knowable is
not, as Mr. Spencer shows, provable by experience.
We cannot by any process of experiment arrive at
a knowledge of the fact, if it be a fact.   In every
experiment we must take for granted the very thing
which is to be proved.   If we measure, the persistence of our standard must be assumed; if we weigh,
the persistence of matter and of gravity must be
taken for granted.   No manifestation of force can be
isolated, so as to be made a separate and distinct
subject of observation and experiment.   To establish

* *First Principles,* § 191.

by any inductive or experimental process, the truth of the persistence of force, is clearly impossible: what we know by experience throughout all the knowable is not persistence, but mutability. No single manifestation of force abides. Mr. Spencer acknowledges that it is so. "We are compelled to admit that Force as it exists out of our consciousness is not force as we know it. Hence the force of which we assert persistence, is that Absolute Force of which we are indefinitely conscious as the necessary correlate of the force we know. By the persistence of Force, we really mean the persistence of some Cause, which transcends our knowledge and conception. In other words, asserting the persistence of Force is asserting an Unconditioned Reality without beginning or end." *

"Once more," he says elsewhere, "we are brought round to the conclusion, repeatedly reached by other routes, that behind all manifestations, inner and outer, there is a Power manifested. Here, as before, it has become clear that while the nature of this Power cannot be known—while we lack the faculty of framing even the dimmest conception of it, yet its universal presence is the absolute fact without which there can be no relative facts. Every feeling and thought being but transitory—an entire life made up of such feelings and thoughts being also but transitory — nay, the objects amid which life is passed, though less transi-

---

* *First Principles*, § 62.

tory, being severally in course of losing their indivi-
dualities, quickly or slowly; we learn that the one
thing permanent is the Unknowable Reality hidden
under all these changing shapes." *

Mutability is the law of the knowable; persistence
in the realm of the known is only persistence of
change. And so into that region of darkness, of
which we are indefinitely conscious, where there is
neither before nor after, neither antecedent nor consequent, neither greater nor less; where it is not
allowable for reason to predicate anything of anything, we are sent to search for the persisting force.
Mistrusting our vision in the dim realm of the
inscrutable, we take the equivalents which Mr.
Spencer furnishes, and we write his fundamental
axiom with equal exactness in any of the forms,—The
Unknowable Reality persists, or the Ultimate Cause
persists, or the Absolute Force persists. Having expressed our ultimate truth in this formula, we have,
according to Mr. Spencer, possessed ourselves of a
principle which unifies all concrete existences, and
compacts into one organic whole the divided limbs
of the entire body of actual or possible knowledge.
But of what value is a principle like this? Will it
bear up a system of philosophy? When we reach Mr.
Spencer's meaning of the term *force*, it is only to find
the signification utterly incomprehensible and wholly

worthless. The thing denoted by the word, when the dry light of criticism falls on it, recedes, like a ghost, beyond the limits of intelligence into the shades of the unsearchable.

Section IV.

Can we Predicate Persistence in any Knowable Mode?

In endeavouring to fix with precision what is meant by Force in Mr. Spencer's ultimate principle, we reach no satisfactory result. Directing our criticism to the predicate of his proposition, let us inquire whether persistence is predicated in any mode that may form a basis for real knowledge.

Persistence, in Mr. Spencer's use of terms, means, continued existence; for he tells us we cannot think existence except as continued. We may, then, take the forms—A is, and, A continues to be, as equivalents. Assuming their equivalence, we write the law of persistence in the form, A continues to be A—a predication of continued identity. If this predication hold good universally, we may transform it into the individual instance—This A continues to be this A. A piece of coal lies before me; I write This piece of coal continues to be this piece of coal. The coal is put into the fire and this piece of coal ceases to be this piece of coal. The predication is proved to be, false : it is clear the predication A continues to be A does not hold universally. It must then be limited. What is the limitation? The answer may be given, It was not the coal, but the force manifested in the coal of which persistence was affirmed. We may, then, write, This A (the force manifested in the coal) continues to be this A (the same force manifested otherwise). At this point we are far removed from the primary dicta of consciousness. We have drawn a distinction between force and the manifestation of force, and we have affirmed the continued existence of the force under varying manifestations. Force is known to us only as manifested : it stands related to our senses. "To conceive" force "is to represent it in some terms derived from our experience — that is, from our sensations." * But our axiom requires that we should separate the manifestation from the force, and think the force apart from the manifestation. Apart from manifestation no definite conception of the force is possible ; unmanifested it is a part of the inscrutable actuality. To individualize this force apart from its manifestations, and think it in the present, to individualize it, apart from its manifestations, and think it in the future, and to affirm continued identity is, on Mr. Spencer's theory, unquestionably illegitimate ; we cannot conceive either term in the proposition — they are alike unknowable. We con-

---

* *Psychology*, vol. II., § 428, note.

clude, then, that the predication of persistence in identity is not valid.

We may take the predication in another sense; it may mean, Force continues to be force : force persists as force and not under any other form. It is, then, predication of continuity in sameness of kind. But is the persistence of force as force a truth ascertainable in any possible manner ? When force is conceived as existing in the unknowable we are, on evolutionist principles, forbidden to affirm of it in any mode. No definite conception is possible. Force, as known, stands related to our senses. Out of relation to nerve-sensibility it is assumed to be out of relation to intelligence. The continuance of force (if it continue) in the incomprehensible in unthinkable modes can, give no validity to an axiom lying at the base of a theory of the knowable cosmos—a cosmos knowable only through the senses. That force continues to be for ever force and nothing else is not a self-evident proposition. Consciousness has no knowledge on the point, and can give no testimony. In what form force existed prior to the coming to be of that universe of which the senses give us means of knowledge, is a problem insoluble by man. Mr. Spencer himself acknowledges it to be so, when he carries force back from the relations of sense and thought into the unknowable actuality. "Force as we know it" he says, "can be regarded only as a certain conditioned effect of the Unconditioned Cause

G

—as the relative reality indicating to us an Absolute Reality by which it is immediately produced."* In that region of the unknowable he will not allow us to form of it any definite concept: whether, in the inscrutable it has uniformly existed as force, or whether it may have existed in some other mode of actuality, we are not warranted either to affirm or deny. We may conclude that the interpretation of the proposition to mean, Force remains force, yields no profitable result.

But the predication may be read with another implication,—one which Mr. Spencer himself has indicated. Persistence may mean continuance "unchanged in quantity throughout all past time and all future time."† That is, the force that persists was a million years ago exactly the same in amount that it is to-day, and so shall be a million years hence. Now it is evident that this affirmation is wholly beyond the reach of experiential proof. We have no means of measuring with exactness any manifested force in the state in which it is, or in the state into which it subsequently passes. Observation cannot assure us that the quantity remains unaltered. At the very moment of observation the process of change is going on. When a gun is fired, a certain amount of force is liberated and a certain amount of effect produced; but these cannot be quantified. The forces

---

* *First Principles*, § 50.   † *Ibid.*, § 191.

contained in the cartridge cannot be estimated; nor can they be summed up in the new forms into which they pass. The persistence, in equality of amount, of a force as manifested, cannot be ascertained experimentally in any instance. To say that any manifested force ever has been and ever shall be the same in quantity is an illegitimate affirmation.

It is supposable, however, that the sum total of manifested force is that the amount of which is to be held constant. This mode of conceiving persistence also fails us. For there can be no experience of a totality stretching beyond the bounds of attainable knowledge. Besides, manifestations are mutations. It is their characteristic to be ever coming into view and ever vanishing from observation. The totality of manifestations cannot be summed; but even if we were able at any one point in time to sum up the total of manifested force, it would be impossible for us to affirm its perpetuity. For the knowable touches the unknowable at every point in space and time; we cannot, therefore, separate the knowable to measure the sum of it. The law of the manifestation of the inscrutable power is hidden from us. Mr. Spencer, no doubt, assumes that the manifestations of the absolute are throughout all time "unchanged in quantity." But another thinker is as free to conclude—and has as much reason on his side—that the amount has not continued constant. The manifestations of the unknowable power may at some point in time have been less or greater than at present. The cosmos, as we see it, may be one throb in the pulsations of a mighty rhythmic movement through which the absolute energy has been revealing itself in a constantly changing totality of manifestations. That the amount remains constant, and has for ever remained constant, is a supposition not only unwarranted, but out of harmony with the evolution doctrine itself. We should, as disciples of Mr. Spencer, be led rather to conceive of the unknowable actuality as revealing itself in modes ceaselessly changing, both in amount and in variety. Out of the depths of the absolute cause all manifested force wells up. The fountain out of which it springs is infinite. As the myriad moving atoms, whirling in systems of inexplicable complexity, rise into view, we can think of them as in continual play of perpetually changing shapes, the totality rising and falling with ceaseless rhythmic mutations, in endless diversity of mode and in continually varying amount. We can imagine also that, in the great cosmic movement, ever moulding it anew, are forms of beauty and forthgoings of power which intelligence can never reach through sense. A vision of this kind is in truer harmony with the whole course of change than Mr. Spencer's hypothesis of a hard line on the one side of which thought has an "indefinite consciousness" of the absolute energy, and on the other, sees an unalterable sum of manifested power. If we take the persistent force to be the absolute actuality, as, following Mr. Spencer, we are warranted to do,—for "by the persistence of force" he says, "we really mean the persistence of some cause which transcends our knowledge and con-ception,"—we predicate the continued existence of the absolute force in equality of sum throughout all time. But to affirm that the incomprehensible "continues unchanged in quantity" is manifestly in-competent to human intelligence. At every point in time it is assumed to be unbounded and ever inscrut-able: we are forbidden to form of it any definite con-cept whatever. To predicate of it persistent equality in amount is doubly absurd.

We make no real advance, then, by taking persist-ence to mean continued sameness of quantity.

Even if it were possible to quantify the totality of force, or to isolate and compare individual instances, persistence could guarantee one thing only, that is, the constancy of the amount. The something might become another thing in all respects save in quantity. For brass we might have gold and for stones iron, provided only the balance of the totals remained undisturbed. For force is with Mr. Spencer the equivalent of all modes of being, spiritual and material, of every mode of motion, or exercise of thought; of everything that exists or has existed. To affirm, then, that the sole ultimate truth is the persistence of force in equality of amount, is to re-move from thought all questions of kind and to

reduce all truth to relations of quantity, all knowledge to measurement. But, as we have seen, exact
quantification is impossible. If all truth be precision
of measurement, truth is forever hidden from man,
and the light of real knowledge can never fall upon
his path. The exact quantification, towards which
science, following the method of experiment, more
and more tends as it becomes perfected, is in every
instance but an approximation. Exactness of quantification, carried backward and forward from an inconceivably remote past to an inconceivably distant
future, is unattainable, whether in the individual
instance or in the totality of things.

We are compelled, then, to reject the predication of
persistence as continued existence, whether in identity,
or in kind, or in quantity. Removing these modes of
predication, what thinkable conception remains ? We
reach as a residual notion the bare thought of *being ;*
and lay at the basis of our cosmic philosophy, as its
fundamental truth from which all other truths are to
be derived, the continued existence of being without
attributes. We are not far from the foundation principle of Hegel—the identity of pure Being and pure
No-thing. But will the knowable universe rest firmly
on such a basis ? We are doubtful of its stability.
Ex nihilo nihil fit.

SECTION V.

COROLLARIES OF THE PERSISTENCE OF FORCE.

There are three truths coming immediately under the principle of the persistence of force which are indispensable to evolutionism and which we shall briefly examine—the indestructibility of matter, the continuity of motion, and the persistence of relations among forces. Without these the evolutionist cannot build up his system: they must be granted him as necessary and universal.

1. *The indestructibility of matter.*

"Our conception of matter reduced to its simplest shape is that of co-existent positions that offer resistance." * It has two essential attributes. We are under necessity of " representing to ourselves the ultimate elements of matter as being at once extended and resistent. . . . . Of these two inseparable elements, the resistance, is primary and the extension secondary." † Mr. Spencer holds the " indestructibility of matter" to be a derivative truth, the persistence of force being the ultimate from which it is derived. Does the persistence of force necessitate the persistence of matter? Clearly not. The persistence of force only warrants us in affirming the persistence of force. Matter is a manifestation, and manifestations are

---

* *First Principles,* § 48.   † *Ibid.*

inconstant. Being a manifestation, matter is not guaranteed continued existence; for the continued existence of force does not necessitate the continued existence of every manifestation of force. Force persists, while its manifestations change. Is the manifestation known as matter so differenced from all other manifestations that the persistence of force should determine its persistence? The two essential attributes of matter are resistance and occupation of space. Now these are not attributes essential to the idea of force, and do not necessarily persist with its persistence. Space-occupying—that is, bulk—is relative; it is capable of more and less. Mr. Spencer speaks of it as a special kind of force. "The first of these," he says—the space-occupying kind of force— "has no specific name." * But we are familiar with the fact that the kind of force manifested in "space-occupying" may be increased or diminished. Now if the space-occupancy may become less, is there a point at which this diminution necessarily stops? Is there a line drawn at which the continuity of movement is broken, and at which it is said to the vanishing process, "Hitherto shalt thou come, but no farther?" If so, then the law of continuity is violated. If, on the other hand, the law of continuity prevail, and the space-occupying mode of force gradually merge in some other mode, then matter has lost one element of

---

* *First Principles,* § 58.

the force manifested in it, and it has been, in so far, destroyed.

Take the other attribute. Resistance is also relative —a question of more and less. It is relative also in this, that it cannot be known except in the relation of matter to matter. If we think of an atom, removing from our thought all other matter, and conceiving it out of relation to all other matter, we are not necessitated to ascribe to it the attribute of resistance. Besides, there is no sufficient reason for excepting matter from the law of the correlation of forces. " Forces standing in certain correlations form the whole content of our idea of matter."* If it be a correlated force, matter may, in the inscrutable cosmic activity, be interchangeable with other modes. Otherwise we set bounds to the principle of the correlation forces, and in drawing the boundary line we violate the law of continuity.

There is, then, no sufficient ground for affirming that matter, whether viewed as resistant or space-occupying, persists. But turning from force as manifestated, which, on Mr. Spencer's theory, does not persist, to the presisting force—the unconditioned and unknowable power — we find no support for the doctrine of the everlasting continuance of matter. The absolute force does not persist in any knowable mode. The persistence of a knowable mode cannot, therefore, be deduced from the persistence of the un-

* *First Principles*, § 48.

knowable; and no warrant is given for affirming the indestructibility of any manifestation. Whether matter does or does not continue to exist, the principle of the persistence of force cannot determine. The permanence of a manifestation in the knowable cannot be established by assuming the permanence of unconditioned force in the unknowable. If the persistence of the unconditioned force necessitated the continued existence of all modes of manifested force, all manifestations would be eternal.

To deduce from the persistence of force the indestructibility of matter is obviously illegitimate.*

(2.) *The continuity of motion.*

By a like process of reasoning, we are led to the conclusion that the persistence of force gives no warrant for affirming the ceaseless continuity of motion. It will not enable us to determine whether or not the sum of motion in the universe remains equal over all the cycles of change. Visible motion is not continuous: the continuity is "the constancy of the total made by adding together actual and potential, molar and molecular."† But we have no means of arriving at a warrantable affirmation of the constancy of this total: these modes of motion are modes of force, and may be interchanged with other manifestations of the unknowable energy. Experientially they cannot be

---

. * The inconceivability of matter ceasing to be is dealt with in discussing the question of creation.
† *First Principles,* § 56.

summed. If the force manifested in them is manifested in any other forthgoing of energy, or if it sink into the depths of the inscrutable, the persistence of force is equally satisfied. This corollary also fails as an axiomatic truth.

3. *The persistence of the relations among forces.*
" The first deduction to be drawn from the ultimate universal truth that force persists, is that the relations among forces persist." * Is this a universal principle ? Clearly it must be, if it be an immediate deduction from the " ultimate universal truth." Now observe, it is not *some* relations, but "*the* relations " that persist. " We cannot assert persistence of this something beyond consciousness without asserting that the relations among its manifestations are persistent."† The relations among the manifestations of the persistent " something beyond consciousness " comprise relations of space, time, number, quantity, quality, and cause and effect. Do all these relations among forces persist ? To answer in the affirmative launches us on a sea of absurdities. Forces are manifested as occupying positions in space, if these spatial relations continue constant, every part of the cosmos must remain eternally in fixed relation of distance to every other, and motion internal to it is impossible : if time relations remain persistent, there can be no succession ; the outflow of change was at the first instant stayed

---

* *First Principles*, § 63.   † *Ibid.*, § 65.

and set in an eternal rest: if relations of number persist, there can be neither union nor division. Two forces may be conceived as becoming one force, as two dew drops may merge in one, or one force may be thought of as dividing into two; but if the one continues one and the plural remains plural, there can be neither union nor division throughout all time. In like manner, if the relations of quantity remain fixed there cannot be either addition or diminution: if relations of quality are constant, the universe is doomed to everlasting sameness; differences of kind cannot arise; the homogeneous can never become heterogeneous.

Passing by all other relations, Mr. Spencer deals only with that of cause and effect, and to it applies his axiom. "Every antecedent mode of the Unknowable must have an invariable connection, quantitative and qualitative, with that mode of the Unknowable which we call its consequent. For to say otherwise is to deny the persistence of force. If in any two cases there is exact likeness, not only between those most conspicuous antecedents which we distinguish as the causes, but also between those accompanying antecedents which we call the conditions, we cannot affirm that the effects will differ, without affirming either that some force has come into existence or that some force has ceased to exist."*

---

* *First Principles,* § 63.

There is an evident fallacy in this reasoning if we take our stand on Mr. Spencer's principles. What is that we call effect? Clearly it is a manifestation of force; that which we call cause—that is, cause within the knowable—is also a manifestation of force. What then, is the relation that persists? Is it the relation of manifestation to manifestation, or force to force? It cannot be the relation of manifestation to manifestation; for the manifestations are ever changing; the course of cosmic movement is ceaseless mutation. The relation of manifestation to manifestation is wholly phenomenal—mutable as the fleeting manifestations. The persisting relation must then be that of force to force. But do the forces that persist stand related? and if so, do they stand related in any knowable mode? The persisting forces are part of the inscrutable energy. A new and interesting question presents itself. Do the inter-related forces exist as constituents of the absolute force, continuing distinct throughout all modes of its manifestation? If so, we shall need to know their law before we can claim to understand their manifestations in the cosmos: if we are precluded from affirming anything of the forces constituting the incomprehensible, how can we assure ourselves that the relations of forces wholly inscrutable, and whose continued persistence as distinct sources of causative energy is doubtful, persist? We can draw no conclusion as to the persistence of knowable relations from the persistence of the unconditioned force—a force that does not exist " under any form cognizable by us."

It may be answered, The causal manifestations are by hypothesis the same: they being assumed the same in every particular, the form of manifestation, called the effect, will be necessarily the same. Let it be remembered, however, that we are engaged—not with speculations as to what *might* be, but with inquiry as to what *is* and *has been.* On what ground do we base the assumption that groups in every particular alike do from age to age recur? We have to face the great experiential inquiry, Do manifestations precisely the same ever reappear? On evolutionist principles the universe is not at two successive stages exactly similar. It is only observation that can assure us whether groups of manifestations that can be identified as the same, recur; and, consequently, every inference carried beyond the ken of observation is to be received with doubt. But even though it were certain that groups phenomenally alike had been observed, we could not, from the persistence of force, conclude with certainty that they contained the same measure of causal efficiency: for the inherent energy is the forthgoing of the inscrutable power, of which, under the same phenomenal appearance, there may be more or less. We are again driven back to the ever-recurring assumption, involved in every part of Mr. Spencer's system, that the law of the unknowable is known, that we have ascertained as an indubitable truth that the visible universe is an ever unmodified manifestation of the Incomprehensible Actuality—an assumption which is not a dictum of consciousness and which is impossible of proof.

Tested in itself or in its corollaries, Mr. Spencer's fundamental axiom is found wanting. It has no validity as a universal truth. Evolutionism founded on it is a pyramid built upon its apex. But no wider foundation is available. "The sole truth which trans-cends experience by underlying it is the Persistence of Force. This being the basis of experience must be the basis of any scientific organization of experi-ence. To this an ultimate analysis brings us down, and on this a rational synthesis must build up." *

---

* *First Principles,* § 62.

CHAPTER IX.

THE Evolution Philosophy requires as its basis certain postulates, without which it cannot be constructed. We shall inquire what these postulates are, and subject them to a critical examination with a view to test their validity. If they are questioned, the entire system is questioned; if they are rejected, the entire system falls to pieces.

1. The theory of Evolution presupposes, as its primal conception, the cosmos coming into the view of science as a force homogeneous or nearly homogeneous. We cannot take a step forward until we have first assumed the existence of a force, described by Mr. Spencer also as a "mass," in a state of homogeneity or something very nearly approaching that condition. The more nearly this first force approximates to a perfect homogeneity, the more complete will be the unification of knowledge. Every trace of heterogeneity accepted in our primal concept, marks a breach of continuity and is evidence that the unity aimed at is not perfect.

Let us examine this conception, that we may

see what is taken for granted as to the force whose existence we posit.

1. Our first question, then, is as to the extent of it. It is either infinite or finite : let us suppose it infinite. If the force be infinite it must be heterogeneous; for an infinite homogeneity does not afford the conditions necessary for cosmic motion in accordance with dynamic law. In a homogeneous mass extending to infinity, every line of force would be counteracted by a line of force equal and opposite, and motion would be impossible. Let us, then, suppose the cosmos in its primal state to be heterogeneous. This heterogeneity may be either of two kinds—the heterogeneity of a universe regulated and shaped in accordance with law, as the universe is in its present condition seen to be, or the heterogeneity of an indeterminate mass in which there is no known or discoverable law. The former fails to unify knowledge, for it begins with the very diversity now existing; we may for the present, then, put it aside, and examine the latter conception. Is this conception one which may form the starting point of scientific knowledge? Clearly it is not. A heterogeneous mass extending to infinity can have no place in scientific thought. An infinite heterogeneity would afford a limitless field for surprises. Traversing this boundless region of heterogeneity, science could never know what she might stumble upon at the next step. Miracles would cease to be wonders. This

H

omnipresent heterogeneity, working on in the unbounded activity of an infinite energy, could never be
fathomed, or the mode of its operation determined:
thought could not set to it any bounds, or lay upon
it any constraint of law.   In face of it intelligence
is bewildered.   Like Noah's dove, reason may for a
time circle in unresting flight over the boundless
waters, but it soon returns, not bearing even an olive
leaf.   If an infinite heterogeneity be taken as the
primary condition, the evolution hypothesis breaks
down in its initial conception.

Let us suppose the cosmos to be finite.   This finite
force may be assumed to be either homogeneous or
heterogeneous, and it must exist under some particular
form.   If it be limited and spherical, and at the same
time homogeneous, every atom will move in a right
line towards the centre; these motions being uniform
and in one direction, circular motion is excluded, and
the conditions necessary to evolution are not given.
If the form be not perfectly spherical, but irregular,
motion may arise, but from the ensuing motion it will
be impossible to deduce a cosmos characterized by
orderly movement.   Physics will fail to furnish any
explanation which will connect the existing condition
of the universe with that original shape.   When we
go back by this line and seek for a firm footing on
which science might rest securely, and, from that solid
ground, work forward in the elucidation of things, we
plunge into the depths of chaos.

Suppose the primal form to be limited and hetero-geneous. Then in going back to search for an explanation of heterogeneity, we are driven to posit heterogeneity as our starting point. We begin with an imperfect unification of the first matter. The law of continuity is violated at the first step: the stream whose divisions are to be traced back to unity is assumed to be divided at the outset. If the hetero-geneity which we posit be that of law as at present operative, we have made no approach towards unification of knowledge. If the heterogeneity be indeterminate and lawless, science can never rest in any assured confidence that the best established generalizations may not be overturned. Law is, in that case, strictly limited to the bounds ˎof observation. A finite heterogeneity does not furnish a starting point from which to work out the complete unification of scientific knowledge.

Whether regarded as homogeneous or heterogeneous, when we think the cosmos as finite, we circumscribe it within a limit. Beyond that limit no force by hypothesis exists. If force existed anywhere beyond, it would necessarily stand related to the cosmic force, affecting it and being affected by it; and the cosmic force is on the supposition wholly insphered within itself. Considering the force then as bounded, we must think it as enclosed within a boundary line, within which all being is included, and beyond it not-being. Let us try to realize in thought this conception. We reach a line of limit, on the one side of it is force, on the other—nothing: that line divides being from not-being. But Mr. Spencer has been at great pains to show that no such mental process is possible; that non-existence cannot be presented in thought. Taking his own criterion as the test of truth, this conception must be rejected.

One other criticism may be added. The unification of knowledge is the answer of philosophy to the craving for unity of thought. That evolution seems to explain nature so as to let the mind pass continuously onward without break in the connection of fact with fact, is a chief source of its hold on men of science. In view of this habit of scientific thinking, it is curious to see how the very first step in the process is a breach of continuity. If the universe be infinite, continuity is broken by every line that marks heterogeneity: if the universe be finite, the mind must fix a circumscribing limit; when thought reaches that line, it is sharply arrested by a boundary beyond which nothing exists. Now, if the law of continuity must be broken when we come to the "walls of the world;" if evolution lays down limiting, or differencing, lines as essential to its initial process in interpreting the universe, it is manifest that breach of continuity lies at the root of all mental activity, that it is an essential necessity of thought, and "to know in part" is the normal condition of intelligence.

One other mode of conceiving the primal form of

the cosmos may be adopted. We may attempt to think it as the bounded manifestation of an infinite force; but we shall then be in no better position. We shall have increased our burdens and gained nothing; for we cannot determine the self-revelation of the infinite, or trace the bounds within which the limitless energy is manifested.

The postulate fails us, therefore, whatever be the mode in which we try to represent it in thought. In the book of Genesis, as written by the evolutionist, the first sentence is unintelligible.

2. The evolution hypothesis assumes the continuance of the evolving force, throughout all time, in invariable equality of amount.

Having already discussed the possibility of quantifying the force of which persistence is predicated, it is not needful to repeat the argument.* We may note briefly that it is incompetent to human intelligence, in any mode of representing the cosmos in thought, to conceive the sum of it. If it be infinite, the total is in terms declared to be immeasurable; if it be finite, it is still immeasurable, for it is practically limitless to thought; if it be the bounded manifestation of an infinite power, we are as far afield as before in the attempt to quantify. The sum of force must, in any case, remain undefined. It is, therefore, impossible to compare the amount of force existing at

---

* *Supra*, Chapter VIII., § IV.

the beginning with the total at any succeeding point in time : both terms in the comparison are beyond the capacity of intelligence, and comparison fails.

Yet the entire chain of reasoning by which it is proposed to establish the evolution doctrine proceeds on this fixedness of quantity. The matter in the universe remains by hypothesis undiminished and un-increased ; " the quantity of motion is fixed ; " the force " remains unchanged in amount throughout all time." If this assumption be rejected, the whole system goes to pieces. But this assumption has no scientific value ; for even if it were true it is unprovable. The new cosmic philosophy, the unification of all knowledge, is not only in its initial step, but throughout the whole course of its interpretation of nature, necessitated to employ a postulate involving affirmations regarding matters of fact in the world of concrete reality, as to the truth of which experience can tell us nothing. Yet the whole process is, at every step throughout, depen-dent on the truth of this assumption : if it be rejected every link in the chain of reasoning is broken.

Has the total sum of manifested force remained equal throughout the ages ? Who can answer ? Not the evolutionist, for he has no knowledge beyond that furnished through the senses : not the experientialist, for he cannot survey the entire universe of being : there is no evidence furnished by the mind itself ; for in mind there is nothing, according to the evo-lution hypothesis, except what individual or race experiences have imparted to it. This postulate, required at every step in the interpretation of nature on the principles of evolution, is one which could be affirmed only by Absolute Intelligence itself.

Whether it be true or not true as a matter of fact that the total sum of force in the cosmos remains constant, the need of taking it for granted, while its truth is altogether unprovable, taints the evolution theory throughout. The conditions in which the doctrine of evolution could be established do not exist.

3. The evolution hypothesis postulates the inclusion, under the law of the continuous redistribution of matter and motion, of every event or change in the universe. This law is taken as covering all activities and all orders of existence. "Existences of all orders do exhibit a progressive integration of matter and concomitant loss of motion."* Mr. Spencer applies his law alike to mechanical, vital, and mental action. It must be accepted as of universal application, for by it all knowledge is to be unified.

In the postulates already examined, we had to do with what we showed to be illegitimate processes of thought. The conceptions were impossible or incongruous with other conceptions necessary to the evolution doctrine. The postulate now in question lies so far within the compass of knowledge of fact that it may be tested by experience. There are whole classes

---

* *First Principles*, § 107.

of facts apparently in direct conflict with it, and which must be got out of the way before it can be accepted. For if there be any fact incapable of being interpreted in terms of matter and motion, the postulate in question is untrue. To bring the intellectual activities, the moral feeling, and the emotions under the law in question, the phenomena of mind must be compelled to take a place among the correlated forces of the cosmos, each of which may be transformed into one of the others. The endeavour to reduce mental operations to instances of the correlation of physical forces, has, as we shall see, failed. If our reasoning on that question, set out in a future chapter prove to be well-founded, this postulate also must be swept away.

4. It is necessary also to grant the evolutionist, that the total amount of matter in the cosmos is never increased or diminished; and that the total amount of motion remains invariable.

If the matter existing in the primal form of the universe were either increased or diminished, the law of the continuous redistribution of matter and motion would not furnish a true account of cosmic change. Let us imagine matter at any moment, increased by the transference of force existing in some other mode into matter, that is, into force "resistent and occupying space;" the doctrine of evolution would be falsified. All the relations of the physical cosmos would be modified; for the proportions of the masses would be altered. All motion must now take a new direction; for being invariably in the line of the greatest force, and the relations of forces being changed, the direction is necessarily changed. The introduction of this new piece of matter sends a thrill through the whole system, and separates, by a clearly defined demarcation, the past from the future series of changes; it cuts the course of cosmic history, by a distinct breach of continuity, in two. A like consequence would ensue were motion either arrested, diminished, or increased. The thorough-going evolutionist will, therefore, contend vigorously for the indestructibility of matter and the continuity of motion, and refuse to admit the possibility of the increase or dimintion of either· The introduction *ab extra* of any alteration of the materials on which his process of quantification proceeds, would be fatal to the accuracy of his results.

5. The evolutionist must be further given, as a fundamental truth, that force as manifested in the cosmos includes in these manifestations all the causes of each change, and of the total course of change. It is essential to the evolution hypothesis, as a complete theory of the universe, that the whole sum of phenomena, physical, mental, moral, spiritual, found at any time existing, shall be taken as the necessary outcome of the immediate past, and that past the outcome of a preceding past, and so backward to the primal condition of the universe, posited by evolutionism

as its first conception. When we go back, then, to that primordial manifestation of force with which evolution sets out—a mass homogeneous or nearly homogeneous, "diffused, uniform, indeterminate." * we are to find in it the causes of all knowable phenomena. That mass contained in it, by hypothesis, all the causes which, gradually evolving, have issued in the unimaginable diversity of the universe at it is. These causes are such as may be comprehended in one moving mass, and have their operation in new modes of the relations of matter and motion. They are generalized in a "dynamic principle." The law expressing their combined operations, is the law of the continuous redistribution of matter and motion. The links of physical causation, on this supposition, bind the present in all its varied phenomena—physical and mental—in one unbroken chain of necessity to that far off past. In this primordial manifestation of force, rising into the view of science, lay the causes that have evolved the heavens and the earth, that have shaped all forms of knowable existence, that have generated all sensate being, that have created Adam and Christ.

Let not our position be misapprehended. We recognize it to be the work of science to search in antecedent cosmic phenomena, for the causes of all that comes within the field of observation. It is the

---

* *First Principles,* § 187.

very business of science to do so. Nothing is to be deemed inexplicable by natural law, unless there be good reason to judge that such explanation is not possible. Even when for a time baffled, it is the part of science to return again and again to the search, in hope of accomplishing, by patient toil, the seemingly impossible achievement. But it is not to be tolerated that there should be buried under the pretence of solution, difficulties that remain still unsolved. Nor are working hypotheses to be raised to the rank of established truths. There should be as much keen-sightedness in recognizing the want of completeness in proof, as there is in noting facts that seem to support a theory. The adverse facts are to be recorded with as much care as those that are favourable. The one class of instances is as precious to true science as the other.

When it is asserted that all the causes of all that may be known are included within the cosmos, the proposition is ambiguous till we have first fixed the limits of the cosmos as conceived in thought. If the cosmos be infinite, embracing all existences—God, the soul, and the world—it includes of necessity all causes. The proposition, read in that sense, is an identical proposition—it amounts to affirming that all things include all things. It does not in the least degree advance our knowledge; for what science has to do is to trace the relations among phenomena within that infinite, in their ᴄo-ordination and succession;

and it serves in no respect, when dealing with any given instance, to carry with us the assurance that in the bosom of immensity lie all the causes of the phenomenon in question. It is drawing water with a bottomless bucket.

If the cosmos be finite and self-enclosed, embracing all being and encompassed by not-being; then equally the postulate is an identical proposition; for we have excluded all causes lying outside the cosmos, when we have included all being within it. In this form it is also equally useless; for it is no aid to us to know that the totality of existence includes the totality of causes. If, indeed, the cosmos were assumed to be within the compass of experience; if observation and experiment could traverse it to its farthest boundary and most profound depths, then to be assured that it contains all causes could have a real significance to the inquirer; but if it go deeper, higher, wider than we can reach, there is still unbounded room in which causes may lie hidden; for the reality and its possibilities are in respect of our intelligence unlimited.

To assume a defined cosmos, therefore, including all causes within itself, secures a merely visionary advantage; but that advantage is gained at an infinite cost; for, in drawing a boundary line inclusive of all being, thought has, according to Mr. Spencer, contravened its primary condition and destroyed itself.

If, again, we hold a cosmos limited in extent, the manifestation of the unlimited power, and including within itself all the causes of the phenomena evolved in its history, we gain no single advantage, and we increase many times the difficulties that meet us. There lie against this mode of conceiving the primal condition of the universe all the objections that lie against the modes already considered, while other inseparable difficulties are added. We begin, in this case, by attempting to draw a boundary line around the infinite by determining how the absolute power must manifest itself: we lay down as fixed that the unconditioned energy, operating as cause, has produced no effects except those emerging in its primordial manifestation; but to fix such a limit pre-supposes, as we have already seen, either that the entire course of cosmic history is experientially known in its totality and in detail, or that we have discovered the law of the manifestation of the incomprehensible and infinite; either of which suppositions is obviously absurd.

Let us take an instance as illustrative of our argument. When the physical condition of the earth was such as to be adapted to the existence of vegetal life, vegetal forms appeared. How did this life originate? Evolution asserts that it was produced as the effect of the physical forces already in operation, being their necessary outcome, and that no cause may be sought outside these physical antecedents: the dynamic action passed into the form we call vital action by physical necessity. Is this an adequate explanation? If the process from dynamic to vital action is found to be inscrutable by science; if every explanation that professes to set out the transition fails, we are thrown back on the inquiry, Is physical science adequate to the explanation of all knowable things? Do the principles of dynamics cover and elucidate all the phenomena of concrete existence? How if the origin of life lie in something outside dynamic law? if the behaviour of matter according to dynamic law be not all that is in the phenomenon? if we are here face to face with another mode of being? Or, to put it more nearly after the fashion of Mr. Spencer's philosophy, in a supposition equally thinkable with that adopted by him and equally scientific, vegetal life may at the fitting moment have arisen out of the depths of the inscrutable power. The existence of an incomprehensible actuality having been postulated as an ultimate datum of consciousness, we are not chargeable with following an unphilospohic method if we see appearing in the first beginning of life a new manifestation of that "absolute Reality by which the relative reality is immediately produced.*

In like manner, the beginning of sentient life presents an inexplicable problem to science endeavouring to solve it by means of dynamic principles. The life of the animal, like that of the plant, arose when physical conditions suitable for its continuance ex-

---

* *First Principles,* § 50.

isted. But science has no evidence on which to affirm that the antecedent mode of being manifested in the dynamic laws of matter and motion and force was its sole cause. No connecting links can be shown to account for the transition from the insensate to the sensate: nothing has been brought to light by science which is fitted to elucidate the origin of feeling. It is an assumption wholly without warrant that the physical causes already operating in the universe, at the moment when feeling first came into existence as a mode of being, were adequate to produce it. It is more reasonable to suppose that it came to be by the immediate operation of the inscrutable first cause, whose continued existence in relation to the phenomenal Mr. Spencer affirms.

But the exception to the universality of physical law, which stands out most clearly and indubitably, is the beginning of self-conscious intelligence. When the universe had reached a state in which it afforded a fitting habitat for such a being, man appeared. Conscious thought, knowing itself and its environment, is the most notable of all phenomena in the cosmos. Till man is accounted for, the first question of philosophy, and the question which gives the key to every other, is unanswered. If the law of the continuous redistribution of matter and motion can account for consciousness, it has won universal dominion, and is the law of all knowable being; but if it does not furnish a true solution of this problem, it has no claim to universality, and evolution fails in the accomplishment of its task. The great central fact still stands apart: the unification of knowledge is not complete. The appearance in the universe of a being who can say, *I am*, is the one fact which, if left unaccounted for, renders any theory worthless, as a complete interpretation of the universe. Do the causes in operation in the knowable, antecedent to man's appearance in the universe, give an adequate explanation of the origin of mind? We shall, subsequently, at some length, discuss the proposed solution, and show that it leaves out of view the most essential features of the phenomenon. It will be found to deal with that which lies *circa hominem*, rather than *in homine*. When a human mind awoke to consciousness of itself and its environment, there occurred an event not explicable by the laws of physical causation. No dynamic principle will cover it. A new realm of existence is revealed, wholly diverse from that ruled by the laws of matter and motion: it is the realm of being conscious of itself, of being whose characteristic attribute is Thought.

Before it will be possible to admit that the cosmos contains within itself all the causes of all knowable phenomena, these unmistakable exceptions must be explained; these separating lines obliterated; these large classes of facts brought within the grasp of physical causation: or we shall have to widen the conception of the universe until it include all concrete being—embracing under that one term God, the soul, and the world. But when the conception is enlarged so as to correspond with reality, it becomes worthless to the evolutionist, and is discarded.

6. To produce the cosmos that is, and as it is, there is needed one other datum. A determinate extent and relation of parts in its primal state must be given, or a wholly different cosmos must have evolved. Inasmuch as the existing cosmos is, on the evolution hypothesis, limited by necessity to the original homogeneity, there must have been a special form and collocation of the diffused mass, and a special fixed quantity of motion distributed in a determinate manner to produce, in the operation of dynamic law, the known result. For the present cosmos is not the only form conceivable—the possible variations are infinite. Nothing can be clearer than that this primordial arrangement must be postulated by the evolution hypothesis: without it the cosmos as it is could not have arisen. The most trifling shade of difference— the oscillation of a molecule in the least degree more or less—the position, by a hair's breadth on one side or on the other, of the line marking the heterogeneity of part from part would, in the lapse of inconceivable periods of change, have wrought out incalcuable differences of result. Any other imaginable condition and collocation of matter, and these are infinite, and any greater or less amount of motion, would have produced a universe wholly different from that we see. The

I

existence of Mr. Spencer's system of philosophy was determined by a nice adjustment in that original collocation of forces: a difference quite imperceptible would have left the thinking portion of the world, if in that case any thinking portion had ever come to be, without the very important addition which Mr. Spencer has contributed to speculative thought.

No doubt we must postulate some mode in which the original matter and motion were distributed in space, and one is as readily taken for granted as another. But by what right does the evolutionist demand that among the infinite possibilities we should posit just that one mode, and no other, which contains the amount and arrangement of matter and motion that will, if his theory is true, evolve the existing universe? From that which is, he may reply, I infer what must have been. The inference is doubly illegitimate; for the point in debate is whether, from a primordial homogeneity to the present form of things, there may or may not have been any intervention of the absolute power, whether the process has been necessarily from the beginning until now the continuous and untouched operation of dynamic law, and he posits an ordered heterogeneity: not only so, but to show that all new manifestations of power and the revelation of being in any mode not the outcome of a dynamic principle are for ever excluded, he assumes a specific and determinate arrangement of the imagined mist cloud. We may with as much warrant take for granted repeated interventions of the absolute energy.

The evolutionist rejects the doctrine of final causes: he refuses to allow, as legitimate, belief in a directing intelligence; yet he requires to have given him an original arrangement of the universe exactly adapted to his hypothesis. When we admire the order, and rejoice in the beauty of the world that is, when we turn to nature and ask, "How have all these exquisite adaptations of one part of the organisation to another part, and to the continuance of life, and of one organic being to another being been perfected?"* When the mind turns back upon itself and marvels at the mystery of that inner world; when we reflect that we live, and that we live in a cosmos with marvellous mutual adaptations between it and our thought, we may well suspect the soundness of a theory which, while rejecting the doctrine of a presiding intelligence, directing all things towards its purpose, needs to assume a special collocation of forces in the original indeterminate mass—a collocation so special and so definite that the very least departure from it would have been fatal to all this order, and would have brought into existence a universe possibly without adjustments, fitting movement to movement, and part to part, without the orderly and the beautiful to admire, and without a self-conscious being to delight in it.

---

* Darwin's *Origin of Species*, Chap. III.

Yet that primal force, endowed with a dynamic potency capable of evolving through inconceivable cycles of change—all the while receiving no fresh impulse and no guidance—this universe whose order science explores—this world peopled by myriad intelligences engaged in the task of its interpretation—Mr. Spencer finds it needful to his philosophy to characterize as "an indefinite, incoherent, homgeneity."

When we consider the number and the gravity of the demands made by evolutionism in the form of postulates incapable of proof, we are justified in dealing with the hypothesis at the outset as illegitimate. The conditions needful for the establishment of it by sufficient evidence do not exist. Even if it were true, it could not be proved true.

But the evolutionist replies, Grant, meanwhile, these postulates; we shall proceed to apply the hypothesis in the elucidation of facts; we shall prove to you that the key is the right one by showing that it fits the lock.

We proceed, then, to examine the detailed explanation of phenomena furnished by evolutionism; we enter upon the examination weighted with a heavy load of assumptions under which reason staggers. But knowledge is to be completely unified. We strive for a high prize. The appeal is to experience. *Solvitur ambulando.* Let us see.

CHAPTER X.

THE FORMULA OF EVOLUTION.

"PHILOSOPHY," says Mr. Spencer, "has to formulate the passage from the imperceptible into the perceptible and from the perceptible into the imperceptible." * "The change from a diffused imperceptible state to a concentrated, perceptible state, is an integration of matter and concomitant dissipation of motion, and the change from a concentrated, perceptible state to a diffused impreceptible state is an absorption of motion and concomitant disintegration of matter. . . . Loss of motion and consequent integration, eventually followed by gain of motion and consequent disintegration—see here a statement comprehensive of the entire series of changes passed through." †

By a succession of tentative applications of the law —gradually filling up the outline, Mr. Spencer moulds it into its final perfected form, which stands thus:—

"*Evolution is an integration of matter and concomitant dissipation of motion; during which the matter passes from an indefinite, incoherent homogeneity to a definite, coherent heterogeneity, and*

---

* *First Principles,* § 93.   † *Ibid.,* § 94.

during which the retained motion undergoes a parallel transformation." *

This formula expresses the one law which covers all the knowable, embraces all concrete being, and is the complete unification of knowledge actual and possible. It must be carefully weighed, and its pretensions tested.

Examining it closely, one is at first puzzled to decide whether it can in any proper sense be characterized as a *law*. It is rather a description of certain processes of change—and a description of a somewhat loose and inexact kind. The terms are wanting in precision. They do not convey any conception sufficiently clear and definite to form a basis for scientific reasoning. It will not enable us to forecast definite results with anything approaching certainty. With this formula as the instrumental aid to vision, the future and the past are alike blurred and dim. No form comes out sharp and clear. We never fully escape out of the original mist-cloud. Let us take the terms and examine them.

The matter evolved is described as "indefinite." But in what sense? It cannot be in the sense of unlimited, or having no defined measure or bounds. To apply the term to the totality of matter in the sense of existence without limit, or with limits unknowable, is to set out with an inconceivable or merely negative conception, by which we can advance nothing towards

* *First Principles*, § 145.

positive knowledge of the cosmos as it is. If we have
in view not the totality of things, but a portion of
matter — say a plant germ — we are in no respect
helped towards a right understanding of its growth
by the implication that it has, at the outset, no distinguishable bounds separating it from surrounding
matter. If we take the term to mean — as seems
intended—that which is undefined in qualities, that is
having no attributes that can be clearly differenced,
we start with a something assumed to possess no
known or knowable properties by which it may be
distinctly and definitely represented in thought.

The conception of this "indefinite" existence within
the knowable has a close kinship with the "indefinite
consciousness" by which the existence of the unknowable is known. But we are entitled to ask whether
this indefiniteness is the absence of definite qualities or
the impossibility of our knowledge of them. If it be the
latter, we begin by positing our own ignorance, and not
a quality of things; if the former, how does it accord
with the assumption that all the causes of the existing
order of knowable things lay in that original homogeneity? It was, on Mr. Spencer's theory, definite in
its relation to the knowable, definite in the amount of
force manifested in it, definite in the collocation of its
forces, definite in the direction of its motion, definite
in the dominion over it of dynamic law, definite in the
possession of just such causal energy, and of just such
operation of that energy under definite law as issue

necessarily in the universe we see. Yet Mr. Spencer defines it to be "indefinite."

But granted that this homogeneity is indefinite, that it has neither defined boundaries nor defined qualities, Mr. Spencer begins with a concept which is only thinkable as the negation of definite thought, and proposes by its aid to clarify the vagueness of unorganized knowledge. He posits matter void of form to produce an ordered cosmos without the aid of a divine intelligence. He bases his philosophy on an impossible idea.

The word "incoherent" does not bring us nearer to a precise conception. What is meant by not cohering? All matter coheres, if there be any quality essential to matter, as we know it, it is this very quality of coherence. The incoherence is then relative—a question of more or less. If so, the evolutionist must have a standard of comparison. What is that standard? The particles of aqueous vapour in a cloud cohere; particles of sand cohere; particles of wax cohere; particles of steel cohere: what degree of coherence is marked by the term "incoherent?" The thought is again found wanting in exactness.

"Homogeneity" is also a vague term. It may express the uniformity of one substance, as gold, or of a compound evenly mixed, as biscuit, or particles of many kinds equally distributed, as in a deposit of mud. Homegeneity furnishes no distinct conception.

Summing up all these ambiguities, we have a total

that could hardly be surpassed in vagueness. It would serve as a more or less apt description of the universe at any stage of its progress, from the imperceptible to the imperceptible again. Such a concept was surely never before laid at the foundation of any system of philosophy.

The unscientific indefiniteness of these descriptive phrases will appear still more evident, when we keep in view Mr. Spencer's hypothesis as to the constitution of that something, as it rises into the view of science, emerging into the perceptible. In the imperceptible state it was not an "indefinite, incoherent homogeneity." It was an aggregate of systems inconceivable in complexity and intricateness; moving not in a chaotic, confused, and irregular manner, but with the orderly, harmonious, and measured movement of system and law. Mr Spencer supposes the combination of atoms into aggregates, with inter-equilibrated motions and standing related to other aggregates, in systems of ever-increasing intricateness, the whole forming a system as extensive and as complex as the visible cosmos at any stage. Surely such a condition of the universe is badly represented in the phrase, "indefinite, incoherent homogeneity." The "indefinite" has, on Mr. Spencer's own theory, defined relation of its parts and aggregates, the "incoherent" is united in an ascending series of systems, and the "homogeneity" is a whole of inconceivable complexity, having within it the sum of the activities to be afterwards made visible. What scientific value attaches to loose use of phrases like this? Yet this is the foundation laid for a system of universal truth.

Turning to the evolved result, we do not find ourselves in clearer light. What do we learn from the expression, "a definite, coherent heterogeneity." In what sense is the product evolved more definite than that out of which it has been evolved? It is not more definite in quantity—Mr. Spencer assumes that the amount remains invariable,—it is not more definite in bounds—evolution is not a process of contraction: it is not more definitely one thing or many things, one force or many forces; for unless some power has intervened, or something has arisen out of nothing, it had, at the very outset, inclosed within it and its law, all that is in it now. The forces were as definite, the law of their operation as definite. An infinite intelligence might bring order out of confusion, might mould the definite out of the indefinite, might give form to the unformed; but it is wholly absurd to conceive of order rising spontaneously out of confusion, or the indefinite of itself becoming definite. This supposition—which Mr. Spencer would most emphatically repudiate—is the only alternative if, without the intervention of intelligence, that which was before "indefinite" is now "definite." In the change it must have become endowed with new qualities; matter without form has given form to itself: something has arisen out of nothing.

In what sense is the evolved cosmos more "co-

herent?" Its parts cohered in the primal state, do
they now cohere more than at the first? Then the
total of attraction in the universe has increased, and
the law of gravity is a fiction. Is the coherence but
the closer packing of the original matter at certain
points, and greater separation of it at others? It then
means only a re-arrangement of positions, and all
science is knowledge of spatial relations. Coherence
yields no knowable modification except that of form.
The troops that had been arranged in open order are
now shown as massed in columns or in squares. But
we have no account of the way in which new arms of
precision have been elaborated, and how the parts
have been endowed with the higher qualities of intelligence and courage, as well as arranged in new
positions. "Coherence," even if we could measure it,
would explain but a small part of the phenomena.

"Heterogeneity" does not help us to any real meaning. What constitutes exactly the difference marked
by the term? Is it altered distribution in space, or
altered arrangement of parts in mutual relation or in
bulk, or is it difference in the mode of motion of the
whole or of the parts? Or is it all these together, or
something else? What it may be precisely, the formula leaves undefined: it is elastic enough to bear a
variety of interpretations. That into which the
universe passes in evolution is left by the formula
as vague as that out of which it proceeds.

When the explanatory clause of the formula fails

us, we need not look for much light from a study of
the phrase which the explanation is supposed to
elucidate. The words "integration of matter and
concomitant dissipation of motion" do not furnish an
instrument of exact reasoning. In dealing with the
relations of matter and motion, we have not reached a
scientific conception till we have formulated definite
relations of quantity. There is no quantitative relation between this "integration" and "dissipation" set
out in the formula. What the relation may be, if
there be definite relation, is left undetermined. We
have elsewhere general statements as to progress from
"the extreme of diffusion to the extreme of concentration," and from the "greatest quantity of contained
motion to the least quantity of contained motion;" but
these phrases give us no material for scientific knowledge. The exactness with which a law of science cor-
responds with reality is proved by the certainty with
which, by means of it, definite results may be predicted.
What prevision of future events does this law furnish ?
What event has it enabled the evolutionist to foresee ?
It will not help us to write out in advance the series
of changes through which the whole universe or any
part of it will pass. It does not supply an instrument
of discovery where observation has not reached; we
cannot determine by it the form of any organism
outside the field of observation. It cannot, except in
a loose use of terms, be called a *law*.

On further examination of this boasted all-comprehending principle, we are left in perplexity by the difficulty of bringing under it two classes of processes differenced by quite opposite conditions. Mr. Spencer lays down his principle as applicable alike to the movement of the totality of concrete being and to the evolution of individual things. To bring under the same formula the totality of cosmic movement and the changes taking place in individual things is manifestly impossible. The conditions are opposite. A lengthened discussion in his *First Principles* establishes as the foundation of the law of evolution, the indestructibility of matter, the continuity of motion, the persistence of force; and from these Mr. Spencer deduces the "law of evolution," which is, "the law of the continuous redistribution of matter and motion." *

Evolution is, then, a continuous *redistribution;* the quantity of matter remains the same, the amount of motion is unchanged : no addition or diminition is supposed to be possible. The doctrine of evolution professes to show how they are redistributed. To increase or diminish the amount of manifested force would be destructive of Mr. Spencer's demonstration, and fatal to his whole theory of cosmic evolution. All depends on the persistence of force. "Persistence of force is the deepest knowable cause of evolution." But when we come to apply Mr. Spencer's formula to individual objects or classes of things, we must dis-

---

* *First Principles,* § 92.

card everyone of those principles which he had so
laboriously illustrated, and applied deductively with
such seemingly conclusive demonstration. The conditions no longer admit of their application. Force
does not persist, matter is not indestructible, motion is
not continuous within the limits of the phenomena in
question. Let us take as an illustration the growth
of the germ out of which an oak is evolved. Without
pausing to dwell on the difficulty of applying the
phrase, "indefinite, incoherent homogeneity," to a germ
which, Mr. Spencer tells us, "is not absolutely structureless, but consists of a mass of cells,"* let us note
the progress of its growth. The plant grows by constant augmentation from without; it is continually
adding, from surrounding matter, to the matter of
which it is composed. The contained motion increases
with the increase of bulk. The process is not integration but aggregation of matter ; not dissipation but in-
crement of motion; not in either case redistribution,
but increase. Redistribution is a misleading name for
the process. The matter does not remain the same in
quantity, nor the same in its parts : new matter is
being continually added and old matter removed.
The sum of motion is ever changing — increasing
during growth and diminishing in decay; and whether
increasing or diminishing, subject to periodical ebb
and flow. Mr. Spencer tells us that "living bodies

---

* *Biology*, Vol. I., § 55.

display in the highest degree the structural changes constituting evolution." Yet it would be as easy to bring the cosmos, viewed after Plato's conception as an animal, and Plato himself, under the same biological laws, as to embrace under one law of the redistribution of matter and motion the living body and the entire universe. In the evolution of any living thing from germ to maturity, every principle of cosmic evolution is violated—the force does not persist, the matter does not remain equal in quantity, the sum of the motion does not continue the same. A law based on constancy of amount cannot be adapted to ceaseless increase and diminution. The process is not one of redistribution of materials, but of ingathering, sorting, and changing. So far as evolution is exemplified in the growth of any living thing, or in the larger group of changes embodied in the development of a species or variety, it proceeds equally whether force persist or not. Any given portion of force ceases to persist as regards the individual or the class, so soon as it has passed out of the environment; it may persist in the vast tracts of space beyond Sirius, but for the living thing it exists no more. If evolution be redistribution of matter and motion, then its formula is inapplicable to the growth of organic forms, and they are exempted from its law; if evolution be not redistribution of matter and motion, then it conflicts with Mr. Spencer's first principles, and the foundation of his philosophy is shaken. Taking it either way, we are driven to deny the exactness of Mr. Spencer's formula as a scientific principle, and its universality as a law. We look in vain to discover in it the basis of a complete theory of things.

An examination of this formula in its relation to thought and sensation would bring to light another vast field in which it proves wholly without significance; but that question, presenting itself for discussion elsewhere, need not engage our attention at this point.

Our criticism of the formula which expresses the law of evolution may be summed up in a few words. We find it to be wanting in precision, incapable of exact application, of no scientific worth, a loose general description of change rather than a definite expression of the law of change; yet we are asked to receive this formula as the embodiment of a principle which is to dominate all thought, shape all doctrine, form the basis of a universal philosophy, and effect "the complete unification of all knowledge."

CHAPTER XI.

EVOLUTION AS IT GIVES ACCOUNT OF INORGANIC MATTER.

THE Evolution Hypothesis, interpreting the universe by means of a dynamic principle, might be expected to throw its clearest light on the processes of inorganic matter. In this region dynamic law is supreme. The law of the redistribution of matter and motion should, therefore, have its most perfect illustration in instances gathered from the changes taking place in matter where vital action does not intervene. In examining Mr. Spencer's system, the critic is placed at a disadvantage in not having the doctrine applied in this field. After discussing the general question in his *First Principles*, Mr. Spencer devotes the subsequent discussion to the application of his theory in the departments of Biology and Psychology, Social Organization, and Ethics. He does not expound in any systematic way the bearing of his hypothesis as an interpretation of the law of change in inorganic matter. This omission is greatly to be regretted. Matter and motion are more clearly seen in operation when undisturbed by vitality or mind, and the principles of mathematical physics could have been more exactly and rigidly applied as a test of the conclusiveness of

K

the reasoning. In this field it is difficult to hide inconclusive thinking under the mist of generalities: mathematical reasoning does not admit of the substitution of illustrations for arguments and doubtful analogies for conclusive proofs.

We are not, perhaps, pressing too far some indications in his works, if we infer that Mr. Spencer has not in this department arrived as yet at conclusions that could be established by incontestable reasoning. We find him admitting that " the antecedents of those forces which our solar system displays belong to a past of which *we can never have anything but inferential knowledge; and at present we cannot be said to have even this.* Numerous and strong as are the reasons for believing the nebular hypothesis, we cannot yet regard it as *more than an hypothesis.*"* But if the nebular hypothesis be still doubtful; if we cannot be said to have even " inferential knowledge " of it, the same dubiety attaches to the evolution hypothesis; for the existence of a nebulous mass gradually passing, by the operation of dynamic law, into the present state of the universe is essential to the evolution doctrine.

Not having before us a detailed exposition of the application of the evolution hypothesis to the processes of cosmic change, we must content ourselves by examining it in its answer to questions that lie at the

---

* *First Principles,* § 68.

root of the doctrine as an interpretation of all forms of concrete being.

The atomic theory of matter is taken by Mr. Spencer as the foundation of his physical system. What account does he give of the atom? Its inconceivable minuteness may be gathered from his statement that by reason we have been helped to explore a " universe compared with which our earth is a grain of sand, and to detect the structure of a monad compared with which a grain of sand is an earth."* The statement is more rhetorical than exact; yet we may infer from it how minute in his view are the atoms forming the ultimate constituents of matter.

The one knowable quality of the atom would seem to be resistance. "A thing cannot be thought of as occupying space, except as offering resistance. Even though but a point, if it be conceived to offer absolutely *no* resistance it ceases to be anything— becomes *no*-thing."† " Our conception of Matter," he says elsewhere, "reduced to its simplest shape, is that of co-existent positions that offer resistance."‡ Again, he says, " this conception uniting independence, permanence, and force, is the conception we have of matter."‖

In so far as the atom has resistance it manifests force ; beyond this its relation to force is left unde-

---

* *Psych.* Vol. II., § 389.   † *Ibid.* § 348.
‡ *First Principles,* § 48.   ‖ *Psych.* Vol. II., § 468.

fined. But if the essential characteristic of the atom is resistance, how does kinetic energy arise? Is the atom a force-bearer, or is the force inherent in the atom? Have we the atom + kinetic energy exerted through it, or are the atom and the kinetic energy one? The distinction here indicated may seem somewhat fine-drawn; but it is important as marking two wholly diverse views of the universe. Is all force immanent in the atom, or is the atom the instrument of force? The difference is a very real one: it marks the discrimination between agent and instrument, between that which acts, and that which is acted upon. Mr. Spencer favours the latter view. It has an important bearing on his hypothesis; for if the atoms that are built up into the cosmos are not themselves the active forces ever working in it, but are only the vehicles or instruments of the operative forces, then have we, besides matter and motion, a something which is not matter, but plays with it. The atoms, forming the stuff of which the universe is built up, are moved and directed by this force, or these forces, for it may be one force or many, and the result is not the outcome of the law of the atoms, but is wrought out by the undiscoverable force or forces behind them: in which case we are not dealing with matter whose law we might be able to discover, but with forces behind matter whose law is wholly inscrutable, except in so far as it may be revealed in the mode in which the atoms aggregated in molecules or masses are moved. But our knowledge of the law of these hidden forces must be arrived at by observation so far removed from the original activities as to be of very doubtful validity. The action of the forces through the atoms may be controlled by higher laws that are undiscoverable; or the force acting through an atom may cease to act through it and pass into some other mode of activity, wholly out of relation to man's sensibility, and therefore according to Mr. Spencer's theory, out of the knowable. Even the atom itself may disappear, if we may speak of the disappearance of what is for ever invisible: for its resistance is a manifestation of force; if that force cease to act through it in resistance, the atom, according to Mr. Spencer, "ceases to be something and becomes nothing." If, then, each atom is not the embodiment of a quantum of force remaining unchanged, but, on the contrary, is the bearer or instrument of force, not immanent in it but exterior to it, the law of "the redistribution of matter and motion" has no rational basis: it cannot be maintained as the law of the successive changes of all concrete existence, and the evolution hypothesis is not tenable. The atom being enthroned as king in the realm of knowledge, it is not satisfactory, when we would ascertain clearly and without ambiguity what this is which is to be to us in the place of God, to be left without a fully reasoned account of it.

But, leaving this point undetermined, we may ad-

vance a step, and inquire what the evolution doctrine
has to say about the combination of atoms in aggregates with definite internal relations. Suppose three
atoms united in such an aggregate: they come
together in motion, and ceaseless internal oscillation
characterizes the little system. These combined atoms
or molecules, with their internal relations, are sur-
rounded by other like infinitesimal bodies, and move
in relation with them; and these combinations go
on increasing in intricateness, forming a more and
more complex system or aggregate of systems. Some
such process is indicated by Mr. Spencer as going on
through countless cycles before evolution has reached
the stage of visibility; while the universe is still in
the imperceptible. What rational account can the evolution doctrine give of this original process in the
building up of atoms into molecules and systems of
molecules? In these systems there is the complete
outline of Mr. Spencer's future cosmos: all coming
changes lay in those first co-ordinated movements.
The universe is not interpreted till they are eluci-
dated. The atoms have not only moved themselves,
or been moved by the forces behind them; but they
have moved, or been moved, in such directions and in
such skilful combination of motions, that the continuance of the process on the same lines gives the universe
as we know it. Here is another question of vital
moment unanswered.

The progress of organization goes on, according to

Mr. Spencer's view, continually increasing in complexity: system is built up after system, till to
conceive the involved combinations of atoms and
movements contained in a particle of matter invisible
under the microscope, exceeds the utmost power of
intelligence. In that molecule lies a little universe.
And all this world of order and energy, in which every
atom thrills in ceaseless swift vibration, and all groups
of atoms balanced in relations internal and external,
are being ever more perfectly adjusted in harmony
with the end towards which all is moving, lies behind
and beneath that visible cosmos which is the field of
scientific research. The evolutionist can give no
answer to the eager questioning of those who wish
to find some reasonable explanation of how there
arose, out of a pre-supposed universe of whirling
atoms, a cosmos which, at its first appearing in view
of science, contains within it all the causes that evolve
into the order, beauty, intelligence, and moral and
religious feeling known to us.

Of the world that lies behind the visible, evolution
can tell us nothing: yet the visible can never be
understood till that world is known; if final causes
be dismissed from thought and a directing intelligence
be denied. Every department of physical science
runs ultimately into problems of molecular physics.
Chemistry, optics, mechanics, mineralogy, physiology, all reach in the last resort problems which,
if they are to receive a scientific solution, must be

solved by a true theory of the ultimate constitution of matter.

Even within the seen, evolution has no light to throw on those differentiations of matter indicated in the long list of elementary substances—a list which has grown with the advance of chemical science. "Much evidence now conspires to show that molecules of the substances we call elementary are in reality compound:"* but of their composition, as a process in the continuous redistribution of matter and motion, evolution can teach us nothing. Take as an instance gold : the continuous redistribution is here at fault for the compound molecules of gold, if experience may be trusted, suffer no redistribution; the continuity of change is broken. Evolutionism fails us. What problem is there, in terrestial or celestial physics, of which the evolution hypothesis furnishes a valid solution? So soon as we reach a question that runs deep into the constitution of the universe, evolution has nothing better than a guess to offer.

It is a barren hypothesis. It adds nothing to our knowledge of the laws that direct the shaping of a dewdrop or the formation of a crystal. If it has anything definite to teach us in the realm of inorganic matter, Mr. Spencer has not given the world the benefit of that knowledge. Suppose a portion of sea water has evaporated, leaving as a deposit the crystal of salt

---

* *Biology*, Vol. I., Appendix, p. 486.

before held in solution, would it not be the merest pretence of knowledge to bring the process under Mr. Spencer's law of the redistribution of matter and motion, and describe it as an "integration of matter and concomitant dissipation of motion?" It would not add much to the information of the dairy-maid, who had separated the butter from milk, to be told that the "indefinite, incoherent homogeneity" which she calls milk, had been evolved into a "definite, coherent heterogeneity," made up of butter-milk and butter.

The whole range of the dynamical operations of nature may be searched in vain, we think, for a single instance of what could be with exact propriety of language described as evolution. There are abundant examples of something that seems homogeneous becoming heterogeneous: the fluid holding a salt in solution may lose its seeming homogeneity and deposit the salt in the form of crystals; but such a case does not exemplify progress towards a new state of heterogeneity; it is reversion to a previously existing form. The instances furnished by inorganic matter are never illustrations of evolution. They are examples of recurrence to the normal condition as soon as the action of disturbing causes is withdrawn. The evolutionist, when he is limited to the inorganic, is thrown back for his illustrations on the operation of vast cosmic forces : he narrates the story of the birth and death of worlds, and traces with the utmost ease cyclic movements of evolution and dissolution. But the proof is not such as would determine the framing of any hypothesis worthy of being regarded as more than the merest guess. There is no practical business in which such evidence as is adduced would be regarded as of any real worth. Why should it not be maintained that a differentiated condition was the original and is the normal state of the physical universe, and that every seeming homogeneity is a departure from that normal condition, possibly through the interactions of forces producing effects analogous to those breaks of uniformity which present an appearance of exception to the known laws of nature? The supposition is as good as its opposite, and it is more nearly conformable to fact; for science has no knowledge in any field of the actual existence of an " indefinite, incoherent homogeneity." If there be such, it is, on Mr. Spencer's principles, unknowable. Differentiation is the necessary form of all definite concepts. Not only is it necessary in thought; it is invariable in experience. There is no such thing known as a concrete existence which is homogeneous; nor is there any existing thing, the explanation of which, so far as it is within the possibility of knowledge, is furthered by supposing a state of homogeneity. Science begins with differentiation. If a Divine Being created the universe, it was as easy for Him to create it in a differentiated form, as in an immeasurable mist-cloud, or imperceptible mass, containing within it the cause and law of all things : if the universe is not the work of an intelligent Power, then it is equally mysterious and incomprehensible whether we contemplate the existing order as science knows it, or posit in a distant past a universe of moving atoms having in them, or in the forces operating through them, the origin of all knowable existences and the law in accordance with which all things as we know them act.

The evolutionist fails to unify the concrete existences lying under view in the field of inorganic matter. His dynamic principle is fruitless in the region of inquiry where dynamic law is supreme. Even in pure physics evolutionism is silent in face of every fundamental question. The veil is not taken away.

CHAPTER XII.

THE TRANSITION FROM INORGANIC MATTER TO LIFE.

MR. SPENCER is too clear a thinker to fall into the absurdities of the advocates of "spontaneous generation." It is a complete misunderstanding of his doctrine, to assume that he has any interest in finding, by experiment or observation, evidence of new forms of life rising into being out of inorganic matter. Supposed instances of this kind are of value only to advocates who aim at catching the crowd. Mr. Spencer strengthens his position by confuting the advocates of "spontaneous generation." His theory of evolution—and every possible rational theory of evolution—would be overturned if it were proved that new forms of organic life could, in a few hours or days, spring out of inorganic matter. "That creatures having *quite specific structures* are evolved in a few hours, without antecedents calculated to determine their specific forms is," he says, "to me incredible. . . . My disbelief extends not only to the alleged cases of 'spontaneous generation,' but to every case akin to

them. The very conception of spontaneity is wholly
incongruous with the conception of evolution, ...
No form of evolution, inorganic or organic, can be
spontaneous; but in every instance the antecedent
forces must be adequate in their quantities, kinds, and
distribution to work the observed effects. Neither
the alleged cases of 'spontaneous generation,' nor any
imaginable cases in the least allied to them fulfil this
requirement. . . . . Granting that the formation of
organic matter and the evolution of life in its lowest
forms may go on under existing cosmical conditions;
but believing it more likely that the formation of
such matter and such forms, took place at a time
when the heat of the earth's surface was falling
through ranges of temperature at which higher organic compounds are unstable; I conceive that the
moulding of such organic matter into the simplest
types, must have commenced with portions of protoplasm more minute, more indefinite, and more inconstant in their character than the lowest Rhizopods,
less distinguishable from a mere fragment of albumen
than even the *Protogenes* of Professor Haeckel. The
evolution of specific shapes must, like all other organic
evolution, have resulted from the actions and reactions between such incipient types and their environments, and the continued survival of those which
happened to have specialities best fitted to the specialities of their environments. To reach by this process
the comparatively well specialized forms of ordinary

infusoria must, I conceive, have taken an enormous period of time."*

Allowing Mr. Spencer thus, in his own words, to clear away misconceptions that have gathered round his doctrine, let us go on to ask how he conceives the transition from inorganic matter to living organisms.

He first prepares the way by setting out at considerable length, and very minutely, the characteristics of the four chief elements comprising living bodies, and shows that their compounds are unstable and conform to "the conditions necessary to that redistribution of matter and motion which constitutes evolution."† But it is not enough to show that the materials of which organisms are composed are specially fitted to the place and work assigned them. On the theory of a creative intelligence, it will be beforehand certain that the material used will be adapted to its end. Bodies designed to grow, but formed of matter extremely ill-adapted to the processes of growth, would be evidence that the world was ordered by something very different from intelligence. To support the evolution doctrine, it is needful to show —not only that the chemical compounds forming the material of organisms are unstable, and therefore well adapted to the changes necessary in vital action—but in what way that which before existed as matter without life has become a living organism.

---

* *Biology*, Vol. I., Appendix, p. 481.   † *Biology*, Vol. I., § 9.

To trace the course of this change, Mr. Spencer goes back to the invisible world of atoms. He supposes them aggregated into molecules, and these into other aggregates, and so onward, in ever more complicated systems, until we reach the molecule of which protein is formed. We have then found a form of matter modifiable with extreme facility by surrounding agents. This protein "is capable of existing under probably at least a thousand isomeric forms; and, as we shall presently see, it is capable of forming with itself and other elements, substances yet more intricate in composition, that are practically infinite in their varieties of kind. Exposed to those innumerable modifications of conditions which the earth's surface afforded, ... this extremely changeable substance must have undergone now one now another of its countless metamorphoses. And to the mutual influences of its metamorphic forms, under favouring conditions, we may ascribe the production of the still more composite, still more sensitive, still more variously-changeable portions of organic matter, which, in masses more minute and simple than existing *Protozoa*, displayed activities varying little by little into those called vital—actions which protein itself exhibits in a certain degree, and which the lowest known living things exhibit only in a greater degree." *

Biology, Vol. I., Appendix, p. 483.

In this way Mr. Spencer reaches actions "called vital." How out of these minute fragments of protein have special kinds of organisms arisen?

"Molecules, perhaps. exceeding in size and complexity those of protein, as those of protein exceed those of inorganic matter, may, I conceive, be the special units belonging to special kinds of organisms. . . . . The existence of such physiological units, peculiar to each species of organism, is not unaccounted for. They are evolved simultaneously with the evolution of the organism they compose: they differentiate as fast as the organisms differentiate; and are made multitudinous in kind by the same actions which make the organisms they compose multitudinous in kind. . . . . . Every physicist will endorse the proposition, that in each aggregate there tends to establish itself an equilibrium between the forces exercised by all the units upon each and by each upon all. . . . . Organic molecules of each kind, no matter how complex, have a form of equilibrium in which, when they aggregate, their complex forces are balanced. . . . The special molecules having a special organic structure as their form of equilibrium must be reacted upon by the total forces of the organic structure. . . . . Setting out with the stage in which protein in minute aggregates took on those simplest differentiations which fitted it for differently conditioned parts of its medium, there must have unceasingly gone on perpetual re-adjustments of the balance between aggregates and their units—actions and reactions of the two, in which the unit tended ever to establish the typical form produced by actions and reactions in all antecedent generations, while the aggregate, if changed in form by change of surrounding conditions, tended ever to impress on the units a corresponding change of polarity, causing them in the next generation to reproduce the changed form—their new form of equilibrium." *

These quotations fairly represent Mr. Spencer's hypothesis of the evolution of organic matter, the evolution out of that matter of living things, and finally, the evolution of living things differentiated into special kinds of organisms.

On the entire exposition of the change from inorganic matter to living bodies differenced into kinds, we would first of all observe, that there is not one step in the process of which it is possible to furnish any proof. The whole is an effort—a very brilliant effort the reader will readily admit—of the scientific imagination. It is as truly an imaginative creation as the "Midsummer Night's Dream." The scientific mind may say it is very like what might have happened, but we have no evidence that it is the actual course of nature. It is a guess after truth, and guesses as to matters of fact are more likely to be wrong than right. He who shoots into a mist-cloud is not likely

---

* *Biology,* Vol. **I.**, Appendix, pp. 486-7.

to hit the mark. A closer examination will confirm
the judgment that Mr. Spencer has not in this instance hit the truth.

1. The hypothesis assumes the evolution of molecules distinct in kinds, as a process prior to the
evolution of protoplasm. Before Mr. Spencer is in a
position to obtain those "portions of protoplasm more
minute, more indefinite, more inconstant in their characters than the lowest *Rhizopods* — less distinguishable from a mere fragment of albumen than even the
Protogenes of Haeckel," there must have been evolved
out of the simplest aggregates of atoms, molecules (*a*)
differentiated into kinds, and (*b*) reproduced in their
kinds. He must show, then, that the persistence of
force will account for the origination of differences of
kind among molecules; he must show further that
the same dynamic principle will account for the reproduction true to kind of these several kinds.

If it be assumed that a universal law of aggregation of atoms determined the formation of molecules
unlimited in number and in variety, we may find the
first requirement. But then we have begun the first
chapter of the scientific book of Genesis with a de-
claration of the existence and universality of law—
and we take for granted in the collocation and law
of the primordial forces all the phenomena of the
universe as it now is.

Waiving this criticism, and accepting the formation
of myriad kinds of aggregates compounded of the

moving atoms that pervade immensity, we inquire how the kinds are perpetuated. It can only be (*a*) by the molecules when formed remaining for ever fixed, or (*b*) by the continuous formation of new molecules of the different kinds in the same manner in which the original molecules of these kinds were produced, or (*c*) by the propagation of successive generations of molecules generating after their kind, in the language of Moses, " seeding seed after their kind." The first supposition is contrary to the principles of evolution ; the persistence of force, as Mr. Spencer applies it, renders such perpetuity impossible. Fixedness of these composite molecules is inconsistent with the continuous mutation constituting the cosmic process. The second supposition is also incongruous with the principles of evolution, according to which the movement of the universe is a ceaseless movement onward: "into the same river no man can enter twice." The third is the only supposition consonant with Mr. Spencer's doctrine; but it lands us in inexplicable mystery. The propagation of molecular structures true to their kind is wholly inconceivable. Mr. Spencer does not undertake to give an account of it. We have, then, at the very outset, the two most difficult problems which meet the student of organic life in its fully developed state—differentiation into kinds, and propagation of each after its kind. The evolutionist begins, where Moses begins, with the seed reproducing its kind. But there is this wide differ-

,ence : Moses begins with life—the living seed. The
evolutionist must be given kinds and the reproduction
of kinds in the primal atomic aggregates, in the
earliest conceivable stage of evolution ; he must find
kinds and the reproduction of each after its kind long
antecedent to the first beginning of life.

Again, there is pressed on our attention an instance
of the manner in which evolution, when one reaches
a point of real moment, leaves the vital question
unanswered.

2. But let us, for the sake of argument, grant Mr.
Spencer his molecules of "extreme modifiability,"
he has still out of these to build up the protoplasm,
portions of which began, as he supposes, to display
actions approximating to those called vital. Now he
is at this point met by an obstacle which lies in the
way of his theory, and which has for so far proved
insuperable. He has to get protoplasm antecedent to
the existence of any living thing. Here he is met by
a uniform experience—an experience without known
exception, that protoplasm is only found in that
which is, or has been, living. Mr. Spencer must, then,
before he can take a single step in his progress
towards organized bodies, obliterate one of the clearest
drawn lines in nature, and postulate the existence of
protoplasm prior to the existence of life, while all
observation and experience bear testimony to the
presence of life as the invariable condition of the
existence of protoplasm. That is, he has introduced

the very property or principle to be accounted for—
life, in assuming the production of protoplasm—which
is a form of living matter—as an intermediate step in
the progress towards life. The assumption is in direct
conflict with a quite uniform experience.

3. But granting Mr. Spencer his "still more composite, still more sensitive, still more variously
changeable portions of organic matter," we cannot
at once allow him that they "displayed actions
varying little by little into those called vital." He
takes for granted that by variations added by little
and little the actions displayed by the minute aggregates of protein molecules would in the end reach
actions properly called vital. This is to take for
granted the very point at issue. To assume that the
addition of a sufficiently prolonged series of changes,
each in itself infinitesimal, to action which is not
vital, will constitute vital action, is to assume that the
difference between mechanical and vital action is one
of minute variation and not of kind. The two kinds
of action are altogether diverse. To assume that they
are similar, that they are but varieties of the same,
is another of the instances so frequently occurring in
the evolution doctrine of obliterating dividing lines
when they run across the doctrine and break its
continuity. It is the business of science not to bury
facts but to explain them.

Motion internal to the aggregates called molecules
may be conceived as changed in many ways: it may

be modified by the growth of new molecules; the inter-molecular motions may be modified by the inter-actions of each molecule and its environment; but no increase or diminution, or composition, or variation of such motion will constitute that difference which exists between vital and mechanical action. No change in the times of oscillation of the atomic constituents or inter-action between molecular aggregates and their environment will produce that which is signified by the word life. Motions that are mechanical (or, if the term be preferred, dynamical) and nothing more will not yield vital actions.

It is not unusual for a disputant to cover a false process in his logic by departures from sound reasoning which escape detection from their apparent insignificance. Mr. Spencer's indiscernable modifications make the contrast between life and the action of inorganic matter less marked; but we repeat, additions may increase motion, variations may render it more complex or change its direction or its mode, but no increase or variation can make it other than dynamic. Minute variations may insensibly change the physical action or alter the chemical qualities of a portion of matter, but can never bridge over the separation between the dynamical and the vital. It is directly in the teeth of all experience to deem it possible to divide and subdivide life by little and little downward until its distinctive characteristics have been pared away, and it has become only a mode of molecular motion:

it is equally in conflict with all knowledge of nature to assume it to be possible, by inappreciable increments of molecular motion added on through infinitesimal stages, to turn it into life. The difference between living bodies and inorganic matter cannot be obliterated by such gradations of change.

4. When the evolutionist has advanced from inorganic matter to life, he has then to undertake the task of accounting for the innumerable varieties of kind which characterize the organic kingdom. From the lowest vegetal and animal forms to the highest, over the whole range of life, the varieties surpass the power of thought. How have all these arisen, and how are they perpetuated? Mr. Spencer answers by introducing the "physiological unit." This special creation fills so important a place in his doctrine that we must examine it closely as to its origin and nature. "Organisms," he says, "are built up of certain highly-complex molecules, which we distinguished as physiological units—each kind of organism being built up of physiological units peculiar to itself." *

---

* *Biology*, Vol. II., § 178.

CHAPTER XIII.

L ET us call up the physiological unit, and examine it as keenly as we can ; for it yields the explanation—the only rational explanation which evolution offers—of organic structure, and of the multiplied forms of life.

1. We, first of all, notice that it is extremely small —so small that we must add another lens to our microscope, the lens called imagination, to bring it within the range of vision. Extremely minute though it be, it may still contain within it the secret of organic life and of sensation ; for these mysteries are not questions of bulk, but of kind. Let us then study closely this minute exponent of the invisible, who holds the mystic scroll, whereon is written the solution of every problem in the range of organized nature.

2. We find that it is a highly organized body—"a definite, coherent heterogeneity." It has parts, and each part is distinctly differenced from every other, and is definitely related to every other. The soaring eagle is not more really a systematized structure. "Molecules, perhaps exceeding in size and complexity those of protein, as those of protein exceed those of

inorganic matter, may, I conceive, be the special units belonging to special kinds of organisms. By their constitution they must have a plasticity, or sensitiveness to modifying forces, far beyond that of protein; and bearing in mind not only that their varieties are practically infinite in number, but that closely allied forms of them, chemically indifferent to one another as they must be, may co-exist in the same aggregate, we shall see that they are fitted for entering into unlimited varieties of organic structures." *

3. A further examination shows the physiological' unit to be composed of system upon system of molecules, in successive degrees of complexity; each system, and each combination of systems, having its peculiar internal motions, and its individual polarity; and each system having the equilibration of its polarity in the perfected structure of the entire unit. " By combination of molecules with one another, and recombinations of the products, there are formed systems of systems of molecules unimaginable in their complexity. Step by step, as the aggregate molecules so resulting grow larger and increase in heterogeneity, they become more unstable, more readily transformable by small forces, more capable of assuming various characters."† "The chemical units combine into units immensely more complex than themselves, complex as they are." ‡

---

* *Biology*, Vol. I., Appendix, p. 486.   † *Ibid.*, p. 486.
‡ *Ibid.*, § 66.

Each unit is, then, a little universe or infinitesimal microcosm, complex beyond conception. The visible heavens, in the correlations of the solar and astral systems, are simplicity itself compared with the intricacy of the correlated motions and equilibrated systems enclosed in each physiological unit.

4. These units differ in kinds as the developed organisms differ in kinds. They " possess the property of arranging themselves into the special structure of the organism to which they belong." *   From the lowest forms of vegetal and animal organizations, to the highest, from the *Amœba* to man, immense as are the varieties of organisms, so immense are the varieties of physiological units—each of them as completely differentiated as the perfected structure of the living thing—each stamping with its own character every kind of living thing.

But the incalculable diversity is still greater than is thus indicated: for not only do kingdoms, genera, species, varieties, and all the other recognized groups of organisms, mark divisions among the physiological units, but the differentiation among the units runs down to the differences which may be seen among the children of the same parent, or in growths from the same seed; not only so, but every organ of the body has its own special kind.   The little world of relations and adaptations in a single living

---

* *Biology,* § 66.

thing are all traceable to modifications of these units. Each one of them is thus complex beyond the power of thought to imagine, and the multiformity in their intricate structure is beyond the power of figures to express. Yet these varieties of character are necessary to the evolutionist's explanation of the diversity seen in organized nature. The explanation is not less complex than the thing explained.

5. The physiological units have "a more or less distinctive character." "The form of each species of organism is determined by a peculiarity in the structure of its units." These units "have a special structure in which they tend to arrange themselves." They have "an innate tendency to arrange themselves into the shape of the organism to which they belong." "A plant or animal of any species is made up of special units, in all of which there dwells the intrinsic aptitude to aggregate into the form of that species." They show a "proclivity towards a particular arrangement."* These characteristics are ancestral: they are inherited. The extreme modifiability of organic aggregates of molecules is the property most frequently brought into view by Mr. Spencer. He has been at great pains to illustrate the instability of the organic compounds. Yet each physiological unit, however mobile, has stability enough to retain the impress of its ancestry, and to perpetuate it by reproduction. At

---

* *Biology*, Vol. I., § 65.

this remote point in the history of organisms we are taught to recognize the principle of heredity. Mr. Spencer calls the sum of these individual characteristics " polarity," taking the term from a phenomenon of inorganic matter, " a power of whose nature we know nothing." *   Under this term in physics, " a name for something of which we are ignorant—a name for a hypothetical property which as much needs explanation as that which it is used to explain "†—he covers all these innate tendencies and proclivities.   The polarity of the units is the original of the law of heredity.   Polarity in physics is the name of an unknown mode of force.   What light does the evolutionist throw on the dark places of organic history, by clothing with the same robe of mist the unit, which the spell of his imagination has summoned out of the unseen world ?

Every observer, from the herdsman of Haran onward, has known that the offspring derives its characteristics from the parent.   Is our knowledge of the fact more clear to us when we are told that there are physiological units lying far below the visible, which, if we could see them, would be found to manifest these same characteristics, and of which the bodies of our cattle are built up ?

But think of the number and variety of hereditary attributes that we must suppose to be stored up in

* *Biology*, Vol. I., § 64.   † *Ibid.*, § 65.

any single unit. When two cells—the sperm-cell and the germ-cell—are brought together and their enclosed physiological units have been brought into contact, on Mr. Spencer's theory, the decaying vigour is revived and a new evolution initiated. These units bring— each of them—into the contact and new relation that ensues the hereditary characteristics of a series carried back through myriads of ages. In all that succession nothing has been lost. Throughout the vast series of births and deaths no part of the family wealth has been squandered : each bequeathed to its sucessor the heritage of ancestral experience unimpaired, en- hancing it with that gained in the space of its own existence, and the physiological units that, coming to- gether in generation, form the germ of the animal begotten, are thus the sum of all the immense com- plexity of moving systems of atoms and molecules from the first beginning of cosmic history till now. But is this science or fancy ? Are we seriously dealing with knowable facts, or building up a universe exist- ing only in the scientific imagination ? Whatever the the reply may be, it is plain the cosmos is not made more intelligible to us than before. The evolutionist has only carried the most distinctive phenomena of organic life back to a mysterious region occupied by myriad whirling molecules whose oscillations and combined motions, though they include the cause of all the visible universe, lie for ever far below the range of observation.　　•

6. Each physiological unit, in addition to its innate proclivities, has its individual characteristics. These are due to the incidence of environing forces. The history of each unit being different from that of every other, and the incident forces in their impact being diverse in each instance, these diversities involve modifications which give a special peculiarity to each. The unit is inevitably dissolved unless it can adjust its polarity to the new conditions. Its internal equilibration must be brought into accord with the incident forces. Hence the constant change in organisms and the evolution of new forms. If this doctrine be true, we have to clear up a new perplexity. The process of adjustment of units is as difficult to comprehend as the adjustment of living bodies; and the difficulty is increased by bringing into view the further consideration, that while the unit builds up the organism, the organism determines the structure of the unit. Each acts and reacts on the other. Evolution undertakes to elucidate the equilibration of unit and organic structure, as a means of elucidating the equilibration of the living body and its environment. Is the equilibrium of a system of invisible molecules more easily determined than the equilibrium of visible masses ?

7. The physiological units possess inherent powers and properties of the most surprising sort. They have " powers of arranging themselves into the forms of the organism to which they belong." " The polarity of the physiological units produces, during

the development of any organism, a combination of internal forces that expend themselves in working out a structure in equilibrium with the forces to which ancestral organisms were exposed." * The form of each species of organism is determind by a peculiarity in the constitution of its units. That is, the permanent characteristics of every organism are determind by the physiological, units, while the forces in the environment tend to produce modifications of the structure.

In criticising the theories of Dr. Erasmus Darwin, Lamark, and Professor Owen, Mr. Spencer condemns the ascription of organic evolution to "some aptitude naturally possessed by organisms." "In brief," he says, "this assumption of a persistent formative power inherent in organisms and making them unfold into higher forms is an assumption no more tenable than the assumption of special creations; of which, indeed, it is but a modification; differing only by the fusion of separate unknown processes unto a continuous unknown process." † Yet Mr. Spencer cannot avoid the use of similar terms. When he is most emphatic in repudiating all discipleship in any school which acknowledges the operation of supra - dynamical powers, his "speech bewrayeth" him. He speaks of proclivities, tendencies, power of arranging themselves, as characteristic of his units. Of these attributes,

---

* *Biology*, Vol., II. § 18.   † *Ibid.*, Vol. I., § 144.

evolution must give some clear account, unless it altogether fail as an explanation of organic nature. Mr.
Spencer is very much displeased if these powers immanent in the units should be confounded with the
" archæus, vital principle, *nisus formativus* and so on."
He rejects such implication as unfounded, and gives
the explanation that " the proclivity of units of each
order towards the specific arrangement seen in the
organism they form, is not to be understood as resulting from their own structures and actions only; but
as the product of these and the environing forces to
which they are exposed. . . . . In its complete form,
the conception is that these specific molecules, ...
have for their form of aggregation in which their forces
are equilibrated the structure of the adult organism
to which they belong, and that they are impelled to
fall into this structure by the co-operation of the environing forces and the force they exercise on one
another—the environing forces being the source of
the power which effects the arrangement, and the pol-
arities of the molecules determining the direction." *
But this explanation does not satisfactorily clear up
the point: the environing forces may be the power
which effects the re-arrangement, but the inherent
proclivities of the units *direct* it. The winds may
drive the ship; the captain and crew steer it: the
course is determined by the intelligence on board.

---

* *Biology*, Vol. I., Appendix, p. 488.

It is no addition to real knowledge to be told that the innate tendencies, inherent proclivities, and powers of directing the formation of organic structure that lie in the physiological units have been derived from the environment in the past, and are due to a succession of minute modifications wrought through an innumerable series of changes. The action of the environment had over against it from the beginning the reaction of the molecular system. On Mr. Spencer's theory there could not have been any organic structure without an antecedent molecular constitution. Go as far back as we will, we must begin, not with the "indefinite," but with a defined order, not with the "incoherent," but with a combined and compacted system, not with "homogeneity," but with a state of differentiation than which nothing higher in kind can be conceived.

Evolution again breaks down when it faces an ultimate question.

The physiological unit is a necessary link in Mr. Spencer's hypothesis; if we doubt its existence we doubt his doctrine. An examination of what is involved in the assumption of its existence leads us to the conviction that it is a "special creation," not of the Supreme Wisdom, but of the Evolution Philosophy.

M

CHAPTER XIV.

THE ORIGIN OF SENTIENT LIFE.

A BEING endowed with sentience is a phenomenon of which the Evolution Hypothesis must give intelligible account, or confess that it is unable to interpret some of the most obvious facts in nature. In this chapter we shall examine the question only in relation to the lower animals, leaving for separate discussion the origin and growth of self-conscious intelligence.

Sentient life is best exemplified in some of its more advanced forms. In the very lowest kinds it may be difficult to distinguish with certainty the animal from the vegetable. But when we turn to the more highly organized beings, the differences between the two kingdoms are so great that we are embarrased to find characteristics common to both. Take the dog as an example. The facts which await explanation are (a) his intelligence, (b) his sense of pleasure and pain, (c) his complex and highly developed organism. Putting aside the question of intelligence, which will be best examined in its highest form in man, we shall test Mr. Spencer's theory by its success in giving account of the origin of the organism and its sensibility. Organic sensibility, feeling; what account can evolution give of these most notable phenomena? The living organism, immensely complex and most skilfully adjusted to its uses, is, by hypothesis, whether in its present activities or in the process of its construction through an incalculable series of changes, to be accounted for by the laws of matter and motion and these only. Given an adequate knowledge of these laws, the entire phenomenon would be comprehended. The living organism is, on Mr. Spencer's theory, in all its activities and properties, wholly mechanical,—using that term in its widest sense, as including all modes of molecular motion.

The dog is struck; he utters a cry of pain. Is the sense of pain seeming only, or real? Is it a dynamic product solely—an effect of the same kind as the vibration of a tuning-fork, or the changed molecular condition of the snowy petal of a lily when it is marred by a touch of the finger? To answer in the affirmative is to accept a thorough-going doctrine of the mechanical structure of animals, making them merely automatic machines of inconceivable subtilty of adjustment and action. On the other hand, we ourselves know what it is to suffer pain; we have a more immediate knowledge of pain than of mechanical effects. Transferring our own feeling to a like instance, we do not doubt that the dog has a real sense of suffering.

What, then, is the exact nature of that activity in

which the sense of pain arises ? There are two aspects
of the phenomenon—a change in the condition of the
organism and a sensation. It is the latter with which
we have to do. The question at issue is not as to the
mode of molecular action in the nerve-tissue. ˙ We
have no controversy with the evolutionist as to his
explanation of nerve-action. We are ready to accept
any theory of isomeric change or decomposing molecular processes that may seem to accord with the
facts. Let the motions internal to the molecules, or
due to the interactions between molecules, or arising
from the relation of molecules and their aggregates be
what it may ; let the disordered movement be of any
kind that may be imagined, there remains still untouched the essential part of the instance—the *feeling*
of these disordered activities. Until this fact is eluci-
dated evolutionism is at fault.

Where lies the source or origin of the feeling ? Is
it a property of matter, or of some special collocation
or movement of matter, or is it an attribute of some
mode of concrete being distinct from matter ? Let us
suppose the entire universe to be composed of forces
manifested in atoms and their motions ; or, if it be
preferred, let the primary constituents of matter be
conceived of as points of force or vortex rings in a
uniform tenuous ether. The same method of criticism
is equally applicable under any one of these suppositions ; but, as the conception of atoms in motion is
more easily represented in thought, and is that adopted

by Mr. Spencer, we shall employ it in our argument. Let us then regard the universe as composed of atoms and their motions; let these atoms be supposed to be arranged in any imaginable order: if in that universe there should arise this most remarkable phenomenon called feeling, how can it be accounted for? Several hypotheses are conceivable. Feeling may be assumed to be latent in every atom, or in special kinds of atoms, or it may be supposed to lie hidden in some peculiar combination of atoms, or to be a mode of atomic motion, or to arise by the combination of atomic motions. No other supposition seems possible., Now, if the sense of pain is not latent in the atoms, it is inconceivable that it could come to be through any combination of them. Aggregates of atoms, each devoid of sensibility, having immanent in them severally no rudiment of feeling, or capacity for feeling, cannot acquire it by being brought into contact. Did feeling arise in such conditions it would be uncaused: something had then come out of nothing. Nor is it possible to imagine that atoms without capacity for feeling could acquire that capacity by being moved in some particular manner, either individually or in groups. We are then driven either to affirm the capacity for feeling to be a property resident in atoms, or to posit the existence of something other than matter. If we choose the former alternative, we ascribe to the atoms feeling, actual or potential: we constitute them monads; and they, in that case, possess properties which are not dynamic. The dynamic theory is abandoned at the very outset, as insufficient to account for the simplest phenomena; and the philosophy based on it is over-turned. If we adopt the latter alternative, and affirm the existence of concrete being other than the forces manifested in atoms and their motions, then, while we can still hold by mechanical law as the law of atoms, and may affirm the universality of dynamic law in so far as the universe is constituted of atoms, we have introduced a supra-dynamical element; we have affirmed the existence of a mode of being other than force as revealed in matter and motion; we stand face to face with another form of concrete existence, and the assumption that the principle of the persistence of force covers the whole realm of the knowable, is by consequence rejected. Choose which of the alternatives we will, in either case, the dynamic doctrine of evolution is found defective as a theory of sentient organic life.

Having reached the existence of feeling, we have touched the boundary of another world. We are as yet on the outer verge of that new mode of being; but even at this point we feel the presence of other powers; we must henceforth take account of feeling as well as force. Pleasure and pain form the most characteristic feature of animal life. Here, within the horizon of experience, a new phenomenon is full in view. In accounting for it the evolutionist is again at fault. He cannot set it in its true place as an integral part of the universal system. His hypothesis compels him to attempt what can never be accomplished — to assign to feeling its place in an order dominated throughout by physical law. If he take refuge in the unknowable, and affirm that feeling is a manifestation of the inscrutable power in a mode not existing potentially in any antecedent manifestation, he transcends scientific knowledge, and derives his doctrine from a source which, if it be not supernatural, lies admittedly beyond nature, so far as nature consists of phenomena that may be known. The cause to which feeling, in that case, is referred is not a cause of which science can take cognizance.

In dealing with the question of feeling, the evolutionist encounters further insurmountable difficulties. At the moment when this new mode of the unknowable power appeared within the knowable, the process of change was profoundly modified. The evolution of animal organisms must have proceeded henceforth in every part of it, in relation to this unique manifestation, which stands related to every molecular movement throughout the range of animal life.

The relations subsisting within the organism are extremely complex: physical forces are related to physical forces, forces to feelings, feelings to feelings, feelings to feelings through forces, and forces to forces through feelings. Take the last set of relations. Where a feeling, say of hunger, is awakened, it calls forth a series of exercises of physical force. Energy is expended in the pursuit and capture of prey. In this succession of states the feeling of hunger is a necessary element. The antecedent actions stand related to the subsequent actions through the feeling: take away the feeling, and the forth-putting of physical energy consequent upon it, is taken away. The feeling is an essential part of the instance. It matters nothing how the physical series may be otherwise related. Without the feeling the result must be entirely other than it is.

Let us examine the fact more closely. A physical change—a manifestation of the absolute cause in a material mode—is accompanied by feeling, which is a manifestation of the absolute cause in a mode not material. The physical process *plus* the feeling determines the next physical process, which is again accompanied by a second manifestation of the unknowable in feeling. The second physical process *plus* the second feeling determines the next physical process, and so on continually—the manifestation in feeling being as necessary to each subsequent determination as the physical process. If, then, the evolutionist is unable to constitute the feeling an integral part of the manifestations cohering by discoverable physical law, but is driven to refer it to the unknowable, organic evolution is condemned as a one-sided and inadequate hypothesis, incompetent to account for the whole fact; for it proposes to formulate the law of all living things in their origin and development, and it is proved incapable of setting in a comprehensible order the most notable of the phenomena. It is compelled to introduce an incomprehensible cause, not at one point only, but along the entire stream of change. But to fall back on a mysterious, inscrutable cause revealing itself in sentient organic life at every instant and everywhere in manifestations that co-operate with knowable causes, and give to the result its special characteristics, is to condemn evolution as a rational hypothesis.

That this conclusion is just will appear the more evident, if we consider the influence of feeling in the growth and development of organisms. The loss of nerve-sensibility is the precursor of decay in the individual; and the sense of pleasure and pain is, perhaps, the most potent factor in the changes wrought in living things in the course of generations. Through pleasures and pains, the modifications which arise are in great part effected. These feelings cannot be either ignored or placed in a position so relatively unimportant that they may be dealt with as incidents, rather than causes in the process. Environing physical forces are, no doubt, continually operating, and must produce their legitimate effect; but the results brought about are not wholly due to forces operating according to dynamic law; they are in great part owing to the activities called forth by the sense of pleasure enjoyed in certain affections of the organism, and the sense of pain suffered in others.

The operative cause is not the physical force alone, but the physical force *plus* the feeling.

To affirm that the modification of organisms is carried on wholly according to the laws of the under-lying absolute energy as revealed in matter and motion, is most evidently an unproved and unprov-able assumption. In animal life physical action can-not be severed from feeling and studied and measured apart; for sensibility is a primary characteristic of a sensitive organization. The manifestation of the unknowable in feeling is as necessary to the forma-tion or modification of animal organisms as the redistribution of matter and motion, or the persist-ence of force.

Evolutionism once more fails us. The evolutionist is unable to assign any knowable cause for the origin of sentient life; he cannot disclose its place in the cosmos or its relations to the universal order: nor does his hypothesis furnish an explanation of the part which sentience plays in the shaping of organs, the growth of bodies, or those modifications of or-ganic forms that have been wrought out in the course of change.

CHAPTER XV.

THE ORIGIN OF ORGANIC FORMS.

THE account which it gives of the origin of organic forms has gained for the Evolution Hypothesis its widest acceptance. Here its advocates put forth all their strength. They claim to have established the doctrine in this department beyond reasonable doubt.

Surveying the realm of organized matter, we see broad and deep lines differencing great classes of instances; and within these lines large groups clearly distinguished by dividing limits—limits never, within the range of experience, obliterated; and so, by successive divisions, until we reach variations that characterize, not the species, but the individual. This vast multiformity, seen in the contrasts between the two great kingdoms and in the incalculable diversities found in either, is to be derived from one primordial mode of living matter. Evolution is bound, not only to show that out of the same original living matter all these organisms *may* have sprung; it is bound to show that they *must* have sprung from it, and to show how: it is bound to account for their present form by setting out the law of a ceaseless onward movement and of modifications that, by hypothesis, have been growing ever more complex. It is impossible to construct a rational theory on other terms. On these conditions only can a philosophy of evolution be established. The evolutionist must not only prove that all organisms have been gradually differentiated through continuous successive changes; he must also account for the process.

The facts open to observation lie within a brief period of the history of the universe. No more than a narrow strip across the pattern which is being woven in the loom of time is visible to man. From this restricted experience he is left to trace the design backward to the far distant beginning. The instances out of which all theories as to the origin of organic forms are framed may be divided into two classes, organisms as found at the present time with their resemblances and differences, and distribution; and the facts of organic history in so far as they are revealed in the geological record. Over the entire field there has not been discovered anywhere direct evidence of transition form a less developed to a more highly developed species. That the earlier are the lower in organization is to be looked for on any hypothesis. If we accept the geologist's account of the history of the earth's crust, a gradual advancement from lower to higher forms is inevitable. No species can exist except in a suitable habitat; and the earlier geological periods did not afford terrestrial conditions adapted to beings highly organized. Over the whole region open to observation, the lowest organisms are as fixed as the highest: they are never modified to such an extent as to change their kind. To draw out a genealogical tree of the totality of species, it would be necessary to find a series of organisms that have passed by direct ascent into more highly organized species. But just as science looks in vain for the common ancestor of man and the monkey, so does it search to no effect for the common ancestor in every case of diffentiated species down to the simplest. The discovery of forms assimilated to allied species on either side, and in part filling up the interval between, will not furnish satisfactory evidence of the transition, unless there is proof that the allied species are its offspring. What is wanted is the immediately precedent organism out of which the more advanced has sprung. Such common parentage is nowhere found. The very thing needed to give an unassailable basis for the hypothesis of organic evolution is, from the lowest point to the highest, along the whole line, invariably and entirely absent: the genealogical tree is altogether made up of branches; it has no stem.

The series embraced in organic evolution includes Man. The proposal to treat him as an exception is fore-doomed. It is a half-way house, which cannot be the permanent home of science. Every argument against the inclusion of the human organism in the evolution process has its counterpart equally effective against the inclusion of any distintely differenced kind. If it be necessary to introduce a Divine directing Intelligence to account for man, it will be also needful to call in the same supernatural aid to account for inferior species. It is conceivable that an evolutionist, believing in a Divine Creator, might take up the position that in the fulness of time God sent forth His son Adam, formed in the womb of one of the lower animals, and endowed with spiritual life; but an attempt of this sort to reconcile the doctrine of organic evolution with belief in the supernatural origin of the human race is not likely to command assent. To accept it would be fatal to evolutionism; for it breaks the continuity by a special creation and acknowledges the impossibility of interpreting all the known phenomena of the cosmos without introducing immediate supernatural agency, which, if admissible in one instance, must be granted admissible in others also. The distinguished naturalist, Mr. Wallace, who shares with Mr. Darwin the credit of having originated the hypothesis of the formation of species by natural selection, regards man as exempt from the great regulative law of organic change. Mr. Darwin has taken, as an evolutionist, a safer position, in boldly including man—body and spirit—in the operation of his principle. His hypothesis stands condemned unless it is adequate to the task of ranging all organic life in one continuous process. Just as, on the other side, the doctrine of the creationist is defective if he fail to trace evidence of intelligence and will everywhere in the organic kingdoms. Mr. Spencer stakes his theory on a single issue. With him the discussion is narrowed to the inquriy whether the changes which matter undergoes in passing from the unorganized to the organized form, and the series of modifications produced in the vegetal and animal kingdoms, from the simplest to the most highly differentiated organisms, are due wholly to dynamic law, or whether fully to account for the phenomena will require that we shall introduce some other principle or cause. The former view is clearly inconsistent with the facts. It is tenable as a provisional hypothesis only by dropping out of sight some of the most significant phenomena. To accept the alternative and hold that a cause other than force operating according to dynamic law is indispensable to account for the whole, is to set aside a fundamental principle of Mr. Spencer's philosophy, which cannot admit of any such causation.

Mr. Spencer examines Professor Owen's "axiom of the continuous operation of creative power, or of the ordained becoming of living things," and condemns it, as no more scientific than the belief in special creations. He says, "Though these highly-general expressions do not suggest any very definite idea, yet they imply the belief that organic progress is a result of some indwelling tendency to develop, supernaturally impressed on living matter at the outset—some ever-acting constructive force, which, independently of other forces, moulds organisms into higher and higher forms.

"In whatever way it is formulated, or by whatever language it is obscured, this ascription of organic evolution to some aptitude naturally possessed by organisms, or miraculously imposed on them, is unphilosophical. It is one of those explanations which explains nothing—a shaping of ignorance into the semblance of knowledge. The cause is not a true cause—not a cause assimilable to known causes—not a cause that can be anywhere shown to produce analogous effects. It is a cause unrepresentable in thought: one of those illegitimate symbolic conceptions which cannot by any mental process be elaborated into a real conception. In brief, this assumption of a persistent formative power, inherent in organisms, and making them unfold into higher forms, is an assumption of special creations: of which, indeed, it is but a modification; differing only by the fusion of separate unknown processes into a continuous unknown process." *

This criticism is, from the standpoint of the thoroughgoing evolutionist, perfectly just. An hypothesis involving the recognition of a cause of this kind, is no more comprehensible by science than the theory ·of special creations. Whether that cause be designated, with Hartman, the Unconscious, or be called God,

---

* *Biology*, Vol. I., § 144.

organic evolution is thereby made of none effect; for, within the ken of science, it is reduced to a merely phenomenal succession of forms, without a causal nexus binding them to one another. Instead of the disclosure of a knowable cause, which may be brought into relation with other known causes, the evolutionist sees ignorance wrapped up in an incomprehensible term, or hidden behind a sacred name.

Mr. Spencer, on the other hand, undertakes to carry his hypothesis through without taking account of any cause unknown to science. The active causes which he finds operative in the course of organic evolution are:—(*a*) An innate tendency or polarity in the physi-ological units of which organized bodies are built up; and (*b*) the play of the incident forces of the environment. The entire process is explained by these two sets of forces. In what proportions they co-operate in producing all known varieties of living things, Mr. Spencer has not indicated. He deals in a hesitating and tentative way with the whole subject. The sum of his teaching is that the environing forces are the source of the power which effects the changes, the polarity of the units directing it. The doctrine is not by any means expounded with clearness and precision. The following fairly represents it:—The physiological unit has its internal structure—its equilibration of forces within itself. All other units in the organism form a part of its environment; while to these groups of units the entire organic structure stands in the

N

relation of environment. The cause of variation in the units is thus in part internal to the organism; but the organic whole, as well as every part of it, is exposed continually to the impact of the forces constituting the larger environment in which the organism lives. We have, then, a series of contrasts between the environed and the environment, running from the individual unit to the organism, and outward to the entire universe, which complicates the question and renders Mr. Spencer's explanation hardly explicable. We may regard it thus: The unit has an internal system of forces equilibrated in harmony with the ancestral form of organism; all other units making up the living thing have similarly their equilibrations; but the incident forces bear in upon the whole and upon the parts, disturbing the equilibrium. Every such disturbance modifies the internal relations of each several unit, and the inter-relations of the units to one another and to the entire aggregate. In regaining equilibrium the organic structure is modified. Now, if the modified form arise in this way, it is not easy to see how the direction of movement is due altogether to the units, the incident forces only communicating the power. The principle in question seems right in the face of Newton's second law of motion — that change of motion is proportioned to the impressed force, and takes place in the direction of the straight line in which the force acts. Mr. Spencer may take refuge in the distinction between molar and molecular motion, and thus try to elude the grip of Newton; if so, we should not care to follow him into the imperceptible.

Searching for a safe starting point anywhere, from which we may advance along the line of causal activity to the results before us, we go back, finding no resting place till we reach the atom and its environment. Each instance of composition of atoms, and further composition of molecules of greater complexity, and so onward to the physiological unit, is to be explained—if explicable—by the equilibration of the constituent parts and the incident forces. We are, then, driven in the last resort to assume, as existent in the original atom and the force immanent in it, or impelling it, the primal source of that power of direction supposed to be inherent in the physiological units. The gleam of light which seemed to break upon us leads us into the darkness of the incomprehensible, and is dispersed in the atomic whirl. Emerging out of this dim region, we are directed to turn our eyes towards the environment, and seek in it the source of the impelling power which produces the continuous development. Mr. Spencer cites an example. "During its earlier stages every embryo is sexless—becomes either male or female as the balance of forces acting on it determines. Each advance in embryonic complication results from the action of the incident forces on the complication previously existing. Indeed the now accepted doctrine of epigenesis neccessitates the conclusion that organic evolution proceeds after this manner. For since it is proved that no germ contains the slightest rudiment, trace, or indication of the future organism—since the microscope has shown that the first process set up in every fertilized germ is a process of repeated spontaneous fissions ending in the production of a mass of cells, not one of which exhibits any special character. . . . . The partial organization is transformed by the agencies acting upon it into the succeeding phase of organization, and this into the next, until, through ever increasing complexities, the ultimate form is reached. . . . . Structureless, as every germ originally is, the development of an organism out of it is otherwise impossible."*

One cannot but admire the intelligence with which the incident forces are supposed to act: for it is noteworthy, that however the balance in families may be, the number of male and female children, if account be taken of the entire population, is nearly equal. It is quite remarkable how, over the entire animal kingdom, the balance of the incident forces works out a numerical proportion between the sexes, which, however it may vary, is always exactly adjusted to the well-being of the species. It is surely to be excused if one feel sceptical as to the completeness of an explanation which ascribes such

---

* *First Principles,* § 159.

intelligent results to the blind forces of the environment. But the evolutionist may not question the doctrine; for "structureless as every germ originally is, the development of an organism out of it is otherwise impossible."

The same principle is stated more generally elsewhere. "The change from uniformity into multiformity in organic aggregates, is caused, as in all inorganic aggregates, by the necessary exposure of their component parts to actions unlike in kind or quality, or both."*

The process of differentiation by which cells are built up into an organized structure is, according to Mr. Spencer's teaching, due altogether to the environment. The fertilized germ, in certain cases, multiplies by simple fission, increasing the number of cells, but without change in the arrangement of the parts. The difference between the cell splitting up into separate cells, each of them a simple cell and nothing more, and the cell developed into an eagle or an elephant, is due wholly to the incident forces of the environment. The physiological unit is dethroned. It is not easy to see how this doctrine accords with the principle of heredity. It would seem that but for the environing forces every fertilized cell would go on perpetually producing new cells by fission; in which case the ancestral characteristics must perish.

---

* *Biology,* Vol. II., § 311.

But it is not enough that the environment initiate the development of structure ; what is begun needs continued causation to carry it forward to future stages. Observation shows that the process is liable to stop short at any point. There are living creatures that are structureless being nothing more than a bundle of cells multiplying by simple fission. There are others slightly more developed — living beings which still retain the structureless condition, and make no advance in organization. Others have an organization of the most rudimentary sort and never advance beyond the point at which the ancestral cell stopped short. These lowly forms of life are no more modifiable than the highest. They are as fixed in kind, and are, in reproduction, as true to kind, as the most highly developed species. How then are we to account for the extremely diverse action of the same environment ?

It may be answered, The environments are not the same. The environment of the fertilized germ-cell in the egg of an eagle, is not identical with that in the egg of an ostrich. But such an answer would not be satisfactory ; for, by hypothesis, there was a time when the germ-cell of what is now an ostrich was identical with the germ-cell of what is now an eagle ; and when two germ-cells of the remote ancestor became differentiated, what ground is there for affirming that they were exposed to dissimilar environments ? We assume the very point in question. But if this supposition be maintained as legitimate and necessary, we may fairly challenge the evolutionist to point out the diversity in the environing forces which causes the diversity in the cell-growth. No relation, either qualitative or quantitative, is discoverable. The cause is wholly unknown.

What, we may ask, is the scientific worth of a theory that tells us to look to the incident forces of the environment for the cause of certain changes, and cannot give us the faintest clue to the precise mode of force in the environment to which the effects under examination are due? Is this science, or is it not rather the merest ghost and shadow of science? Look again at these living germs. One remains destitute of any trace of organization, a second developes the simplest structure, a third grows into a highly developed organism. They are, at the outset, indistinguishable in chemical composition; their molecular constitution, so far as known, is the same; yet they evolve into the most widely separate structures. If we go back through successive countless generations till we reach the ancestral germs, indistinguishable in their composition or constitution and with the same cosmic and terrestrial surroundings, we are entitled to ask by what causes these germs have passed to such opposite destinies. What dynamic law accounts for their movement onward to that point which they severally reach? Mr. Spencer replies: The law of the continuous redistribution of matter and motion. But when pressed for a more definite explanation, he answers with two discordant voices. The *direction* of the movement, he tells us, is due to the polarity of the physiological units forming the contents of the cell : the directing power lay wrapped up in the germs themselves. This is one answer. Elsewhere he accounts for the direction of movement by the operation of the incident forces of the environment: these have determined whether the primal cell should evolve into a Newton or an ox. This is a second and quite conflicting answer. It is for the evolutionist to reconcile them.

It is the special claim of the evolution hypothesis that it traces all the changes wrought in the organic kingdoms to causes known to science—rejecting all other ; but though the causes by which it is proposed to account for all change may be of a kind embraced in scientific knowledge, there is an utter failure in the attempt to show, in any comprehensible way, the mode of the operation of these causes in producing the forms we see. It is no more unscientific to assume a cause otherwise unknown to science, where it is needful to do so in accounting for ascertained facts, than it is to present as scientific a theory which refers phenomena to known causes, but can furnish no explanation as to how the results arrived at have been reached. In that case, though the causes are known causes, the law of their operation in the in-stance under examination is unknown ; and science is equally at fault. Mr. Spencer's own doctrine is fairly open to the condemnation pronounced by him on the view of Professor Owen: it is "a shaping of ignorance into the semblance of knowledge . . . . the fusion of separate unknown processes into a continuous unknown process."

But if the dynamic hypothesis hold good, it affords the basis for a theory of the origin of species markedly different from that of natural selection. In accounting for the variety of organisms, the Darwinian theory proceeds on the supposition that sameness of structure proves identity of origin. The various groups of vertebrates, for example, are assumed to be differentiated descendants from the same stock; just as all the varieties of pigeons have sprung from one pair. It is taken for granted that sameness of structure implies community of parentage. If the kangaroo and the fox are alike in having a vertebral column, it is concluded they must have had a common ancestor. But the principle is not self-evident: on Mr. Spencer's theory, it is not even probable. The advocate of community of descent is liable to be charged, as Mr. Spencer charges the creationist, with an imperfect appreciation of the great principle of causation. For the vertebrate structure is an effect; and similarity of effects is due to similarity of causes. In so far as the causes operating on living matter are the same, the effects will be the same. If, as Mr. Spencer holds, variation of incident forces determines variety in the

organisms evolved, it is equally certain that sameness
of incident forces will produce similarity in the resulting forms: for to affirm otherwise is to deny the
persistence of force. The vertebrate structure may,
then, be the effect of similarity of causes operating
in the environment and not the outcome of identity
of descent.

The evolution hypothesis supposes a moment in the
gradual cooling of the earth, when organic matter in
the form of protein was produced, out of which, after
a vast series of minute changes, there arose particles
endowed with vital activities. The principle of causation renders it inconceivable that such dynamic
processes should be limited to one spot, or to one
particle of organic matter. Like the formation of
crystals of salt in all parts of the globe where water
containing salt in solution has evaporated, the production of protein matter must have spread over the
whole earth, as zone after zone reached the precise
degree of temperature required. And so soon as protein was evolved, then began everywhere the further
changes that result in organized life. To doubt this
—if the dynamic theory is true—is to reject the
principle of causation. Now the incident forces are
the same, yet not absolutely the same, over the whole
earth. The law of gravitation operates everywhere
and ceaselessly. If it be of advantage in the development of animal forms that the strength and flexibility
of a vertebrate skeleton should form the framework

of the living body, that result will necessarily arise
everywhere. The force of gravity is continually
active and the organism is exposed to constant strain.
Why then search in the distant past for a common
ancestry to account for similarities necessarily involved in the problem in physics which the cosmos is
supposed to be engaged in solving—to find the organized structure best adapted to the forces operating in
its environment, most perfectly adjusted to the mechanical conditions of organic life? All these elaborate efforts to show how the varieties of living
things have arisen from the same primordial living
matter, is evidence that the evolution doctrine has
not thoroughly penetrated and shaped the thinking
of men of science. Every system of natural classification is framed on the principle that likeness of
structure is evidence of community of descent. No
inference could be less in harmony with cosmic
evolution. Similarity of causes will of necessity produce likeness of form in organisms as well as in
crystals. A thorough-going acceptance of causation
will lead the student of nature who proceeds on the
principles of evolution to turn his eyes to the environment, to discover in dynamic law operating therein
the origin of resemblances as well as of differences
among living things. If the vertebrate skeleton be
that best suited to the conditions of animal life in
its highest forms, there can be no sufficient ground for
tracing back to one vertebrate ancestor what must

necessarily have come into being as the effect of uniformity in the causative action of the environment.

In the Darwinian theory the "incident forces" play
a part that is negative rather than positively operative. Nature sweeps out of the way the less fit,
and so makes room for the fittest to live and multiply.
All are more or less adapted to the environment;
the incident forces bear against the ill-adjusted, and
thus indirectly favour those better suited to their conditions. But the "survival of the fittest" will not
account for the production of the fittest. Nothing can
survive till it has first been brought into existence. If
an organism is nearly balanced in adjustment to its
environment, it will probably "increase and multiply"
and very largely "replenish the earth." But there is
a very important antecedent inquiry: we want to
know first how these fittest have come to be. Here
Mr. Darwin's doctrine of natural selection fails us, the
interval between the fit and the more fit is not bridged
over. He cannot show us how those very qualities
that give advantage in the struggle have been produced. When the living creatures that are to wrestle
for the crown of life have been presented in the arena,
appearing with their acquired attributes and adaptations, nature, sternly just, may judge of their worth,
perpetuating the meritorious and punishing with
death those that do not deserve to live. But the real
question is not touched by a theory which can account
only for the removal of the less fit: organic evolution

breaks down unless it tell us how the competitors have been reared and trained, and have been endowed with the qualities and requirements that bring them into competition.

For at bottom the question is not the survival of the fittest, but the origination, development, and continuance of any. How has any portion of matter came to be a living thing? How did the life of one individual pass on into another? How has the broad difference between animal and vegetable been produced? How did all the complex adaptations of organs and the nice adjustments of organisms to environment arise? "Is there not a cause?" Evolution must disclose it or confess all vital problems are left unsolved. If dynamic law covers the whole ground and elucidates all the facts, let its applicability be exhibited with reasonable explicitness. No such scientific precision is attempted. When we ask for definite conceptions, or look for explanations that will have something approaching scientific exactness, we get vague generalizations, far fetched analogies, an imposing array of abstract principles, and are in the last resort conducted into the eternal darkness of the unknowable. Evolution, as a rational theory of organic nature, is fatally defective. The new cosmic philosophy is found wanting in its own chosen field.

An illustration may make more evident the justness of this criticism. The growth of a single germ presents to the dynamic theory of organic evolution a wholly insoluble problem. Take an example from incubation. With no special operation of incident forces beyond the maintenance of a certain degree of warmth, the fertilized cell passes in a few days through a complete process of evolution; and the chick comes forth a highly developed organism, capable of free motion and of acts that simulate intelligence. Has all this vastly complicated process been initiated and carried out solely by the operation of dynamic law? Is it an instance of the redistribution of matter and motion, and nothing more? The persistence of force is, as we have seen, in such cases, inapplicable; for the forces are being constantly altered in their sum, and in their inter-relations. Mr. Spencer is not able to reduce to a mere dynamic process the development of a living germ into an organized structure. If he prove himself able to reduce to the redistribution of matter and motion the series of changes by which the "uniform mass of matter" forming the germ passes into a highly organized living creature, then he may hope to explain by a like process the modifications exhibited in the whole breadth of the vegetal and animal kingdoms. The difference is one of degree, not of kind. Science is never repelled by consideration of the magnitude or difficulty of the task set before her. The most involved and intricate problems, if within the limits of science, yield to patient and well-directed effort. It is not that the evolution of kingdoms and kinds is a vast and immensely complicated question that any thinker will regard it as a hopeless one. Evolutionism is challenged because, in the individual instance no less than in the inmeasurable aggregate of organic life, it attempts to solve the problem on principles which are demonstrably defective. No single pulsation in the circulatory system, has been, or can be, explained, if the solution be rigorously limited to dynamic principles, and every other cause excluded. Life in its simplest manifestations, in its least intricate activities, cannot be reduced to molar and molecular motions; which, if we had a complete knowledge of them, might be written out in the formulæ of mathematical physics. It is here that the antagonists who take firm hold of each other must join issue. The simplest obtainable instances should form the subject of experiment and illustration : let it be fairly discussed by the experts whether there be any vital activity, the phenomena of which can be fully exhausted by a knowledge of dynamic law, and if it can be proved that a dynamic principle accounts for the whole, then we shall admit that the evolution philosophy has a strong presumption in its favour. But we are convinced that no such conclusion is possible. There are causes, or a Cause, working, in the whole realm of organic nature—notably in sensation and the phenomena of intelligence—directing and controlling all things, which may not be confounded with that force whose law the physicist expounds. That which affords to thought the truest representation of this unseen Power is not the operation of any dynamic principle, but the energy of self-conscious mind.

CHAPTER XVI.

THE EVOLUTION OF MIND.

Section I.

The Origin of Consciousness.

WHEN a being arose to whom it was given to say " I AM," there appeared in the cosmos the most marvellous of its phenomena. "On earth there is nothing great but man: in man there is nothing great but mind." The science of mind lies at the foundation of philosophy. In any rightly ordered attempt to combine all knowledge in one system, self-conscious intelligence is the first subject of study. It is incumbent on the evolutionist to set consciousness in its place in that vast flow of change, and show how it has arisen through the operation of the great cosmic law. A philosophy may be fairly tested by the mode in which it deals with this fundamental question. The issue in the case of evolutionism is not doubtful; incompetent to answer any vital question in the realm of inorganic matter or organized life, the evolution hypothesis is wholly inadequate to the task of solving the problems that arise in the investigation of the intellectual and moral nature of man.

o

When human consciousness first came into being, how did it stand related to the antecedent modes of concrete being? Consciousness did not exist within the knowable at that moment. Human consciousness, when it arose, was a unique phenomenon. All knowable relations were, by hypothesis, relations of persisting forces, directed solely by the laws of matter and motion. How, as the outcome of that immediately precedent condition of the universe, did consciousness emerge? A universe existed without thought; a universe now exists with thought. Has the unconscious become conscious? and if so, how? The evolution hypothesis is bound to explain the mystery by exhibiting the transition as a phase of its continuous process. If it can do this it has triumphed: the priest of the coming dispensation has vindicated his authority; Aaron's rod has budded.

An immediate operation of the first cause may be assumed, but at the cost of sacrificing the very principle of evolution; for the supposition implies a direct intervention within the knowable, a distinct breach of continuity, in effect a special creation.

Criticising the opinion laid down in his *Physical Ethics* by Mr. Alfred Barrat, that consciousness "must be considered as an invariable property of animal life, and ultimately in its elements of the material universe," Mr. Spencer says: "Without questioning that the raw material of consciousness is present even in undifferentiated protoplasm, and everywhere exists

potentially in that unknowable Power which, otherwise conditioned, is manifested in physical action
(*Principles of Psychology*, § 273-4), I demur to the
conclusion that it at first exists under the form of
pleasure and pain."* Mr. Spencer does not question
that "the raw material of consciousness is present
even in undifferentiated protoplasm." Out of this
raw material evolutionism undertakes to produce the
manufactured article. Let us scrutinize this undifferentiated protoplasm: What do we find? Only
processes of physical change—atoms and their motions,
atoms and their motions only. Along that entire
series, exceeding in extent, multiplicity, and intricacy
all powers of thought, there appears nothing having
knowable kinship with self-conscious intelligence.
The atoms whirl in ceasless eddies, combine and re-
combine, form system after system of molecules, ever
growing in complexity until they arrive at the stage
of protein compounds. They aggregate into protoplasm; but no thrill of atom or internal throb of
molecule contains, so far as intelligence can judge, the
promise of self-conscious life. If the raw material
of consciousness is there, it is indistinguishable; if
the process of manufacture is going on, it is undiscoverable.

But when physical law fails, the incomprehensible
is at hand to rescue the evolutionist from manifest

---

* *Data of Ethics*, § 39, Note.

absurdity. "The raw material of consciousness . . . . everywhere exists potentially in that unknowable Power which otherwise conditioned is manifested in physical action." This is a striking instance of the method of evolutionism when it faces a question that goes deep into the nature of things. "The raw material of consciousness is present even in undifferentiated protoplasm:" "the raw material of consciousness everywhere exists potentially in that unknowable Power." Choose either answer, you are left equally unenlightened. If the raw material of consciousness "everywhere exists potentially" in the unknowable power, it exists potentially in that power wherever and however manifested: it exists potentially in the inscrutable actuality that manifests itself in the sands of the Sahara, or in the red granite of Aberdeen. We learn nothing from being told that the raw material of consciousness exists in the unknowable reality. Everything that has come to be has existed potentially in the great First Cause. But there may be a gleam of light in the statement that this raw material exists in that power "which *otherwise conditioned* is manifested in physical action." We have here two contrasted modes of conditioning of the unknowable energy,—"variously conditioned modes of the universal immanent force."* One is the physical universe, with uniformities of action which

---

* *Biology*, Vol. I., Appendix, p. 491.

science formulates in physical law. In this conditioning the persistence of force is found everywhere exemplified : dynamic law everywhere prevails. But the unknowable is conditioned otherwise. This other conditioning is contrasted with the former and cannot be brought within it. The law of the conditioning in physical action is not applicable in the new order. The present is, therefore, not the outcome of the precedent cosmic state : the series of continuous manifestations is broken, science cannot connect the one conditioning with the other.

In having recourse to the unknowable cause, the evolutionist confesses that the origin of consciousness is not discoverable by his methods ; he acknowledges the presence of another form of being in the elucidation of which the work of the laboratory is of no avail. To refer the inquirer to the inscrutable reality is, from the standpoint of scientific knowledge, meaningless : it is to admit philosophic impotence. To say with the intellectualist that consciousness had its origin from the Supreme Intelligence, is to give an answer consistent with itself, and having on the face of it the semblance of truth, but to account for consciousness by carrying it back into the incomprehensible, is simply to take refuge in the outer darkness. No doubt, if there be an intelligent power behind all we know, that infinite Mind will be competent to furnish not only the " raw material of consciousness," but consciousness itself. The theist holds a clear and tenable position: the agnostic is hopelessly at fault. If the evolutionist is compelled to have recourse to the unknowable, conditioned otherwise than in physical action, to explain the origin of consciousness, what has come of his boasted all-embracing principle?—his unbroken operation of dynamic law? The continuous redistribution of matter and motion has been proceeding with unceasing flow: a point is reached where consciousness comes into view of thought. It emerges as a direct emanation from the unknowable power "otherwise conditioned." It is not, then, the outcome of that power as conditioned in physical action. The universality of the dynamic principle is denied; and the evolution hypothesis falls with it.

Consciousness in every intellection testifies against the proposal to constitute of the knowable one organized system cohering by physical bonds. Self, conscious of itself, stands apart; *in* the physical universe, but not *of* it. The chasm cannot be bridged over. It is impossible to embrace all experience in one coherent process of evolution. Mr. Spencer states, with great force, the contrast between the two realms. "There lies," he says, "a class of facts absolutely without any perceptible or conceivable community of nature with the facts that have occupied us. The truths here to be set down are truths of which the very elements are unknown to physical science." *

---

* *Psychology*, Vol. I., § 41.

"Psychology is a totally unique science, independent of and antithetically opposed to all other' sciences whatever. The thoughts and feelings which constitute a consciousness, and are absolutely unanswerable to any but the possessor of that consciousness, form an existence that has no place among the existences with which the rest of the sciences deal. Though accumulated observations and experiments have led us by a very indirect series of inferences to the belief that mind and nervous action are the subjective and objective faces of the same things, we remain utterly incapable of seeing and even imagining how the two are related. Mind still continues to us a something without any kinship to other things; and from the science which discloses by introspection the laws of this something, there is no passage by transitional steps to the sciences which discover the laws of these other things." *

Evolutionism has, at this point, reached a demarcation so clear and deep that it would appear hopeless to attempt to combine in one the two classes of facts. But if they cannot be brought into one coherent organic whole, the unification of knowledge is still incomplete; the principle of continuity is violated the knowable is parted into two distinctly differenced realms; dynamic principles do not rule all experience; the totality of concrete existences cannot be made to form parts of one unbroken stream of change; and a philosophy on the basis of evolution is impossible.

SECTION II.

IN WHAT DOES CONSCIOUSNESS INHERE?

Granting for the moment that consciousness is not existent in any knowable mode until a wave of molecular motion thrills through a nerve centre, and that it is then startled into being in the form of a nerve-shock, we ask, In what did consciousness lie hid up to that moment? and where is it concealed till it reappears when the nerve-pulse throbs again? It was not latent in the matter of which the organism is composed; for Mr. Spencer very strongly repudiates the charge of being a materialist: nor can we go behind the matter to the force which is manifested in it to find consciousness there; for the portion of matter is a fixed quantum of manifested force, no part of which can be transformed into a new mode called feeling. Under the guidance of Mr. Spencer we have recourse to the unseen to look for that in which consciousness inheres; it lies hid in the unknowable actuality. But then the question arises, What relation does that actuality bear to the organism and its activities? Let us try to see the fact quite clearly. A wave of molecular motion passes through a nerve centre : consciousness comes into being out of the inscrutable. Does the inscrutable power, in response to each pulsation that runs along a nerve, reveal itself in consciousness for an instant, and when the nerve-thrill ceases, fall back again into a condition of incomprehensibility ? It would appear so. The conception is a most curious one, and deserving the closest scrutiny. It may be represented in this way. The laws of dynamics regulate the eternal whirl of atomic motion. In the process of change certain molecular orbs, in these vast atomic systems, come into conjunction. At that instant the molecular movement is answered by the inscrutable power flashing forth into consciousness, vanishing and returning in response to the rhythmic pulse of physical force. Now note the consequence: if it be that the dynamic law of matter and motion is that which, without interference and without cessation of its continuous operation, directs all motion throughout the universe; if throughout all processes the knowable causes and effects are calculable with rigid mathematical certainty; if every throb of physical force is determined in a fixed physical succession, then every occasion of the manifestation of the unknowable in consciousness is an effect determined not by intelligence, but by inflexible physical necessity, is due not to the infinite power revealing itself in consciousness, but as " otherwise conditioned " in the physical law of its manifestation through matter. The evolution philo-

sophy is, on this supposition, founded on an entirely
materialistic basis. What is latent in the incomprehensible we cannot discover; what lies in the knowable is the law of physical force dominant everywhere.
It is a mere evasion of a conclusion repugnant to
reason to carry us back to an ultimate actuality
which is neither matter nor spirit, but is manifested
in both; seeing that the manifestations of the unknowable in mind are wholly conditioned and are
irresistibly determined by the laws of matter and
motion, and stand in a relation to the thrill of the
nerve centres as definitely fixed as a musical note to
the vibration of a harp-string. Conditioned in one
mode the inscrutable reality is matter, conditioned
otherwise it is mind: but as mind the law of its
manifestation is subsumed under and wholly shaped
by the laws in which it is conditioned as matter. It
is clear that evolutionism is, as a philosophy of the
knowable, in principle and in effect, thoroughly
materialistic: it enthrones physical force as sovereign
over the whole extent of knowledge.

SECTION III.

THE UNIT OF CONSCIOUSNESS.

On the evolution hypothesis mind is a growth.
To bring the growth of mind into harmony with the

evolution of material forms, it is necessary for Mr. Spencer to obtain a unit of intelligence analogous to the chemical and physiological units which play so important a part in his doctrine of inorganic and organic evolution. This "unit of consciousness" is indispensable to his hypothesis. Without it, he can no more build up a mind than he could build up an organism without his physiological units. We shall examine this unit of consciousness somewhat closely.

"There may be a single primordial element of consciousness, and the countless kinds of consciousness may be produced by the compounding of this element with itself, and recompounding of its compounds with one another in higher and higher degrees; so producing increased multiplicity, variety, and complexity . . . It is possible then—may we not say probable?— that something of the same order as that which we call a nervous shock is the ultimate unit of consciousness; and that unlikeness among our feelings results from unlike modes of integration of the ultimate unit. . . . Our typical case of musical sound will exhibit the agreement. . . . . Here the nerve pulses and the pulses of feeling clearly answer to one another; and it can scarcely be doubted that they do so throughout." " Mind is certainly in some cases, and probably in all, resolvable into nervous shocks; and these nervous shocks answer to the waves of molecular motion that traverse nerves and nerve centres." . . . .

"Mind is certainly in some cases, and probably in all, resolvable into nervous shocks." *

Though Mr. Spencer seems to speak with confidence that he has found the unit of consciousness, out of which mind may be built up; yet there is considerable hesitancy in his treatment of the question. "The subjective effect," he says, "produced by a crack or noise that has no appreciable duration is little else than a nervous shock. . . . . The state of consciousness so generated is in fact comparable in quality to the initial state of consciousness caused by a blow . . . which state of consciousness may be taken as the primitive and tpyical form of the nervous shock. It is possible, then—may we not say probable—that something of the same order as that which we call a nervous shock is the ultimate unit of consciousness." †
The subject is dealt with in a hesitating and tentative way. Possibilities and probabilities will not suffice. The doctrine of the evolution of mind lies at the very heart of evolutionism. Mr. Spencer cannot evolve mind without his unit of consciousness. Whatever doubt attaches to this primal element, attaches to the composite whole built up out of it. If the evolutionist is not fully confident about his unit, he needs to be much less confident when he proceeds to compound his units with one another, and recompound

---

* *Psychology*, Vol. I., § 60, § 61, § 62.
† *Ibid.*, Vol. I., § 60.

their composites. The doubt does not diminish in the process: it is multiplied.

In inquiring into the nature and reality of this primordial constituent of mind, I would first observe that a nervous shock is not a feeling till it is felt. It is the consciousness of it that constitutes it a feeling. A nervous shock, without consciousness, is a nerve-thrill and nothing more. Two successive waves of molecular motion may pass through the brain, one of them is felt the other is not; of the one we are conscious, we are not conscious of the other. The characteristic fact, the consciousness, is not accounted for by the wave of nerve-action. The analysis of mind into nervous shocks, as its elementary constituents, does not avail to bring within the compass of the dynamic theory the consciousness which is the most distinctive feature in the phenomena. At this point in advancing along the forward movement of the cosmic force, thought is arrested. An invisible, but very real line of separation divides the self-knowing *I* from the vast stream moving onward according to dynamic law. Evolutionism is, confessedly, for Mr. Spencer repeatedly acknowledges it, unable to bring consciousness within its sweep. When it touches one of the most vital questions in philosophy, it acknowledges itself unable so much as to to attempt an answer. In the proposed unification, the central factor in knowledge stands out the great exception.

But, to return to the point immediately before us,

we reject, as inconsistent with what consciousness itself testifies, this theory of a unit of consciousness corresponding to a nervous shock. Whether violent or gentle, nervous shocks have reality to me, as a fact of my experience, in no other way than by my consciousness of them. "I know,—I desire,—I feel. What is it that is common to all these? *Knowing* and *desiring* and *feeling* are not the same, and may be distinguished. But they all agree in one fundamental condition. Can I know, without *knowing*, that I know? Can I desire, without *knowing*, that I desire? Can I feel, without *knowing*, that I feel? This is impossible. Now this knowing that I know, or desire, or feel,—this common condition of self-knowledge is precisely what is denominated consciousness."*

Whether I perceive, or feel, or will, whatever be the mode of experience of which I have direct knowledge, consciousness forms its primary element. To search for a unit of consciousness is to assume that there is some elementary form of consciousness which can be distinguished and dealt with as a distinct and definable part of the whole. It is to ignore the fact that consciousness is essentially cognitive and is in every case the same. To be conscious that I feel is the same in respect of consciousness as to be conscious that I will. The consciousness itself cannot be broken up into units: it is identical in all forms of experience.

---

* Sir W. Hamilton's *Lectures, Metaphysics*, Vol. I., p. 158.

To break up consciousness into units, we must deal
with the object of consciousness, not with consciousness itself—not with the knowing that I feel, but with
the thing felt. But to make this the principle of
discrimination is to seek, not the unit of consciousness,
but the primary object in experience. We are no
nearer the unit of consciousness by the process. We
cannot go back and find what is the first object of
consciousness; and if we could, we should not have
laid a firm foundation for the superstructure of intelligence. Mind is best studied in its highest and
most perfect state; not in the dim beginnings of
cognition in undeveloped childhood. But another
difficulty presents itself. Given the unit, it must be
multiplied and compounded either as an act of consciousness or as an object of consciousness. It cannot
be dealt with in this fashion as an act of consciousness; for consciousness is simple and remains simple.
Throughout all complex intellectual operations, it remains one and unchanged. The boy who feels the
rod knows that he feels; the boy who works out an
abstruse problem knows that he reasons. The consciousness viewed simply as consciousness is the same.
Taken as the object of consciousness the unit cannot
be built up into the structure of developed intelligence. There is no one object of consciousness :
experience is manifold: the objects revealed in experience are endlessly varied ; and unless there be one
thing the sole constituent of all things, no process of

compounding and recompounding the proposed unit will yield a body of intellection corresponding with reality.

Even though the pulse of feeling could be shown to answer in every case to a nerve-pulse, even though it were granted that they are inner and outer faces of the same, Mr. Spencer's attempt to find a unit of consciousness in the pulse of feeling fails: it is not the pulse of feeling, but the consciousness of it, with which he must set out.

But we deny that "nerve pulses and pulses of feeling clearly answer to one another," as "inner and outer faces of the same." The correspondence of mind and body is a commonplace of psychology in all schools. That nerve-action and feeling correspond is proved in every twinge of toothache. But that the correspondence is that of the outer and inner faces of the same thing is not proved: on the contrary, there is grave doubt of its truth. If the nerve-thrill and the feeling are two sides of the same they should invariably exist together: where the outside is discovered the inside should be found with it. But this is not the case. Thrills of nerve-change pass through the nerve-centres often, and no feeling answers them. The outer face is there, while the inner face is wanting. The nerve-thrill has no counterpart in feeling unless we are conscious of it. Consciousness is, then, the characteristic element in this instance. It is not a wave of molecular motion, but *knowing* to which we come in the ultimate resort. Consciousness is the primary attribute of mind: we begin with knowledge.

Evolutionism is again at fault. It cannot build up mind without a primal constituent which may be brought into correlation with the physical forces of the cosmos. Mind, conscious of itself, rejects as illusive and unreal—as a mere creature of imagination —the unit whose composition into ever more complex modes is to exhibit the law of the formation of mind and the history of the growth of thought: but if the unit of consciousness be discarded, the edifice into which it has been so laboriously built up, disappears with it.

SECTION IV.

THE RELATIONS OF FEELINGS.

Let us grant the evolutionist his unit of consciousness and accept his hypothesis that feeling and waves of molecular motion in the central ganglion are inner and outer faces of the same, and let us inquire how he proposes to build up mind out of these materials.

"The proximate components of mind are," on his doctrine, "of two broadly contrasted kinds—Feelings and the Relations between feelings. . . . . Each feeling, as we here define it, is any portion of consciousness which occupies a place sufficiently large to give it a perceivable individuality. . . . . A relation between feelings is, on the contrary, characterized by occupy-

P

ing no appreciable part of consciousness. Take away
the terms it unites and it disappears along with them;
having no independent place, no individuality, of its
own. It is true that, under an ultimate analysis,
what we call a relation, proves to be itself a kind of
feeling—the momentary feeling accompanying the
transition from one conspicuous feeling to an adjacent
conspicuous feeling. And it is true that, notwithstanding its brevity, its qualitative character is appreciable; for relations are (as we shall hereafter see)
distinguishable from one another only by the unlikeness of the feelings which accompany the momentary transition." *

Let us see how this theory will work. A molecular
wave passes through the central ganglion. Its inner
face is a feeling sufficiently large to constitute a perceivable individuality. A second similar wave follows,
and a feeling like the first ensues. The feelings being
alike, if they are co-terminous they cannot be distinguished ; they flow together and constitute, not two
feelings, but one : no perceptible relation subsists between them. To be distinguishable, they must be
separated either by the intervention of a dissimilar
feeling or by the lapse of an interval of time. The
separation cannot be by the former; for in that case
the immediate succession would be that of two unlike
feelings, and the relation would be between these two.

---

* *Psychology*, Vol. I., § 65.

Like feelings must, then, be parted by an interval of time—an interval sufficient to discriminate the one feeling from the other. An insuperable difficulty now comes into view. How is this interval to be bridged over? The feeling that has just vanished cannot do it; for it has ceased to be: the new feeling cannot help; for it has not yet come into being: the waves of molecular motion are of no avail; for the one wave has ceased and the other has not arisen: the organism cannot accomplish the transition; for it can only make itself felt by a new wave, with its inner face of feeling. This, feeling, again is either like or unlike those in the original relation. If like, it runs into continuity with them, and the three merge into one: if unlike, we have then to compare feelings that are dissimilar, a second series of difficulties present themselves, and we are no nearer the relation sought. We are, of course, precluded from introducing something having consciousness of both waves of molecular change, and so knowledge of the resemblance; for that would be to introduce Mind, which has yet to be built up of feelings and relations of feelings.

Once more the evolutionist is at fault. In his hypothesis there is no place for knowledge of the likeness of successive like feelings.

Take now the occurrence of dissimilar waves and concomitant dissimilar feelings. Suppose one feeling to be followed by a second of unlike quality; in which case the feelings may come together without a dividing interval. How in this instance does the knowledge of relation arise ? "The requisite to the existence of a relation is the occurrence of a change—the passage from one apparently-uniform state to another apparently-uniform state, implying the momentary shock produced by the commencement of a new state." *

The relation is "itself a kind of feeling," and we are necessitated to ask, How does this "kind of feeling" arise ? It is not accounted for by either of the related feelings. The first cannot yield it ; for the first has just passed away : the second will not yield it ; for the second cannot give the transition to itself from the first. We shall look in vain to the organism. It can only furnish a new wave of molecular motion with its inner face of feeling : a third feeling then comes into view, and the relation of this third feeling to the original pair augments the complexity. The new feeling cannot intervene between the other two ; for they are assumed to be contiguous : it must come after the second ; but to compare it with the second presents all the difficulties involved in comparison of the second with the first, and enhances the perplexity ; for we have then to compare it with the first through the second. A third shock is added, and the complication is increased.

Another supposition is conceivable : the initial part of the second feeling may be the feeling required.

But how is this part of the feeling felt as a distinguishable shock ? It is absurd to imagine that the initial portion of a feeling could feel the shock arising on the coming of itself into being. It may be maintained, however, that the feeling sought is not the initial moment of the second feeling, but the passage from the first to the second. We ask, then, what is that which passes from the one feeling to the other ? What is it that feels the transition ? Not the first feeling; for it does not pass into the second—it ends as the second begins : if it passed into the second the result would be continuity of feeling and a shock could not arise : not the nerve-thrills; for these have their inner faces in the related feelings, and to change the relation of the thrills would be to change the relation of the feelings : not the organism ; for it cannot pass consciously from feeling to feeling except by a nerve-thrill and its corresponding feeling ; in which case this feeling must also be brought into relation to that preceding and following, and the original difficulty recurs.

We make no advance by supposing the case of related feelings that are co-existent. If the feelings are alike and co-existent, they are indistinguishable; they merge in one. If they are unlike, the old difficulty reappears. " The requisite to the existence of a relation is the occurrence of a change . . . . implying the momentary shock produced by the commencement of a new state." To call up the feeling of relation there must be "the commencement of a new state;" that is, there must be a transition from the one feeling to the other. But this passage from the one state to the other implies an order of succession, and we are involved in exactly the same perplexities as before.

The evolutionist is again face to face with an insoluble problem : he cannot account for the knowledge of relations. Feelings are related; but these relations can become a part of knowledge no otherwise than by being known. Molecular action and concomitant feelings will not yield known relations. We must postulate something, call it what you will, having the faculty of comparing and taking knowledge of like and unlike, of equality and difference, of greater and less.

SECTION V.

REASONING.

We have seen that the evolutionist cannot on his hypothesis obtain the feelings out of which he proposes to create mind; and given the feelings, he cannot account for the knowledge of their relations. But let us suppose that this fatal blank is filled up; he is still only at the beginning of his task : he must now, out of feelings and relations of feelings, frame intelligence and build up the whole edifice of reasoned thought.

"Reasoning is but a formation of cohesions among

manifestations."* The evolution of mind is a process of grouping. Feelings are arranged in clusters; these clusters grow more definite, more coherent, more heterogeneous, in accordance with the universal law of the evolving cosmos.

Now it is to be noted that the most elementary grouping requires the presence of the relational element; but relations can have no place in consciousness without comparison : something must exist beforehand having a faculty of comparing. We can begin the process of grouping only by assuming the existence of intellectual power. "All thought involves the consciousness of likeness :" † consciousness must " be a competent judge of the likeness and unlikeness of its states." ‡ It is just in proportion to the presence in experience of this element of knowledge that feelings are found capable of being grouped; and the grouping consists of "decided mutual cohesions" that "cling together with tenacity"§ in proportion to the definiteness of the relations. The absence of "the relational element of mind" leaves the states of consciousness altogether incoherent.

When tracts of consciousness are distinguished by predominance of the relational element, "the compound feelings can unite into coherent and well-defined clusters." ‖ But this amounts to saying that

---

* *First Principles*, § 45.   † *Ibid.*, § 44.   ‡ *Ibid.*, § 41.
§ *Psychology*, Vol. I., § 69.   ‖ *Ibid.*, § 70.

where the intellectual element predominates, the feelings are thereby constituted a part of thought. The very thing to be evolved is assumed as conditioning the evolution.

"In tracts of consciousness where the relational element predominates, and where the clustering of feelings is consequently well-defined, the clusters themselves enter into relations one with another." * Here, again, as we advance to a higher stage in the composition of mind, the coherence of groups with groups is determined by the relational element— that is, by the faculty of perceiving relations. The intellectual power by which objects are compared, is the condition that regulates the clustering of groups with groups. Once more, the very thing to be evolved —the ultimate goal of the operation—is the most important factor in working out the higher degree of mental composition.

Feelings of one order enter into relation with those of another; but those of "different orders which enter into definite relations and cohere most strongly, are those in which there is predominance of the relational elements," † and "the method remains the same throughout." Throughout the whole process of the evolution of mind, the relational element determines the grouping; in other words, the intelligence involved effects the advance and is the measure of it:

---

* *Psychology*, Vol. I., § 71.   † *Ibid*, § 72.

the amount of mind already existing is the amount of mind evolved. The grouping does not originate intelligence; intelligence regulates the grouping: mind is not the fruit of the clusters; the clusters are the product of mind.

These groups are separated into real and ideal. What we call knowing an object is the assimilation of a group of real feelings with one or more ideal groups.* Grouping implies the distinction between what Mr. Spencer calls real and ideal feelings—that is, between presentative and representative knowledge. The evolutionist cannot take a single step forward in his clustering of feelings, unless there be granted him the existence of some means by which what has been presented in perception can be retained and reproduced and compared with the new object. Here we have cognition of objects, retention and reproduction of percepts, knowledge of relations, and comparison of the objects of consciousness conditioning the evolution of mind. " The feelings called sensations cannot of themselves constitute Mind, even when great numbers of various kinds are present together. Mind is constituted only when each sensation is assimilated to the faint forms of antecedent sensations." † This "consolidation of successive sensations to form what we call a knowledge of the sensation as such," is needed "to form the smallest

---

* *Psychology*, Vol. I., § 73.   † *Ibid.*, § 73.

portion of what we call thought, as distinguished
from mere confused sentiency." * Throughout the
entire range, from the simplest recognition of likeness
or difference up to the most complicated and profound
intellectual process, ·the one characteristic, essential
at every step, and which determines the whole, is the
knowledge of relations, or in Mr. Spencer's language
" intellection" which " comprehends only the relational
elements of mind." In intellection there is implied
(1) a faculty of perception of external objects, (2) a
faculty of reproducing the object in thought, (3) a
faculty of comparison of object with object, either
directly or through the representative faculty, (4)
ability to group objects according to known resemblances. The exercise of all these powers is necessary
to the simplest beginnings as to the greatest achievements of thought. It is of little moment what name
we give to that which is assumed to be in active
exercise throughout the whole range of intellection.
Call it mind, or by what name you will, it is not a
product of evolution: it is there alike in the first
dawn of consciousness and in the mightiest efforts of
intellectual power. Ever revealing itself in the conscious life of each man is that something which hears,
and sees, and feels; which remembers, and imagines;
which compares, and judges; which links concept to
concept and group to group; which, acting according

to its own laws, builds up slowly from generation to generation the vast, complicated, orderly, and imposing edifice of knowledge. At every stage in the reach of human progress that something is seen in exercise; it is not in process of being evolved : on the contrary, it is that which is continually evolving, out of the raw material of experience, the marvels of disciplined thought.

When we enter the world of mind we know ourselves in a realm which dynamic principles do not rule; we see another system of laws in operation. Man is not a ripple on the stream of cosmic mutation : he derives his origin from another source.

SECTION VI.

SELF AND NOT-SELF

What account does the evolution philosopy give of the fundamental cognition of *self* as contrasted with *not-self?* How does this essential element of experience arise as a product in the course of cosmic change ? It will not suffice to say : the origin of this essential characteristic of thought is inscrutable—it has emerged out of the unknowable; for that is to affirm that so far as knowledge reaches consciousness of self is not a part of the evolving process—is not an integral part of the totality of the universe as it passes from stage to stage continuously, in an unbroken evolution. •

In dealing with this subject, Mr. Spencer is not so lucid in his exposition as is his wont: he writes like one carefully guarding against difficulties. The knowledge of *self* and *not-self* he classes among the intuitions which must be accepted provisionally—" Those fundamental intuitions that are essential to the process of thinking " and that " must be temporarily accepted as unquestionable, leaving the assumption of their unquestionableness to be justified by the results." * We are quite willing to grant that the fundamental intuitions "are to be accepted" as unquestionable; but to do so is fatal to evolution as a doctrine to be held true universally; for the evolutionist is bound to find the place of these fundamental truths, as they arise of necessity in that universal movement which the evolution hypothesis undertakes to formulate. Results may justify the intuition, but cannot justify the evolutionist. The intuition is called as a witness against him: its absolute veracity only renders its adverse testimony the more damaging.

While classing it with fundamental intuitions, Mr. Spencer speaks of the cognition of the *ego* as "a primordial product of consciousness" † "a cumulative result of persistent consciousness of likeness and differences among manifestations;" ‡ that is, he distinguishes between consciousness and consciousness of self, and regards the latter as resulting from conscious-

---

* *First Principles*, § 39.   † *Ibid.*, § 45.   ‡ *Ibid.*, § 44.

ness of those likenesses and differences that group all manifestations into the two great divisions—the *ego* and the *non-ego*. But is this a valid distinction? Can there be a consciousness without consciousness of self? Let Sir W. Hamilton answer:—" I know, I feel, I desire, etc. What is it that is necessarily involved in all these? It requires only to be stated to be admitted, that when I know, I must know that I know,—when I feel, I must know that I feel,—when I desire, I must know that I desire. The knowledge, the feeling, the desire, are possible only under the condition of being known, and being known by me. For if I did not know that I knew, I would not know. Now this knowledge, which I, the subject, have of these modifications of my being, and through which knowledge alone these modifications are possible, is what we call *consciousness.* The expressions *I know that I know,—I know that I feel,—I know that I desire,* —are thus trranslated by, *I am conscious that I know, —I am conscious that I feel,—I am conscious that I desire.*

" Consciousness is thus, on the one hand, the recognition by the mind or ego of its acts and affections; in other words, the self-affirmation that certain modifications are known by me and that these modifications are mine. . . . . Though the simplest act of mind, consciousness thus expresses a relation subsisting between two terms. These terms are, on the one hand, an I or Self, as the subject of a certain modification,—and on the other, some modification, state, quality, affection, or operation belonging to the subject. Consciousness, thus, in its simplicity, necessarily involves three things,—1°, A recogizing or knowing subject; 2°, A recognized or known modification; and 3°, A recognition or knowledge by the subject of the modification." *

We have found the evolutionist chargeable with obliterating dividing lines where they run across his hypothesis: we have here an instance of the opposite error. He discriminates consciousness from the consciousness of self, representing the former as in full exercise without the latter. Sir W. Hamilton clearly establishes the fact that they are one. To distribute experience into successive morsels, so as to avoid a breach of continuity, the evolutionist splits up consciousness into separate fragments: he creates a difference where no difference exists.

At the foundation of his philosophy Mr. Spencer lays these postulates:—"An unknowable Power; the existence of knowable likenesses and differences among the manifestations of that Power; and a resulting segregation of the manifestations into those of subject and object."† Accepting the existence of an unknowable power and of knowable likenesses and differences among the manifestations of that power, we are no nearer a reconciliation of the consciousness of self with the evolution hypothesis. Likenesses and

---

* *Lectures. Metaphysics*, p. 192. † *First Principles*, § 45.

differences are found in every part of nature. Their existence is co-extensive with concrete being. Each thing is either like or unlike every other. It is evident, then, that the emphasis is to be laid on the word *knowable*. The possibility of our knowing these likenesses and differences is the real thing postulated; in which case the assumption is of man's ability to know the like and the unlike; that is, the evolutionist grounds his "fundamental cognition" on the possession by man of a faculty of comparison. He must find a power of comparing like and unlike, and of classifying objects accordingly, prior to the differentiation of con-sciousness into consciousness of self. Given an un-knowable power, and given a faculty of comparing and classifying, there will follow "a resulting segrega-tion of the manifestations into those of subject and object." But what the power is by which this segre-gation is effected is left undefined. Elsewhere we are told that "the manifestations of the unknowable *fall* into the two separate aggregates," and again it is said that "strictly speaking it is in great part *spontaneous*." Mindful of Mr. Spencer's repudiation of everything like spontaneity, we are somewhat puzzled to fix the exact meaning; for "the very conception of sponta-neity is wholly incongruous with the conception of evolution."* Nor are we helped by learning that "it is a legitimate deliverance of consciousness elaborating

---

* *Biology*, Vol. I., Appendix, p. 480.

its materials after the laws of its normal action;" †
which certainly involves the implication that consciousness is an operative element in the process of
evolution, and that in so far as consciousness is a
manifestation of the unknowable diverse from its
manifestations in matter and motion, the dynamic
movement is directed from a source extern to it.

The salient characters by which the two orders are
discriminated are seven. "Manifestations of the one
order are vivid and those of the other are faint.
Those of the one order are originals, while those of
the other are copies. The first form with one another
a series or heterogeneous current, that is never broken ;
and the second also form with one another a parallel
series or current that is never broken: or, to speak
strictly, no breakage of either is ever directly known.
Those of the first order cohere with one another, not
only longitudinally, but also transversely ; as do also
those of the second order with one another. Between
manifestations of the first order the cohesions, both
longitudinal and transverse, are indissoluble; but
between manifestations of the second order, these
cohesions are most of them dissoluble with ease.
While the members of each series or current are so
coherent with one another that the current cannot be
broken, the two currents, running side by side as they
do, have but little coherence—the great body of the

vivid current is absolutely unmodifiable by the faint, and the faint may become almost separate from the vivid. The conditions under which modifications of either order occur, themselves belong to that order; but whereas in the faint order the conditions are always present, in the vivid order the conditions are often not present, but lie somewhere outside of the series. Seven separate characters, then, mark off these two orders of manifestations from one another."*

I quote this enumeration at length, as a full state-ment of Mr. Spencer's position is necessary to justify my criticism. He bases on this ground his doctrine that the unknowable power is conditioned in mani-festations of two orders—mental and material—and repudiates either material or spiritual unitarianism.

What are here called manifestations, vivid or faint, are elsewhere spoken of as feelings—"primary or vivid feelings," and "secondary or faint feelings."† It could not be otherwise; for manifestations can have place in consciousness, on the evolution hypothesis, only as feelings. This fact has an important bearing on the doctrine that "each order of manifestations carries with it the irresistible implication of some power that manifests itself; and by the words *ego* and *non-ego* respectively, we mean the power that manifests itself in the faint forms, and the power that manifests itself in the vivid forms."‡ At first

---

* *First Principles*, § 43. • † *Psychology*, Vol. I., § 73.
‡ *First Principles*, § 44.

Q

sight the language might seem to indicate that there
are two unknowable powers manifested in the two
classes of phenomena. But such a supposition is so
entirely alien from Mr. Spencer's system that we are
not entitled to draw the inference. The underlying
power is the one unknowable energy immanent in all
things. It is only the manifestations that may be differenced. Let us fix our thoughts by citing an example.
A soldier passes: the perception of him constitutes a
feeling of the vivid order. The image remains in the
memory and can be recalled at pleasure : when recalled
it appears as a feeling of the faint order. Next day a
soldier in similar uniform passes. Again a vivid feeling is produced. This feeling forms a cohesion with
the faint feeling that remains from seeing the soldier on
the preceding day. Now, according to Mr. Spencer's
doctrine, the vivid feeling is a manifestation of the unknowable in the *non-ego*, while the faint feeling is a
manifestation of the unknowable in the *ego*. A relation subsists between the two manifestations : we may
ask to which aggregate does it belong ? So far as it
is a relation of the vivid feeling it is a part of the
non-ego; so far as it is attached to the faint feeling
it must be taken as belonging to the *ego*. But waiving minute criticism, we ask, How does the manifestation in the aggregate called *self,* differ from that in
the aggregate called *not-self,* as a manifestation of the
unknowable ? A nerve-thrill is the outer face of the
vivid feeling: a nerve-thrill is the outer face of the

faint feeling. The mode of manifestation in either instance is a certain molecular action in the central ganglion. The actions are localized in the same part of the organism: the molecules are the same; they are the constitutents of the brain substance: the mode of action is the same—the only difference conceivable being one of degree. The manifestations of the unknowable in the vivid and faint feelings are not distinguishable in any intelligible manner: as feelings, the manifestations are the inner faces of nerve-thrills; as nerve-thrills, they are modes of molecular motion. The exciting stimuli may be in the one class external to the organism, and in the other internal to it; but these are no more than variations in the operation of known or knowable causes of the same kind and set in one series, the links of which evolution forbids us to break or to search for a new beginning in the unknowable. Is it not, then, altogether futile to lay it down as a first principle that there are two orders of manifestation clearly segregated one from the other, each order carrying with it the irrestible implication of some power that manifests itself; "and that by the words *ego* and *non-ego* respectively are meant the power that manifests itself in the faint forms, and the power that manifests itself in the vivid forms?"

Mind conscious of itself can never be evolved by the clustering of aggregates of feelings. In the process every characteristic of mind is brought into play, not as the result of the grouping, but as its condition. Mind directs the work. See how much is implied: a sentient organism, feelings, relations of feelings, knowledge of relations, composition of feelings and of relations of feelings—all that which is included in the word thought. To borrow our terms from another school of psychology—we find sensation, perception, memory, imagination, comparison, judgment, reasoning; and yet, with all these in exercise, we are supposed to be but in the process of evolving a self-conscious mind.

Evolutionism is necessitated to assume an order that will admit a gradual and unbroken advance from the lowest form of sentience to the highest powers of reasoning: the consciousness of *self* as contrasted with *not-self* breaks the continuity. The cohesion of the whole can only be effected by accounting for this fundamental distinction as having arisen in the gradual clustering of feelings into the two groups above described. But there is nothing in experience to warrant such a theory of the origin of self-consciousness.

The evolutionist is unable to give account of any vital fact arising in the study of mental science. The evolving mass, working in limitless energy through its perpetual mutations, has no promise in it of a self-knowing mind. However varied the multiplicity of change, there cannot emerge out of it a being conscious of self, and who, surveying the world in which he lives, is able to reduce its varied phenomena to order in his thought.

SECTION VII.

INNATE PRINCIPLES.

The Evolution Hypothesis cannot admit the existence in man of a source of intellectual and moral power, intimately united to, but not identical with, the sentient organism, having relation to its environment by means of the organism through which it affects and is affected by the external world. If man be constituted with a dual nature—mental and physical — he cannot have arisen in an unbroken course of cosmic mutation. It is essential, therefore, to evolutionism to account for his mental faculties, and for those axiomatic truths which are accepted by reason as soon as their terms are understood, in a way that will prove congruous with the supposed ceaseless dynamic process.

The mode in which the evolutionist deals with our knowledge of the external world is a crucial instance of his treatment of the question. Rejecting what are called faculties of the mind, he interprets the relation of consciousness to the surrounding universe from a quite different point of view. According to Mr. Spencer the gradual evolution of organs, becoming more and more perfectly adjusted, is accompanied by the gradual formation of correspondences between associated groups of feelings, that is nervous shocks, and the physical changes in the environment. Sense-perception is, then, the answer of the nervous organism to the impact of an external force, and is the setting up of a series of composite nerve-actions corresponding with the external order. Ultimately and essentially every perception is a group of nervous shocks co-ordinated so as to be in more or less exact accord with the relations existing in nature. The "unit of conciousness" has been compounded and re-compounded: the organism has registered these waves of molecular change; and the cognition of an external object is the bringing into play of the accumulated experiences, through impact of the object itself in direct contact, or mediately, as in vision through the agency of light.

But perception of the world around us cannot be generated by nerve-shocks. Something with faculty of knowing must exist before there is any cognitive act. Some one with a faculty of perceiving exists before anything is perceived. We must start in the study of mind with knowledge. Cognition of external objects is not the consequent; it is the condition of experience. The knowledge may be of the most rudimentary kind; but it is knowledge. Without it no play of nerve-thrills, no composition of nervous shocks will build up the cosmos in our experience. A mind with power of perceiving, and that power in exercise, is necessary on the one hand; an organism, endowed with sensibility, and affected by a wave of molecular motion, is indispensable on the other, that in the combined result there may be experienced what we may regard either as a sensation or a percept—as a sensation, if the sense element is predominant in consciousness, as a percept if the intellectual prevail. In this case, and the same criticism holds good throughout, Mr. Spencer pushes into the background the primary mental characteristic—*knowing*. He groups units of feeling, and constructs an objective world in this fashion in thought : but he loses sight of the fact that to know is the first and most distinctive' attribute of mind.

Passing from the discussion of these inborn modes of composite action displayed in the cognition of external objects, and in the higher exercises of intelligence operating on the materials furnished in sensation, we proceed to inquire how evolution deals with those attributes of mind, which the intuitionist holds to be essential to all reasoning, innate principles —not derived from without, not generated by experience, brought by the mind with it as it comes into existence—the law 'of its distinctive form of being. These primary intuitions, operative without consciousness of them, when analyzed and formulated, are axiomatic truths—*a priori* synthetic judgments. The experientialist denies that there are such principles native to intelligence ; affirming that these axioms are nothing more than generalizations from a uniform experience. Mr. Spencer, on the other hand, claims for his theory that it brings into harmony the two great schools: while holding that all knowledge is derived from experience, he maintains that organized experiences constitute forms of thought. Axiomatic truths are innate to the individual, but experiential to the race. The space-intuitions which are recognized as necessary and universal "are the *fixed functions* of *fixed structures* that have been moulded into correspondence with fixed outer relations. .... The truth that a straight line is the shortest line between two points lies latent in the structure of the eyes and the nervous centres which receive and co-ordinate visual impressions. .... Just as it has become impossible for the hand to grasp by bending the fingers outwards instead of inwards; so has it become impossible for those nervous actions by which we apprehend primary space-relations to be reversed so as to enable us to think of these relations otherwise than we do." *

This view is expounded more fully in another passage:—

"What is the meaning of the human brain? It is that the many *established* relations among its parts, stand for so many *established* relations among the psychical changes. Each of the constant connections among the fibres of the cerebral masses, answers to some constant connection of phenomena in the ex-

---

* *Psychology*, Vol. II., § 332.

perience of the race. . . . . All the organized arrange-
ments subsisting among the nerves of the infant's
brain, not only make possible certain combinations of
impressions, but also imply that such combinations will
hereafter be made—imply that there are answering
combinations in the outer world—a preparedness to
cognize these combinations—imply faculties of com-
prehending them. . . . . In the sense, then, that there
exist in the nervous system certain pre-established
relations answering to relations in the environment,
there is truth in the doctrine of 'forms of intuition'
—not the truth which its defenders suppose, but a
parallel truth. Corresponding to absolute external
relations, there are established in the structure of the
nervous system absolute internal relations—relations
that are potentially present before birth in the shape
of definite nervous connexions. . . . . . These pre-
determined internal relations, though independent of
the experiences of the individual, are not independent
of experiences in general : they have been determined
by the experiences of preceding organisms. The corollary here drawn from the general argument is that
the human brain is an organized register of infinitely
numerous experiences received during the evolution of
life, or rather, during the evolution of that series of
organisms through which the human organism has
been reached. The effects of the most uniform and
frequent of these experiences have been successively
bequeathed, principal and interest; and have slowly

amounted to that high intelligence which lies latent
in the brain of the infant—which the infant in after
life exercises, and perhaps strengthens or further
complicates—and which, with minute additions, it
bequeaths to future generations.   And thus it happens
that the European inherits from twenty to thirty
cubic inches more brain than the Papuan.   Thus it
happens that faculties, as of music, which scarcely
exist in some inferior races, become congenital in
superior ones.   Thus it happens that out of savages
unable to count up to the number of their fingers and
speaking a language containing only nouns and verbs,
arise at length our Newtons and Shakespeares."*

There is no mistaking the significance of this doctrine.   It makes the evolution of the nervous organism the origin of those innate principles that lie at
the basis of experience, and regulate all reasoning.
Intuitions are organized ancestral experiences registered in the brain, and become " the fixed functions of
fixed structures."   Truth is the accord of the "absolute
cohesions" among the fibres of the cerebral masses
with constant connections among the phenomena of
the environment.   Reason has no more to do with
these organized experiences than to read the record:
nor, indeed, is its part even so active as reading would
imply: the brain works out the result; consciousness
means no more than our being aware of it, sometimes

---

* *Psychology*, Vol. I., § 208.

in the process, more frequently only when the work is completed. The physical laws of the organism dominate and determine the whole. The intuitions of space relations, the principles that form the conditions precedent to experience, the primal elements of reason, as well as the laws of discursive thought are, on this theory, fixed functions of fixed nervous structures which have been organized through the invariable experiences of ancestral organisms reaching back to a time long antecedent to the differentiation of the human race.

Let this doctrine be called materialism or not—it assumes that the laws of the physical organism, not only correspond with, but *are* the laws of thought. Just as the "physiological units" are supposed by their polarity to build up new particles into the specific structure of the animal, or as the equilibration which has been correlated with the ancestral structure, fixes the colour of the hair or the contour of the face ; so do these same units mould the nervous system into those modes of nerve-action, which are the forms of thought—the regulative principles of reasoning. The processes of thought are pre-determined by the inborn forms of thought, the forms of thought are determined by the inborn law of organic action, that law is a mode of molecular motion of the physiological units— their equilibration as constituents of the organized body—and is the resultant of the entire series of incident forces which have impinged upon the organism from its primeval state, cycles of ages before the differentiation of man, onward until now. If this be not materialism, it at any rate ascribes all that is distinctive in intelligence to the physical forces operating in the environment. Man's mind is on the hypothesis as necessarily shaped in the mould of physical nature as is the rounded pebble on the beach.

Note the consequences that inevitably follow. The innate principles that lie at the basis of all reasoning are not on this theory to be accounted universal and necessary. truths. They are, in the narrowest sense, relative. They are functions of the organism, and hold good only in the relations of that organism and its environment. Carried beyond the environment that has shaped them, they are inapplicable and invalid. If the brain has been envolved through physical causes only, then the evolved product has only physical correlations. Its intuitions are limited to the physical: they have no wider validity or meaning. Besides, the adjustment of organism and environment has been a constant process of equilibration, and is not at any two points in time exactly alike. The adjustments of the past are not precisely congruous with the conditions of to-day. The congruity between the organized forms of thought and the environment, continues constant only through the continued harmonious changing of both. No doubt some elements are comparatively stable: still the present adaptation cannot be taken as the measure of the past or as a sure forecast of the future. All mental phenomena are "incidents of the correspondence between the organism and the environment." There are, no doubt, sequences that seem to be constant: so far as our limited experience reaches, in space and time, we find the adjustment true; but experience is, on the point, an unreliable witness; for organized experiences are antecedent to conscious experiences and direct them. We are always looking through an elaborately constructed series of lenses which are being constantly modified. How far they can be relied upon as, at any given point in human history, representing a correct adjustment of vision to object we have no means of testing. We only know with certainty that there has been a continuous course of adaptation, and that every adjustment was temporary, being no more than a moment in a ceaseless process of equilibration. True for that moment, the adjustment must be untrue at every other point in time.

Mr. Spencer's doctrine of first principles involves the denial of the universal validity of any truth. Truth is, on his theory, never fixed; it is a ceaseless moving equilibration. Evolutionism is an essentially sceptical theory.

But the consequences reach still further. This doctrine of innate principles overturns the imposing edifice which Mr. Spencer has erected with so much labour. Evolutionism is based on the validity of dynamic principles throughout all cosmic change. Mr.

Spencer founds his philosophy on a dynamic law whose applicability throughout all time is founded on the first principles underlying experience. Reject these and the whole structure falls to pieces. But first principles are on his hypothesis functions of the nervous organization, formed by interaction of nerve and environment. Now the formative period, during which the human organization has been evolved, is but a span, and the environment whose incident forces have shaped it, is but a hand-breadth in the limitless universe. Myriad forces are continually playing around the nerve tissue; of these some, perhaps, the largest part, are imperceptible and unknowable. The adaptations of the organism are only adjusted to such of them as may tend to further or hinder its organic life. But evolutionism is not narrowed to the adjustments and experiences of the human organism in its environment, in so far as these bear relation to its maintenance in life. It proposes to embrace the whole movement of manifested force. It reaches back to a condition antecedent to the origin of any organic form, covers the whole extent of inorganic matter, and undertakes to recount the past and forecast the future of all concrete being. Yet its only basis is the record of ancestral experiences in the fixed structures of the brain.

If the central ganglia are not a true and complete record of the past in the law of its immeasurable movement, Mr. Spencer has no foundation for his system and no material out of which to build it. Granted that the organized sensibility of man registers with exactness the invariable sequences in its environment, granted also that philosophy can correctly decipher the inconceivably complicated record, the validity of the testimony is, as we have seen, narrowed to the physical surroundings of the organism, and has no meaning beyond that range. Take out of Mr. Spencer's philosophy every proposition affirmative of any fact except such facts as are vital to the continuance of man as a living organism; narrow it strictly to its own field—its only possible field—and his system, so vast and so elaborate, will shrink into a few truths in physics and physiology.

To grant the evolutionist his own first principles is the destruction of his hypothesis. In truth, evolutionism is a parasitic growth living on the sap of more vigorous organisms. Deprive it of this stolen nutriment and it dies.

SECTION VIII.

THE CORRELATION OF MENTAL AND PHYSICAL FORCES.

To bring the activity of mind within a universal law of physical change, it is necessary to establish the correlation of every exercise of mental power with the forces of the material universe. No one will seriously dispute that there is a relation subsisting between the forces of the organism and the mental operations embodied in thought. The fact that in connexion with and through a bodily organization, the spiritual nature of man receives knowledge of and acts on the external world, renders it certain that there will be found remarkable correspondences between the activities of the mind and the functions of the body; but it is quite a different thing to assert that mental operations and physical forces are embraced under one law of correlation and equivalence. "Yet," Mr. Spencer says, "there is no alternative but to make the assertion: the facts which justify, or rather which necessitate it being abundant and conspicuous." "Between the physical forces and the sensations there exists a correlation like that between the physical forces themselves." * This view is reasoned out both in his *First Principles* and in his *Principles of Psychology* with much fulness of argument and illustration. The cogency of the reasoning is, however, greatly weakened by Mr. Spencer's repudiation of the materialist theory. If it were maintained that intellection is a mode of molecular motion; if the mental were accepted as merely physical,—or if monism were reached from the opposite side and the material held to be spiritual,—one could readily comprehend how the operations of mind might be set in a series of correlations of physical force.

* *First Principles*, § 71.

But within the knowable Mr. Spencer rejects the monist doctrine: he holds that the immanent energy is conditioned in two modes; it is conditioned in matter otherwise than in mind. He must, therefore, bring the manifestations thus distinctively conditioned into a unity of relation such that mental activity may be interchanged with physical action. If we look closely at the correlation assumed to exist, it will be seen to be impossible, unless on a unitarian basis,— either that of sheer materialism or thorough-going idealism.

The use of steam as a driving power furnishes a good example of correlation. Coal generates steam; steam produces motion. The coal is expended in raising the steam, and the steam in causing the motion: the one form of force passes into the other —the amount expended being balanced by the work done. The principle of correlation involves—(a) the expenditure of force which passes into a new form, (b) equivalence in the amount of the force under both forms. If mental activity be brought within the correlation of physical forces, there must be—(a) the passing of physical force into intellectual force, and *vice versa;* and (b) the amount of physical force expended must balance the mental force produced. When a nerve-thrill passes into the sensorium, and a cognitive act ensues, has the physical force operating in the molecular motion in the brain passed into the cognition and been wholly, or in part, expended in

R

producing it? Either the cognition is a physical phenomenon—a new mode of matter and motion, or the physical force which has passed into the intellection, and which has been expended in producing it, has ceased to exist as physical force. If the physical force continue to exist, then, on the principle of correlation, the cognitive act cannot take place: the persistence of force forbids it. If the physical force operating in the brain pass into intellectual energy, it must expend itself in the work, and we have so much force taken out of the physical universe, and transformed into an immaterial form in intellection. This intellection may, in like manner, be transformed back again into molecular motion; in which case the spiritual mode of being is robbed of so much existence, while the material universe has restored to it the former amount. Is not such an interchange of the intellectual and physical — of cognition and motion, absurd? Yet there is no other supposition possible, if while we reject materialism we maintain the correlation of mental and physical forces. The correlation cannot come into play unless by the expenditure of so much physical force in the production of so much spiritual force, and *vice versa*—the force in either case passing into the new form. We conclude that it is not possible to bring into correlation with physical forces the exercise of intellectual and moral power. But if it be impossible to do so, it is impossible to establish a universal law of evolution.

CHAPTER XVII.

I OUGHT; I will: these words express the most noteworthy of all experiences—the obedience of law in conscious freedom. We are now at the opposite pole of being from the whirling molecule or the revolving planet. We have entered a realm altogether diverse from that ruled by physical law. The whole scene is changed. Life is here directed towards an end voluntarily chosen as an object of pursuit. Motives—not forces — are the impelling power: reason—not dynamic law—determines conduct. Consciousness of liberty is the condition under which obedience is rendered.

No philosophy can long command a wide assent that does not deal in a satisfactory way with the problems of morality. The worth of a system may be fairly judged by its account of the principles that regulate conduct. Moral life is everything to man: it is the man. In his best moments he feels that it will profit him nothing, if he gain the whole cosmos, and lose himself, or be cast away. Mr. Spencer cannot be charged with under-estimating this great theme. His ethical doctrine has been, he tells us, the final aim

of all his labours in philosophy. "This last part of
the task it is, to which I regard all the preceding
parts as subsidiary. Written as far back as 1842, my
first essay, consisting of letters on *The Proper Sphere
of Government*, vaguely indicated what I conceived to
be certain general principles of right and wrong in
political conduct; and from that time onwards my
ultimate purpose, lying behind all proximate purposes,
has been that of finding for the principles of right and
wrong in conduct at large, a scientific basis."*

It is Mr. Spencer's aim to establish moral principles
on a rational basis. The foundation has been laid in
his philosophy. He is consequently precluded from
expounding any ethical doctrine that is not the legitimate fruit of his system. We are not prepared to
deposit in the ark of the coming dispensation the
tables of a new law, till we have tested their scientific
worth: we must also see how they follow, as a
necessary outcome of the philosophy from which they
derive their authority.

"Critics of a certain class," he says, "far from re-
joicing that ethical principles otherwise derived by
them, coincide with ethical principles scientifically
derived, are offended by the coincidence. Instead of
recognizing essential likeness they enlarge on super-
ficial difference."* We question if the defenders of
Christian ethics are chargeable generally with this

---

* *The Data of Ethics*, Preface, p. iii.   † *Ibid.*, Preface, p. v.

offence. They do not commonly disparage moral lessons drawn from nature. The testimony of nature to the spiritual and moral law of God, is a favourite topic with apologists. To discover a fundamental antagonism between scientific, or natural, and supernatural, or revealed, morality, would be fatal to the doctrine of a divine revelation; for if natural morality were opposed to revealed morality, the claims of revelation to be from God could not be maintained: conscience would be bound to reject as false ethical teaching in conflict with the first principles of morals. But it is fair and right to point out that a system of ethics derived exclusively from natural law is inadequate; that something more, something higher, is requisite for the guidance of human life. Still more needful is it to examine the ethical teaching of a philosophy which claims to embody all truth. So far as the merit of Mr. Spencer's doctrine is concerned, the question is not whether an ethical code can be framed apart from revelation; but whether the evolution hypothesis can, consistently with its principles, provide it. Religion has heretofore been the most important source of moral impulse, and the chief light for its guidance. The Church of God is the great school of ethics. A high standard has been set before mankind —a standard approached in but few instances. Yet there have never been wanting in the Christian society some who have exemplified in a high degree the noblest qualities—devotion, self-sacrifice, patience, gentleness, courage, purity, charity. Soldiers unsurpassed in valour, scholars pre-eminent in learning, statesmen illustrious for wisdom, have reverenced a divine ideal and submitted themselves to the revealed law of God. Out of a supra-natural source the water of life has flowed, refreshing and reinvigorating the moral strength of the greatest and best of men. We have to inquire what the new philosophy has to offer in the stead of this venerated authority.

1. Moral law is obeyed, and can be obeyed, only in conscious freedom. Moral obedience is willing obedience. The evolution hypothesis cannot account for the consciousness of liberty; and if accepted as the true philosophy would inevitably destroy it. Evolution cannot create the conditions requisite to conduct that lies under a sense of responsibility; it cannot furnish the requirements indispensable to the coming to be of moral life. For evolution proceeds on the assumption that inflexible physical law dominates everywhere, directing all the activities of the organism. "Mental acts are nervous functions." It is dynamic law that moulds the innate truths of reason, and shapes the fundamental principles of morals : the law of the organism is the law of mind. Nerve-action is correlated in the bonds of physical necessity with the forces of the environment; so that the physical law of the universe governs absolutely the conscious life. These are not conditions in which action that deserves the name of moral is possible ; let them be realized in

thought, and for that mind morality can have no longer any real meaning. The evolutionist may reply that his is not the only system of determinism; that he lays no greater constraint on man's freedom than the Calvinist. But the fact is not so: the Calvinist does not deny liberty, he contends for it.* What he rejects is an imagined liberty that can have no existence in a real world—a liberty which divests the individual of every trace of character, deprives reason of all decisive judgment, and robs motives of their power. Moral action is no more possible *in vacuo* than vital action.

Exception is taken to the evolution hypothesis in the interests of morality, on the ground of its doctrine of physical causation in mental operations. Man knows himself to choose and to resolve: it is when he would carry out his intention through the organism that he becomes conscious of the control of physical law. He recognizes in this realm the fixed physical order of the world, and by obedience accomplishes his purpose. It is not correct to say that moral action is, on the intuitional theory, uncaused. The intuitionist seeks a cause, but looks for it in the man himself—in his intellectual and moral nature. Man in his own inner

---

* In his *Dissertatio de Libertate Humana, contra Spinozum,* Turretin gives the following definition of liberty :—" Libertas, juxta simplicissimam et receptissimam ejus notionem, est *facultas eligendi,* seu, quod idem est, *facultas agendi ut libet;* vel, ut aliis verbis rem eandem exponamus, *imperium quod quis habet in proprias actiones.*"

experience knows that he acts freely. "If that sense of liberty is deceptive," says Turrentin, "and we cannot trust it, nothing human is certain, and universal scepticism must follow." * Evolutionism treats as illusive this consciousness of freedom. It frames a theory of the correlation of organic and mental action which fixes every purpose in a necessary physical succession. The law of molecular motion in the physiological units rules "the thoughts and intents of the heart." But liberty and responsibility are crushed out by this physical necessity. In the evolution hypothesis there is no room for moral life. Its ethical doctrine is sheer dynamic determinism.

2. Having seen that evolution does not furnish the conditions requisite for free and responsible action, let us inquire what account it gives of the sense of obligation, and whether under its sway that moral intuition could survive.

Mr. Spencer arrives at the sense of obligation in this way:—In the evolution of animal organisms race-needs render it inevitable that at times " the pleasures of the present must be sacrificed to the pleasures of the future." In this is found the essential characteristic of the moral consciousness — "the control of some feeling or feelings by some other feeling or feelings." "This conscious relinquishment of immediate and special good to gain distant and general good, while it

---

* Turretini *De Libertate Humana.*

is a cardinal trait of the self-restraint called moral, is also a cardinal trait of self-restraints other than those called moral—the restraints that originate from fear of the visible ruler, of the invisible ruler, and of society at large. . . . . Eventually the moral control, with its accompanying conceptions and sentiments, emerges as independent. . . . . As with the restraints thus generated is always joined the thought of external coercion, there arises the notion of obligation ; which so becomes habitually associated with the surrender of immediate special benefits for the sake of distant and general benefits."*

There are two elements in this " notion of obligation : " (*a*) the surrender of a present pleasure for the sake of a future benefit, and (*b*) the coercive sense of obligation to do so. Now there is little doubt that men would in any circumstances soon discover that some present pleasures must be sacrificed that more distant benefits might be gained ; but this implies forethought, comparison, preference, choice—the very qualities that characterize the developed moral nature. Just as in the supposed evolution of mind we found it necessary to assume in every instance the exercise of the mental power to be evolved.

The second element in the "notion of obligation" originated in a different way. It was driven into the primeval man by the club of his chief, while alive, and

---

* *The Data of Ethics,* § 44.

by the ghost of the chief, when dead ; by the dread of
the avenging gods ; and by the stern action of society
putting down conduct that proved injurious to it.
Created in this fashion, the sense of obligation was
originally an illusion—a falsehood. The poor savage
in whose breast it was engendered was the dupe of
his own fears. In passing, one may be permitted to
notice how familiar the evolutionist is with the
feelings and experiences of the primitive savage man :
he speaks of him as if he were his next door neighbour.   Our dusky African brother will not, on
evolution principles, serve as a true specimen of
primeval humanity; for through myriad ages the
evolution of the race has been going on—each new
experience marking some change, however slight.
The fixedness that would assimilate the savage of
to-day with the human being of the first ages is a
phenomenon wholly at variance with the assumed
unceasing process of change.

We shall suppose, however, that the simple primitive man had thus imposed on him a coercive sense of
obligation : How will it be with the more highly
evolved man, who sits in judgment on his chiefs,
relegates his God to the unknowable, and delights in
dissecting with keen scalpel the nerves and ligaments
of society ?   Will he continue to allow himself to be
coerced by the authority of moral law ?

Mr. Spencer answers by bringing into view what
he regards as the sanction of moral action—the neces-

sary issue of every act in pleasure or pain. A penalty or reward attaches to everything we do: either the individual or the race is benefited or injured thereby. Personal desires and the interests of humanity often conflict; but the rival claims are being continually adjusted in the equilibration which evolution is ever more perfectly working out. Let us grant all this: still the difficulty is not removed. If we were dealing with objects without reason, we might calculate with some confidence as to the operation of seemingly conflicting forces; we might compute their resultant; but we have to do with men, who are impelled by many motives, whose moral sense has to keep strong passions in control. Let every member of the social organization know and believe that the sole moral quality of actions is to minister pleasure, and that the claim of moral law is nothing else than a demand that the individual should sacrifice a present and certain to a distant and uncertain pleasure in his own experience; or that he should bear pain—sometimes to the extent of sacrificing his life—that a modicum of pleasure might be ultimately added to the sum total enjoyed by the race: what will his response to such ethical doctrine be? He is not bound to do or to refrain from doing because of any penalty attaching to conduct; if there be penalty affecting the individual at all, he may judge, perhaps, that in his present environment it is as often against the right action as in favour of it: he is not bound to subordinate the lower feelings to the higher; if the lower—being for the most part more intense—yield him a greater sum of pleasure in this life, it is his duty, as well as privilege, to indulge in them: he is not bound to be truthful or honest; for though society is much injured by roguery and deceit, the harm wrought by his conduct would affect him little in comparison with the many advantages to be secured by his dishonestly gotten wealth.

The ethical doctrine of evolution is exposed to the same criticism that lies against every form of Hedonism: it cannot give a rational account of the origin of moral obligation, or reasonable assurance of its perpetuity. As in the case of intellection, so in morals, we must recognize the existence of something with faculty of comparing, judging, choosing—conscious that there is that in conduct which is right or wrong —in many instances seeing dimly, or not at all, the true relations of things; yet in experience, as in language, acknowledging all the while the *ought* and the *ought not.*

3. Moral life works out a purpose: through proximate ends it strives towards some chief end. What object can the evolution hypothesis set forth as the supreme aim of human action? The perfectly evolved life is one perfectly adjusted to environment: this completeness of adaptation is the only ideal state conceivable on the principles of evolution. "The acts adjusted to ends, ... become, as evolution progresses, better adjusted; until finally they make the

life of each individual entire in length and breadth,. at the same time that they efficiently subserve the rearing of young, and do both these not only without hindering other individuals from doing the like, but while giving aid to them in doing the like." * This completing of the life in length and breadth is more fully stated elsewhere. " The type of nature to which the highest social life affords a sphere such that every faculty has its due amount, and no more than its due amount, of function and accompanying gratification, is the type of nature towards which progress cannot cease till it is reached." †

That the state of humanity on the earth will yet be elevated and improved, so as to attain a fulness of life and satisfaction in living not now known, is a reasonable hope. But in procuring that blessedness other influences must be brought into exercise, of which evolution can give no account. It can only set before man, as his ideal condition, a perfect equili- bration of the personal life in the harmonious action of all the faculties, and the constant accompaniment of their activity with a sense of pleasure ; a perfect adaptation of the individual life to the social organi- zation, enhancing the personal enjoyment by a com- munity of pleasurable feelings ; and therewith a perfect adjustment of society in its members one to another and to the whole, and the whole to the

---

* *The Data of Ethics*, § 15.   *Ibid.*, § 67.

environing cosmos, thereby securing the greatest fulness of life possible of attainment by man. It is not conceivable that such a result could be reached by the sole operation of the forces recognized in the evolution hypothesis; but if it were conceivable, we must bear in mind that at the moment when that ideal state is perfected its dissolution begins. The persistence of force forbids its continuance for one hour. The forces that have slowly accomplished the perfect adjustment cannot rest: they must work on: further change towards adaptation is precluded; the movement can only be towards the disturbance of the equilibrium—which is dissolution. The fulness of life is the beginning of death.

Now we may fairly ask, what is it in the history of the race, from the present moment to the final destruction, that is to form the supreme end of action? If we strive toward the consummated equilibration, we pursue a shadow; for when the harmony is complete, it forthwith perishes in discord: if our aim be not the perfected state, but the progress towards it: then inadequate adjustment is a thing to be desired; for it is that very lack of adaptation which prolongs the process, and so lengthening out the life of humanity, increases the total sum of enjoyment.

But for the individual member of society this ideal fulness of life can have no practical significance. He is destroyed in the progress towards it: it can profit him nothing. The evolution of his personal life is a brief process of adjustment, which soon reaches its climax; and then, the adverse influences predomina-ting, the struggle is speedily ended. The great social organization itself is overmastered by forces that are sovereign over the direction and mode of its corporate life. The sweep of these causes is beyond the reach, or even the vision of the members. Why contend for an evanescent dream? Why wrestle with or seek to aid the vast forces of the cosmos? Let them drift onward to universal disintegration. His own satis-faction in life is for every man the main concern: can evolutionism help him to a greater sum of plea-sure? Conflicting motives toss him to and fro; impulses are strong; passions turbulent: what ideal can evolution furnish to the individual life, whereby these conflicting influences may be set in their due order? What ultimate personal aim to regulate all proximate aims? Around us there is a ceaseless struggle: more of pleasure than of pain, perhaps; but the pleasures and the pains very unequally dis-pensed. Escape pain and seize pleasure, is the dictate of self-indulgence. Evolutionism has no countervail-ing persuasion to offer—no "chief end" imperative over all balancing of conflicting feelings; no moral nature capable of being developed in strength and beauty; no future in which there may be reaped the seed here sown in tears.

4. The evolution hypothesis leaves man without

effective moral guidance. It has no means of devising rules of conduct that might constitute a permanent ethical code. Pursuing the method followed in accounting for the innate principles of reason, Mr. Spencer finds in man moral intuitions which are the organized experiences of the race. But just as he cannot on his own principles discover any truth that is universal and necessary, so is it incompetent for him to lay down any moral precept as binding on all men everywhere. No precept derived from the principles of evolution can be a universal and authoritative rule of moral action. The great ethical principle of Mr. Spencer's system is adjustment to environment for the individual and the race, so as to secure the fullest attainable life for each and for all. Moral action is, then, a process of continuous adaptation—a ceaseless changing. No code can be framed, whose precepts will have more than a temporary value. " Eternal and immutable morality " is but a fine phrase. Life being adjustment to conditions, the rule of right-living, true for a time, must fall into desuetude. The ethical code is for ever changing to suit the continuous movement towards equilibrium. Designed to be perpetual, the moral law given to Israel was graven on the granite of Sinai; but the precepts delivered to man under a dispensation of evolution, need to be inscribed on waxen tablets; for the lawgiver must turn his stylus often and, as conditions alter, amend his work.

5. The ethical doctrine of evolution is characterized

throughout by dominance of the pleasurable. It is pleasure that furnishes the end, the impulse, the standard, the rule, the sanction. " Life is good or bad according as it does, or does not, bring a surplus of agreeable feeling." " Conduct is good or bad according as its total effects are pleasurable or painful."* " Pleasure, somewhere, at some time, to some being or beings, ... is as much a necessary form of moral intuition as space is a necessary form of intellectual intuition."† This is thorough-going hedonism, tempered by the theory of a natural codification, or digest, of the laws of pleasure in the organized experiences registered in the nervous system.

To discuss adequately the ethical value of pleasure would necessitate an examination of what is conveyed by the term. As Mr. Spencer uses it, he includes every form of gratification—the joy of one who bears suffering for the benefit of another, and the delight of the glutton in his feast. Give width enough to the meaning, and it may embrace at once paradise and the pothouse.

But, passing from this point, note the confusion between the moral quality and the consequences of its exercise. It may be true that the right always results in a surplus of pleasure; while it may be false that the surplus of pleasure constitutes the rightness of the right. The evolutionist is bound to show that the

---

* *The Data of Ethics*, § 10.   † *Ibid.*, § 15.

moral quality of the action is its tendency to produce agreeable or painful sensations.

It is clear no moral teaching could spring from the evolution hypothesis except the ethics of pleasnre. Out of the primordial homogeneity no other doctrine could be evolved. Is'it a sound theory of life ? Is there nothing better within the range of human experience than pleasure, and nothing worse than pain ?. Is the good nothing more than that which imparts enjoyment ? and is the essence of evil that it entails suffering ?

The whole question will appear in a different light if we approach it from the opposite standpoint : if we hold that there is that in man which is in its nature moral—that which is capable of moral growth or decay, of being perfected or debased. The moral attributes of mind give man a sovereignty over agreeable or painful sensations : pleasure is not to him the very substance of his life—the form of moral intuition. The relations of experience are still further modified if we cherish belief in a future state. Weal and woe are not measurable within the limits of the present world : there are results that do not lie within the visible; and the hedonist computation of the worth of actions is manifestly false. The broken life is perfected : the seemingly complete is seen to be defective. In the hope of another life, all things appear in a new light.

Mr. Spencer has in his ethics, as in his sociology, presented many questions of conduct in a novel and

striking manner: but as a whole his moral system is
unsound. It has no solid basis and no imperativeness.
In accordance with his cosmic hypothesis he can present no other. Man is a passing phase of a vast mutation. The individual perishes; so also does the race.
All things hasten to dissolution. Why strive to gain
for man a little increase of length or fulness of life?
Let the mighty forces sweep on and evolve what
result they may: we shall soon disappear, merged in
the great cosmic stream.

CHAPTER XVIII.

CREATION.

THE bearing of the Evolution Hypothesis on belief in creation, and especially the creation of man, has at once aroused antagonism and won support. The doctrine of creation lies much nearer the central truths of revealed religion than might at first sight appear. It shapes our creed as to the Divine Being in Himself and in His relation to those who are thought of as His creatures: His creatures they are not, if He is not Creator. Deny creation and you profoundly modify the idea of God—an idea determining all religious dogma and prevading all devotion. But we are not here concerned with the theological bearings of the question: our business is to examine the doctrine of evolution in contrast with that of creation, that we may judge which presents the great mystery in most complete harmony with what reason accepts as assured truth.

The denial of the possibility of creation is a denial either of its possibility to thought or its possibility in fact. The evolutionist challenges the legitimacy of the idea of creation, alleging that it is unthinkable. Mr. Spencer says, " Our inability to conceive matter becoming non-existent, is immediately consequent on the nature of thought. Thought consists in the establishment of relations. There can be no relation established, and therefore, no thought framed, when one of the related terms is absent from consciousness. Hence it is impossible to think of something becoming nothing, for the same reason that it is impossible to think of nothing becoming something—the reason, namely, that nothing cannot become an object of consciousness. The annihilation of matter is unthinkable for the same reason that the creation of matter is unthinkable."* Again, "Those who entertain the proposition that each kind of organism results from a divine interposition, do so because they refrain from translating words into thoughts. The case is one of those where men do not really believe, but rather *believe they believe.* For belief, properly so called, implies a mental representation of the thing believed; and no such mental representation is here possible."†

Lange is still more emphatic. "The creation of the world from nothing is at least a clear and honest theory. It contains so open and direct a contradiction of all thought, that all weaker and more reserved contradictions must feel ashamed beside it."‡

Creation is, then, alleged to be impossible to thought —"a mental representation of the thing" is impossible

---

* *First Principles,* § 53.   † *Biology,* Vol. I., § 112.
‡ *History of Materialism,* Vol. I., Second Section, Chapter I.

and this inability to think creation "is immediately consequent on the nature of thought."

It would be easy to turn the edge of Mr. Spencer's criticism upon himself. The relation which he substitutes for that of Creator and creature, is no more thinkable. It is as difficult to represent in thought the relation of noumenon and phenomenon, reality and appearance, absolute cause and conditioned effect, as it is to conceive of "God, the Father Almighty, maker of heaven and earth."

But there is an obvious fallacy in assuming that no conception can be thought unless it can be represented to the mind in an image or other sensible form. Nothing could be more completely unfounded than this assumption. A great part of the matter of thinking, and above all of exact thinking, is such that it cannot be presented to consciousness in any visual or sensible mode. Mr. Spencer's test would remove from the range of knowledge all relations of relations; none of which can become objects of consciousness by an image or "mental representation of the thing." It is as impossible to conceive a point, or a line, or the millionth power of six, or the equality of ratios, as to conceive not-being. Mr. Spencer's criterion would also exclude from thought all conception of mind. Here is an object of knowledge of which we cannot form any "mental representation;" yet men reason with precision, taking mind, or a faculty of mind, as one of the terms. Abstractions constitute the greatest part of the material of thought, and the more completely abstract the relation is—the more entirely apart from concrete things—the more definite and exact the process of reasoning. If the criterion in question were valid, arithmetic should get rid of *0* as being the sign of a concept of which no mental representation is possible. Symbolic representation, it may be said, furnishes the means of thinking abstract relations: if so, we can equally well think under a symbol the relation of Creator and creation. But is not-being, is no-thing so far removed from experience? Does it not rather run alongside of all experience? The school-boy becomes alive to it when he puts his hand into an empty pocket; we find it laid as a competent mode of thought at the basis of his philosophy by one of the greatest thinkers of this century. How can that be said to be unthinkable which is being constantly thought? "Note the ambiguity of saying that the idea of destruction is unthinkable, in the face of the fact that for centuries it has been thought. This has been evaded by the assertion that 'men did not really think the idea, they only thought that they thought it.' But this is to confound conception with imagination. In almost every thought, idea, conception, there are, over and above the condensed perceptions capable of definite expression in terms of sense, elements incapable of such expression."*

---

* Lewes, *Problems of Life and Mind*, Vol. II., p. 270.

But though creation be granted thinkable, its reality may be denied on the ground that it is impossible in fact. This impossibility may be founded on either of two grounds—(*a*) a supposed inability in God to create, or (*b*) a supposed inability to create the universe that is.

(1.) God may be so conceived in thought that the idea of God is inconsistent with the idea of creation, and creation concluded to be impossible. We may think of God as the Absolute, as existing out of all relations,—altogether self-contained,—His whole activity immanent. If we so think of Him, we exclude of necessity the possibility of creation. But such a mode of representing the Divine Being in thought is contrary to the revelation of Him in Scripture : self-communication, not self-inclusion is His characteristic. His activity does not remain immanent: it is manifested. His "goings forth have been of old from everlasting." * If, then, we have formed any idea of God inconsistent with the exercise of creative power, we are not to discard the belief in creation, but to amend our idea of God.

(2.) It may be supposed that the universe that is, could not have been created by God. A lurking doubt of this kind is often discoverable. If God be a *Spirit*, how, it is asked, can He be the Creator of that which is so entirely diverse from Him as matter ?

---

* Micah v., 2.

To harmonize in thought the belief in God as a Spirit, and belief in the origin of matter by His creative power, it is open to the thinker to modify his conception of God, or of matter, or to bring them together in an act—not of knowledge, but of faith.

The conception of matter may be modified. Berkeley, seeing that the atheism of his day lurked in matter, attempted to remove the shelter for unbelief by denying the existence of matter, except as an idea, laying down the principle that its essence is to be perceived. Minds with power of intellection so conditioned as to yield a world, subjective in its origin, but objective to consciousness, can be readily thought of as created in the likeness of the supreme Intelligence, and the difficulty of the origination of matter is evaded. But every system of idealism must encounter the ineradicable belief that a world external to the mind exists. There is, however, a quite needless use of disparaging epithets when matter is spoken of in contrast with spirit. The physicist has done much to alter this tone of thought, and to elevate the conception of the material universe as a work of God. It is impossible to study the visible cosmos without having our admiration excited at every step. There is nothing foul in the world apart from the depravity of moral evil. This mass of ice melts into a running stream; it rises into vapour; touched by the morning sunlight it glows with the most brilliant hues; the cloud vanishes into the azure sky: the solid mass is changed into a form so far removed from grossness that the air into which it has passed furnishes the very term in which the thought of God is clothed, when me speak of Him as "a most pure Spirit." But we have not yet reached a full conception of the marvellous subtilty of matter, when we have looked into the translucent clearness of the sky. Matter is a mode of force. However constituted — whether composed of atoms; or of vortex rings; or of points of force — its ultimate constituents present to the scientific imagination a tenuity immeasurably surpassing anything revealed through the senses. The ultimate form of matter is not an inert thing: it thrills with unceasing movement; its pulsations are the continuous play of all-pervading and limitless energy. In accordance with Mr. Spencer's terminology, matter is a manifestation of force, and force is a mode of power, and power is an attribute of God.

On the other hand, obstacles in the way of the acceptance of the fact of creation, are raised by misconception as to the divine nature. The idea of God comprises many attributes. These attributes the limits of intelligence compel us to think separately. In accurate thinking the divine idea will be presented in that aspect which stands related to the experience at the time in question. When the mind is engaged about the creation of matter, we think of power. Whatever power in kind or in amount is implied in the work, that power is to be ascribed to the Creator.

But even though we should remove every misappre-
hension that tends to render difficult our conception
of the relation, when we try to represent in thought
the creative act, we reach at that point a breach of
continuity over which knowledge cannot carry us.
The transition from power immanent in a "most pure
Spirit," to energy as we know it operative in the
physical universe, cannot be effected by science. We
must believe; we cannot see: "By faith we understand that the worlds were made by the word of
God." * There is, however, within experience, an
instance which helps us to conceive, though we cannot comprehend, the transition. We know ourselves
as willing, and we see that act of the spirit embodied
in the origination of physical change. The transition
from the act of the spirit of which we are immediately
conscious, to the external operation revealed to us by
sense, is not cleared up by any known or conceivable
explanation. Science is here, in our most constant
and intimate experience, as much at fault as in the
attempt to conceive that primal act of the Infinite
Spirit which "in the beginning" issued in the existence
of manifested energy—which "created the heavens
and the earth."

Maintaining that creation is both possible to thought
and possible in fact, we advance to the affirmation
that creation is consonant with experience. This posi-

---

* Hebrews xi., 3.

.tion will be strenuously assailed by the evolutionist. It will be maintained that there is nothing in experience in the least favouring the belief in creation.

Of course experience is unable to testify to its own origin; it cannot transcend itself. A witness has no evidence at first hand to give as to the date or manner of his own birth. His presence, however, is conclusive proof that he has come to be. At the same time experience has relevant and important testimony to offer on the question at issue. There lie in it regulative principles that are proof of a something prior to it— its mould and law. These principles, indispensable to experience—not its outcome but its condition, we may call into court and receive from them valuable evidence as to the first origin of the things we see.

(1.) The knowledge of effects compels us to believe in an ultimate cause. "We cannot think at all about the impressions which the external world produces in us, without thinking of them as caused, and we cannot carry out our inquiry concerning their causation without inevitably committing ourselves to the hypothesis of a First Cause." *

(2.) Over the whole range of observation we find form and order. At the earliest moment when the universe comes into the view of science it emerges in thought under the reign of law, orderly in its arrangement and movement—a cosmos, not a chaos. This

---

* *First Principles,* § 12.

conception is, indeed, a notable characteristic of evolutionism: for it must assume that the universe at the first moment of its existence in the knowable, contains the whole law of its future history, including implicitly the entire order now existing. But the cosmos has not originated the law that moulds it: it is no more credible that it should have originated the law in accordance with which its movements are directed, than that it should have produced the matter of which it consists. This order must also be referred back to the ultimate cause.

(3.) A necessary condition of experience is a self-conscious intelligence; where there is no one to see, there is nothing seen. Man is himself one of the concrete existences in the universe, and his thought is the most notable of its phenomena. How has intelligence come to be ? we seek an adequate cause and find none till we have ascended to the Primal Cause.

(4.) Experience shows everywhere adjustments of means to ends. It will not satisfy reason to turn, as the evolutionist does, from these adjustments to the mode in which they have been produced, and to argue that having been brought about in this or that manner they are not to be regarded as adaptations—that there is in them no evidence of purpose. Suppose, with the evolutionist, that the order of the movement of things produces necessarily in process of time manifold adaptations; suppose a tendency to adjust the balance of each thing with its environment to be the very principle of progress; we are bound to take notice of this order, and look for that in the cause which will account for this universally operative principle of adaptation.

The adaptation of mind to that world in which it dwells and of which it has knowledge, is the most wonderful of all adjustments. The most significant of all the characteristics of the universe, is the existence in it of that which answers to intelligence. The possibility of nature being *thought* involves the implication that there is *thought* in it. Mind answers to the manifestation of mind. The intelligible in the cosmos leads irresistibly to the recognition of an intelligent author.

The existence of a conscious *ego*—knowing self and the environment of self—cannot be a product of the Unconscious. Nothing comes of nothing; there is no more in the effect than there was in the cause. If it be given me to say "*I am*," I cannot but believe that the great First Cause can also say, "I AM."

But if the Primal Cause be a self-conscious Intelligence, His I AM differences Him from human intelligence; as my *I am* differences me from Him. His intelligence is not one with the intelligence of man. My intelligence is a form of being face to face with the Infinite Intelligence. I am not enclosed in the Divine Being. God is not all things, for He is not *This I.* The First Cause and the cosmos are not one throughout. If they are not one throughout, there is no ground to suppose that they are one at any point in immensity. We cannot identify the world with

God. God is, then, the cause of nature, and at the same time not one with it; the cause has not passed into the effect, but co-exists with it. The primal causation, therefore, differs from all known instances of causation: it is Creation.

To sum up the argument: we are compelled, in every process of reasoning as to concrete existence, to reach back to a First Cause. We must recognise that Cause as the author of order and law—a cause having as effect a cosmos with numberless adaptations of means to end, and in which the principle of adjustment is the universal condition of progress. This cause is the source of human intelligence and the origin of a world in which there is everywhere that which answers to intelligence, and, when apprehended, constitutes Thought. Intelligences, countless in number, have been called into being—self-knowing agents, in every conscious act differenced from their cause. How may we most justly represent in the light of experience this beginning? How express the relation of the universe to a First Cause, almighty, self-knowing, intelligent, not passing into—not becoming—the effect, but abiding co-existent with it? How may we think such a cause in relation to the effect? Not by a pantheistic theory of identity, not by the physicist's conception of continuity; not as noumenon and phenomenon: it is Creation.

If, then, creation be competent to thought, and possible in fact; if the regulative principles of experience are so congruous with the conception as to bring it within the probable; if the religious conviction is thus found to be in accord with experiential truth, we may take a step in advance and place the doctrine of creation over against the hypothesis of evolution.

The term creation will cover theories which, within the knowable, differ from evolution in no important respect. With such theories we have, for the present, nothing to do. Creation, as contrasted with evolution, implies not only a beginning of the universe in its matter, force, and law, but such a conception of its constitution and history as sees everywhere traces of intelligence, everywhere the embodiment of thought and purpose; and which, recognizing the vastness of the problem and the limitation of thought, admits the impossibility of interpreting the whole as a continuous process, whether physical or spiritual, and accepts the intervention of divine power as the only rational solution. The conditions of that intervention transcend human knowledge; they lie hidden in the purpose of God.

The question of origins within the cosmos may be approached from opposite points of view. The evolutionist begins with the law of the physical order on the side most remote from the acts of intelligence, and depends for his solution entirely on dynamic principles. The creationist begins with the exercise of intelligence —the side most remote from the physical order, and proceeds from that in nature which reveals the operation of mind ; he seeks a key to the problem in thought. Wherever he sees existences differenced as a new kind he finds a special creation : that which was not and now is, is as a new manifestation of divine intelligence and power. It matters nothing at what moment in time this kind may have come to be ; it matters not what was antecedent to it, or at what point of contact it touched the forms of being already existent, or how close its kinship to them : what the creationist sees is a new manifestation of the all-comprehending mind ; in so far as the conception is separate or special, he sees in it a special creation.

But the evolutionist will urge that the question for science is the mode of the divine operation on the side of the phenomenal. There has been a visible embodiment ; show us, he may say, what was before and after, and its relation to what has preceded, that we may discover the outward and sensible effect. When, for example, a dog first came into existence, picture to us the process. The creationist replies that he cannot. There are no materials to enable him to do so. The scanty records of the past do not warrant any definite representation of the fact. He cannot trace the history of any living thing back to the moment when it emerged within the visible in its primal form. But the evolutionist is in no better case ; he is equally at fault. He has not been able to show in any satisfactory manner the powers of nature at work in originating any given species. How the primordial

T

form has been modified into clearly differenced
structures he has failed to show. His one continuous
process is not more comprehensible or more congruous
with well established truths than special creations.
Over against his one process, continuous, uniform, we
place the endless variety of nature. The evolutionist
professes to begin with uniformity and end with
variety; the creationist sees variety everywhere—at
the beginning as well as at the end of the cosmic
record. The evolutionist postulates an unknown uniformity that he may evolve known variety: the
creationist ascribing to the great First Cause an
infinite wealth of wisdom—an inexhaustible fulness of
life, feels it to be more in consonance with his belief
to recognize, from the outset, in the works of God an
unbounded plenitude of power, conditioned in its
endlessly varied activity by wisdom, justice, goodness.
He can ill brook such limitation of the Absolute
Cause as is set up by the evolutionist, who will have
the Author of all things eternally occupied with the
task of working out an infinitely complicated problem
in mathematical physics.

The doctrine of creation, applied to account for the
origin of the multitudinous varieties of living things,
does not entail the necessity of supposing that differentiated species are to be held as having a clearly-defined
beginning separate from all antecedent forms of life—
a first pair rising into view without kinship with any
former living thing, a wholly separate root from which

a new genealogical tree springs. The creationist is not driven to assume that the various organic forms have been caused in this way. Nor does he come into conflict with what is called the uniformity of nature. He accepts as fully as the evolutionist that there is no lawlessness in the operations of the Inscrutable Power; but he refuses to determine the whole law of God's working by the "parts of His ways" that are discovered or discoverable by man—he refuses to attempt to measure the infinite in hand-breadths. He finds in Moses a precedent and example which commends itself to his reason as congruous with experience—a method of handling the question whose most marked characteristic is the recognition of variety of operation.

The successive changes formulated in evolution are divided into an incalculable series of modifications extending over immeasurable cycles of duration. The conception is so vast that it cannot be definitely represented in thought. It embraces the unimaginable variety of nature in the sameness of one method of mutation; but it stretches the process back to infinity in a measureless series of infinitesimal modifications. We gain nothing in extent or clearness of vision by adopting this standpoint. If we try to summarize the whole, we may note three zones of change, the first from the primal molecule to the condition in which it appears in protoplasm, the second from protoplasm to the cell, the third from the cell to the fully differentiated structure. Now it is noteworthy that these reaches of change, which, on the evolution doctrine, extend indefinitely, are being traversed every day before our eyes in brief spaces of time.   Inorganic matter is being changed in vast quantities into protoplasm, cells are being evolved in immense numbers at every moment, and growth from germ-cell to the perfected organic structure is accomplished in instances of slowest development in a few years.   From molecule to protoplasm ; from protoplasm to cell ; from cell to organism —is not this an epitome of the age-long process of evolution ?   What power is working out at every moment such marvellous results ?   It is the power of living things : the condition of the accomplishment of these inexplicable effects, is the possession of that mysterious attribute called Life.   Surely what is being done every day by living creatures, may have been done in the origin of these creatures by that Being who is the source of their life.

It is charged against the creationist that he degrades the idea of creation to the likeness of human invention—that God is represented as a skilled artificer constructing the universe after a plan.   But the charge may, with greater effect, be retorted on the evolutionist, and with this difference—that he likens the cause of all things to a workman with a very limited amount of skill.   He takes human progress as his pattern of the method of cosmic activity.   Limited in intelligence, in experience, and in power, man is ever advancing by tentative efforts.   He makes many failures before he achieves a complete success. His first rude steam-engine is exhibited that workmen may follow the slow steps of progress, and see how far mechanical skill has advanced by gradual improvement; how the idea has been by degrees more fully explicated and the difficulties of adjustment overcome. It is in the likeness of human progress reaching achievement through failure, that the evolutionist pourtrays the advance in nature from lower to higher organizations. The failures are buried, the successes survive.

To conceive the cosmic process as an endless weaving, out of a uniform, homogeneous first matter, the myriad forms of design traceable in the universe, is an unfounded representation of the course of things. We maintain, on the contrary, that however the pattern may be involved or evolved, however this particular form or that may grow out of or run into other forms, the design is along the whole course of time various, manifold. We are free to hold in the face of science that creation is special, as well as general—that there have been beginnings within the cosmos as well as continuous operation—that the continuity of one ceaseless and unvarying movement is possible to thought only by transcending the visible and finding it in the forth-going of energy from the unseen. Unification is attainable not by knowledge, but through faith. The unity is in God; the uniformity in His law; the continuity in His purpose. When man transcends the visible to account for an origin or change; when he refers it back to the Ultimate Cause and arrives at his explanation through belief in the source of all things; whatever be the name under which he presents that Power—however he may express in words his conception of the relation of that Power to the event, he affirms an origin which is, in so far as intelligible meaning is conveyed, in effect a "special creation."

CHAPTER XIX.

THE Evolution Hypothesis builds on the material cosmos. It looks outward to discover in physical nature a principle of change shaping thought and constituting the law of concrete being. It sees matter and mind cast in one mould and under the same law: it finds one principle dominant throughout experience: it interprets the phenomena of mind in terms of matter and motion and force: it regards reason, conscience, duty, responsibility, emotion, will—all mental and moral phenomena—as modes of experience determined by physical necessity: it extrudes the Creator of all things beyond the range of intelligence—outside the compass of knowledge. A God, of whom man may have even an " indefinite consciousness," there is none in the new philosophy, other than the incomprehensible immanent energy revealed in the universe. That Being comes into the view of reason only in manifestations forming the subject-matter of science, and which philosophy combines in a continuous process. The evolutionist teaches us to see that unbounded Power ceaselessly at work, labouring under the rigid yoke of a* dynamic principle. From an

" indefinite, incoherent homogeneity " it evolves into a " definite, coherent heterogeneity." Then when the evolution is complete, there remains for it but to undo what has been so laboriously done : it works universal dissolution, and reappears an " indefinite, incoherent homogeneity," or an inert compact mass. If it take the latter form, it is doomed to remain in eternal quiescence, solid, insensate—without life or motion for ever. This result the evolutionist cannot accept as probable. Will not the limitless energy energize? How can it be thought as entering into everlasting repose? The persistence of force forbids it. The conception of a resulting indefinite, incoherent homogeneity seems alone congruous with the hypothesis. When dissolution is complete, the evolving process must once more begin. How it will be shaped in the future condition of things, man, a product of the present evolution, cannot conjecture. But amid much that is doubtful this is clear, that if the principles on which the new philosophy is grounded be valid, they carry with them the certainty of either an eternal dynamic process, without meaning or purpose, through which the infinite First Cause passes from everlasting to everlasting continually; or perpetual quiescence in undisturbed inaction—an unbroken stillness of death, neither living God nor living creature existing thenceforth for ever.

It may seem to some that the naked statement of a theory so repugnant to reason is a sufficient confutation. It must, however, be kept in view that, proceeding from well established scientific truths, the hypothesis carries with it the apparent sanction of physical science. It is necessary, therefore, to bring it to the test of criticism. This I have endeavoured to do in the foregoing discussion. How far the argu- is valid and effective it is for the reader himself to judge. The sum of it is this :—

We have challenged the aim of the evolutionist, as transcending the limits of intelligence and inconsis- tent with the nature of the objects with which intelligence is conversant. His hypothesis is, we maintain, from the outset, illegitimate, as attempting an impossible task—the bringing of all concrete being and its activities within a single formula, and that formula derived from one department of experience. Examining the limits of physical science and natural law, we have seen that they do not furnish material for constructing a system of universal truth. We have discussed Mr. Spencer's doctrine of the unknow- able and the knowable, and have argued that it renders his philosophy nugatory, and reduces his hypothesis to a mere unprovable guess. We have seen that to bring the moral and the physical—the soul and the world—together under one regulative principle, and constitute them parts of one process, all concrete existences and all activities must. be embraced within the compass of dynamic law. We have disputed this narrowing of existence within dynamic bonds, and have claimed for intelligence a realm peculiar to itself, and in which the laws of mind, and not those of matter and motion, are the discoverable order. We have examined critically the fundamental axiom of evolution—the persistence of force; and have demonstrated that it is illusory as a basis on which to rear a system of philosophy. We have tested the formula which expresses the law of the cosmic movement, and have shown it to be wanting in precision and of no scientific value. We have inquired what are the postulates involved in the hypothesis, and have proved that from its initial step evolution is burdened with unwarranted assumptions. By this criticism of first principles, we have been led to the conclusion that evolutionism is not tenable as a philosophy; that if accepted it must lead to universal scepticism.

Having dealt with the fundamental principles underlying the hypothesis, we then proceeded to test its worth as an interpretation of known phenomena. Our first inquiry has been as to the origin of the forms and activities of inorganic matter, and we have shown that in this field evolution fails us in every vital question. We then examine its account of the transition from inorganic matter to life, and we find it incompetent to give any rational answer to the questions that arise in discussing the origin of living things. We have subjected to criticism the physiological unit, by whose polarity all forms of organisms are supposed to be explained; and we have seen that this invisible creation of the evolutionist, is as inexplicable as the visible forms themselves. Seeking for some account of the origin of sentient life, we have found that the hypothesis is wholly at fault when called upon to show how feeling could arise out of cosmic mutation. We have examined the evolutionist theory of the origin of the various kinds of living things, and have proved it to be defective and altogether inadequate as a solution of the problem. Tested as to its competence to explain the origin of consciousness and of intellection, or the growth of mind, or the moral nature of man, evolution is demonstrated to be a worthless—a barren hypothesis. The allegation that the conception of creation is unthinkable has been examined, and the doctrine of evolution placed in contrast with the belief in creation; and the latter has been shown to be most in accord with the regulative principles of experience, and most in harmony with the evidences of mind everywhere seen in nature and self-known in consciousness.

Over the entire range of this discussion the questions dealt with have been questions vital to any system of cosmic philosophy. In one or another point the conclusivenesss of the reasoning may be challenged; but the cumulative effect of the whole is, we think, irresistible.

The aim has been critical throughout. No attempt has been made to define the limits within which, in

groups of instances, evolution may be accepted as expressing a law of nature. How far, for example, the
nebular hypothesis is a true theory of the formation
of the heavenly bodies, and whether evolution furnishes an adequate statement of its law, can be determined only by those who have made the question a
special study; but it is intolerable that the experts
should lay down as an article of our scientific creed
any doctrine that is merely conjectural, or but a
fiction—however truthlike—created by the scientific
imagination. How far existing organisms are to be
taken as descended from a common stock, is also a
question to be settled by careful and candid examination of all available facts. That many variations now
established as specific differences have arisen in the
course of change, seems unquestionable; but that all
organic kinds have been so created by differentiation
of the same living matter, is by no means proved; and
it is indubitable that neither the dynamic principle of
Spencer, nor the "natural selection" of Darwin will
account for all that is to be explained in the simplest
and plainest instances.

Our conclusion is, that the Evolution Hypothesis is
incompetent to interpret the most obvious facts in
nature, and is wholly illegitimate and utterly indefen-
sible, as a philosophy embracing the fundamental
principles of all departments of knowledge. Man
cannot recognize in it the goal of his labours, or find
in it the rest of his spirit. It is out of harmony with

his best feelings and truest thoughts: it is in conflict with himself. He knows it to be more in accord with reason to lift up his eyes, and see around him traces of intelligent purpose, and delight himself in the communion of mind with mind. The new cosmic philosophy is an imposing edifice, constructed with great and painstaking labour; but it has neither foundation nor top-stone: it sets forth no discoverable origin; nor is it directed to any conceivable end. Claiming to be the crown of scientific knowledge, it is a poor result of the intellectual industry of the ages. The student of nature, eager to frame for himself some intelligible conception of the world in which he lives, will not accept it as a satisfactory response to his questioning. The more keenly it is criticized the more inadequate will it appear: its dominance is but a passing fashion of opinion. Men whose best thoughts wither at its touch will turn away and seek elsewhere a home for the spirit; they will look for a temple of truth established on a wider and surer basis;—they will choose as their abode " a city which hath foundations, whose builder and maker is God."

LIST OF SOME RECENT PUBLICATIONS

OF

JAMES GEMMELL,

GEORGE IV. BRIDGE,

EDINBURGH.

LONDON............HAMILTON, ADAMS, & CO. ; SIMPKIN, MARSHALL, & CO.
EDINBURGH........................OLIVER & BOYD ; J. MENZIES & CO.
GLASGOW......................J. MENZIES & CO. ; PORTEOUS BROTHERS.

Lectures and Sermons by Martyrs. Containing Sermons and Lectures by Richard Cameron, Alexander Peden, Donald Cargill, William Guthrie, Michael Bruce, Alexander Shields, John Livingstone, John Wellwood, John Welsh, John Guthrie. With Prefaces by JOHN HOWIE, of Lochgoin ; and Brief Biographical Notices of the Authors of the Sermons by the Rev. JAMES KERR, Glasgow, and the following Illustrations :—Grassmarket of Edinburgh, Canongate Tolbooth, Martyrs' Monument, Greyfriars ; House where Cameron was born ; Netherbow Port, Edinburgh ; Greyfriars Churchyard ; Monument at Airsmoss ; and Bothwell Bridge. Demy 8vo, *cl.* (674 pp.) 7/6.

"The volume contains a mine of doctrinal and experimental wealth. It cannot be read without both pleasure and profit. It is worth tons of what passes now-a-days for sermonic literature."—CHRISTIAN AGE.

"No one that values the contendings of Scotland's martyrs should be without a copy."—THE COVENANTER.

"This volume is fitted to prove a genuine memorial of the humble yet truly illustrious band who jeoparded their lives for Christ's crown and the nation's weal. The book is very creditably got up."—R. P. WITNESS.

History of the Westminster Assembly of Divines. By Prof. WM. M. HETHERINGTON, D.D., LL.D., *Free Church College, Glasgow.* Edited by ROBERT WILLIAMSON, D.D., *Ascog.* With Notes and Fac-similes of Title-pages of the Original Editions of the Confession of Faith, the Catechisms, Larger and Shorter, and the Directory of Church Government and Ordination of Ministers. *Fourth edition,* cr. 8vo, *cl.* (499 pp.) 6/.

"The value of the present edition has been greatly enhanced by the care and judgment with which Dr. Williamson of Ascog has readjusted its contents, and added what brings its information into accord with the light of the latest discoveries."—F. C. RECORD.

"An admirable edition of a valuable work at a reasonable price."—THE R. P. WITNESS.

Four Prize Essays on the Sabbath, by Rev.

Mr. HAMILTON, Belfast; Rev. W. C. WOOD, Boston, U.S.; Rev. Dr. ORR, Hawick; and A MEMBER OF THE COLLEGE OF JUSTICE, Scotland. *Thick 8vo, cl., price* 7/6.

To the Authors of these Essays were awarded Prizes of £100, £50, £30, and £20, by the Sabbath Alliance of Scotland. The Adjudicators were: Professor Mitchell, D.D., St. Andrews; Rev. A. Thomson, D.D., Edinburgh; Principal Rainy, D.D., Edinburgh; Rev. J. Marshall Lang, D.D., Glasgow; Rev. J. C. Burns, D.D., Kirkliston.

"Of the first essay we have already spoken in commendation. . . . . The other essays are well worthy of a thoughtful perusal."—*The Nonconformist Independent.*

"These essays are all of them well written, ... they are a storehouse of facts and arguments to all who may have to defend the Rest Day from the attacks sure to be renewed from time to time."—*Dundee Advertiser.*

"In the four treatises now on our table, we can say that each essayist has thought for himself, and in their combined labours they have done more than reproduce the arguments and defences of former authors. . . . . Constitute an encyclopædia of facts and arguments which criticism will only prove to be in harmony with the Bible and science."—*Presbyterian Messenger.*

Our Rest Day: its Origin, History and

Claims, with Special Reference to Present Day Needs. By the Rev. THOMAS HAMILTON, A.M., *Belfast.* Being the Essay to which was awarded a Prize of One Hundred Pounds, offered by the Sabbath Alliance of Scotland. Crown 8vo, *cloth,* 3/.

"His style is lucid, terse, and vigorous. . . . . We most cordially recommend all our readers to procure this able and masterly treatise."—WITNESS.

"It deserves a foremost place amongst the somewhat extensive literature of the Sabbath. . . . . It is clear, concise, and conclusive."—PRIMITIVE METHODIST WORLD.

"A storehouse of fact and argument."—ECCLESIASTICAL GAZETTE.

"Written in an excellent spirit, abounds in learning, is marked by never-failing candour, and contains much practical council, as well as valuable information."—THE CHRISTIAN ADVOCATE.

"The Work is ably done."—LIFE AND WORK.

"Knowing how many valuable manuscripts were submitted to the adjudicators, we were prepared to expect something unusually good, and we have not been disappointed."—FREE CHURCH MONTHLY.

"Other works may have been good, but none could have been better. It is as interesting as it is instructive, and we give it our hearty praise."—SWORD AND TROWEL.

"We consider the book the best and most useful on the subject in the English language."—PRESBYTERIAN MESSENGER.

The Homes, Haunts, and Battlefields of the

Covenanters. By A. B. TODD, Author of "The Circling Year," "Poems, Lectures, and Miscellanies." Cr. 8vo, *cloth,* 3/6. *Second Series in Preparation.*

"The volume is a very interesting one."—*Scotsman.*

"The work of a thorough man of genius. . . . . He has a full knowledge of his subject and a love for it; and he has a fervid poetical temperament, a sympathy with all that is good and true. . . . The topographical sketches with which the book abounds are beautifully drawn."—*Dumfries and Galloway Standard and Advertiser.*

The Scottish Church and its Surroundings

in Early Times. By ROBERT PATON, *Minister of Kirkinner*. Cr. 8vo, *cl.* 2/6.

"His sketches are vigorous and animated ...... writes very well."—THE SCOTSMAN.

"A clear narrative which sustains the reader's attention all through."—NORTH BRITISH DAILY MAIL.

"Fascinating work from beginning to end."—IRISH BAPTIST MAGAZINE.

"We will find here a great deal of information, the result of much research and careful study, presented in a very attractive form and style."—THE CHRISTIAN AGE.

"The style is lucid and the contents interesting."—THE SCOTTISH CONGREGATIONALIST.

Protestant Missions (Outline of the History

of), from the Reformation to the Present Time. By Dr. GUSTAV WARNECK, *Pastor at Rothenschirmbach*. Translated from the *Second edition*, by Dr. THOMAS SMITH, *Professor of Evangelistic Theology, New College, Edinburgh*. Cr. 8vo, (232 pp.) 3/6.

"Dr. Smith's translation of Dr. Warneck's able and valuable treatise will prove of great value, and cannot fail to stimulate and encourage."—ABERDEEN JOURNAL.

"It presents a careful summary of Protestant Mission Work, from the Reformation to the close of the eighteenth century, and deals more fully, though in a sort of statistical and commercial fashion, with the operations that have been carried on in the mission field during the present century."—SCOTSMAN.

"A deeply interesting work."—CHRISTIAN AGE.

"The work is not only a valuable one for the private reader, it is fitted to be an excellent class-book, and in this respect meets a decided want."—THE BAPTIST.

"An encyclopædia of Missions."—LITERARY WORLD.

The Story of Daniel : His Life and Times.

By P. H. HUNTER, *Minister of Yester*. Crown 8vo, 357 pp., *second edition*, 5/.

"The difficult task has been skilfully done. It has resulted in a graphic and vivid historical biography as engrossing as a volume of Macaulay ; and proving that, whatever else there may be, there is at all events a warm interest in the ancient documents. If books like the 'Story of Daniel' were more common, modern faith in the flesh and blood reality of the Old Testament saints would not be so exclusively an intellectual effort as it now often is."—SCOTSMAN.

"Mr. Hunter has done his work very thoroughly, laying under contribution a throng of writers, ancient and modern, and gathering into a focus the scattered rays of light which they send upon one of the dimmest periods of history."—GLASGOW HERALD.

"He has grasped the main features in the character and career of the prophet with penetrating insight, and he presents them to the reader with graphic force and felicity."—CHRISTIAN LEADER.

U

History of the Canon of the Holy Scriptures

in the Christian Church. By EDWARD REUSS, *Professor in the University of Strasburg.* Translated from the Second French Edition, by Rev. DAVID HUNTER, B.D., Partick. In 1 thick vol. (416 pages), 9/.

"A book I highly value."—Prof. A. B. BRUCE, D.D., *Free Church College, Glasgow.*

"A most valuable and useful book."—Prof. WM. MILLIGAN, D.D., *University, Aberdeen.*

"I have found it very stimulating."—Prof. A. H. CHARTERIS, D.D., *Edinburgh University.*

"A most scholarly and comprehensive work. The most complete on the subject we know of."—CHRISTIAN AGE.

"Wide knowledge of Church history, impartial judgment of the evidence of facts, keen historical insight, are certainly not lacking in the History of the Canon.....Its accuracy is guaranteed by the fact that all the proofs have been revised by the author himself."—LITERARY WORLD.

The Atonement : In its Relation to the

Covenant, the Priesthood, and the Intercession of our Lord. By HUGH MARTIN, D.D. *Fourth British edition,* demy 8vo, *cl.* (324 pp.) 7/6.

"Written with remarkable vigour and earnestness."—BRITISH QUARTERLY REVIEW.

"In these days of lax and shallow theology, it is refreshing to come upon a volume like Dr. Martin's. The subject is one of surpassing importance, and upon the treatment of it the author brings to bear extraordinary powers of reasoning, warmed and animated by a soul that has felt the blessedness of an interest in the blood of the atonement......The whole volume is one of no ordinary kind."—ROCK.

"Something like theology. We wish our young divines would feed on such meat as this."—SPURGEON.

The Prophet Jonah : His Character and

Mission to Nineveh. By HUGH MARTIN, D.D. *Second edition,* demy 8vo, (369 pp.) 7/6.

"A good specimen of the author's power of exposition, and is certain to be useful to those who intend to devote special study to the book whose contents are discussed."—GLASGOW NEWS.

"The book is no less rich and varied in matter and earnest in spirit than it is vigorous in style."—R. P. WITNESS.

"Dr. Martin is well-known as an able author. His Jonah is a work of considerable merit,......and is written in an attractive and interesting style."—EDINBURGH COURANT.

Chalmers' (Thomas, D.D.) Select Sermons,

with Tribute to his Memory, by Rev. Dr. LORIMER. Cr. 8vo, *cl.* 1s. 6d.

"Judiciously selected, and will serve, as far as printed words can serve, to convey to a new generation an idea of the power and eloquence which entranced their fathers. It is fitting, too, that Dr. Lorimer's funeral sermon should escape any hostile criticism. From an evangelical and Free Church point of view it is a noble *eloge.*"—SCOTSMAN.

Candid Reasons for Renouncing the Principles of Antipædobaptism. By PETER EDWARDS. Cr. 8vo, cl. 2s. 6d.

RECOMMENDATORY NOTE.

"The following treatise, written by a man who was for ten years a Baptist minister, we very earnestly recommend to the careful study of those who desire to make themselves acquainted with the argument in favour of infant Baptism. The book contains this argument summarily stated, and most logically defended. There is probably no treatise in the English language on a theological subject in which the reasoning is closer. We consider that its careful perusal is fitted, by the blessing of God, to lead Christian parents to understand clearly the ground on which the ordinary doctrine of the Church is maintained, and to value, more than many do, the privilege of obtaining the Church membership of their children."

To the above Note are subscribed the signatures of Eminent Clergymen of various denominations, including the following:—

Principals Rainy and Douglas; Professors M'Gregor, Smith, and Smeaton; Drs H. Bonar, Kennedy, Wilson, and Begg.

Principal Lindsay Alexander, Dr James M'Gregor, *St. Cuthbert's, Edin.*; and Dr Robert Jamieson, *St Paul's, Glasgow.*

"Furnishes sufficient materials wherewith to meet and demolish the arguments of the opponents of infant-baptism."—*The Reformed Presbyterian Witness.*

Willison (late Rev. John, *Dundee*). An Example of plain Catechising upon the Shorter Catechism. New Edition, cr. 8vo, cl. 3s. 6d.

———— The Afflicted Man's Companion; or, A Directory for Families and Persons afflicted with Sickness, or any other Distress. 12mo, cl. 1s. 6d.

———— Sacramental Meditations and Advices for the Use of Communicants, fcap. 8vo, cl. 2s.

These valuable books have been long out of print, difficult to get separately, and have now been reprinted at the request of many.

Begg (James, D.D.), Memoirs of, Minister of Newington Free Church, Edinburgh, by THOMAS SMITH, D.D., *Professor of Evangelistic Theology, New College, Edinburgh*. With Portrait and views of Dr. Begg's Birthplace, etc. 2 vols. 8vo, 15/.

"Will be read with keen interest and enjoyment."—DAILY REVIEW.

"The book........will be eagerly read by the admirers of this polemical worthy."—THE BOOKSELLER.

"The volume is a most interesting production, and one which is certain to command a wide circulation."—GLASGOW NEWS.

"To say that this volume is full of interest is little in praise of what bids fair to be a most elaborate and important work."—PROTESTANT TIMES.

"The charm of the volume will be found in the racy sketches Dr Begg gives of the old ministers whom he knew, whose very names are now passing out of remembrance."—AYR ADVERTISER.

"The volume is exceedingly entertaining, ... it cannot fail to afford much gratification to all classes of readers."—IRISH CHRISTIAN ADVOCATE.

"This volume will be popular with Scotch people everywhere."—*Liverpool Mercury.*

The True Psalmody; or, the Bible Psalms
the Church's only Manual of Praise. With Prefaces by the Rev. Drs. COOKE, EDGAR, and HOUSTON; and Recommendations from Eminent Divines. Cr. 8vo, cl. (220 pp.) price 2/.

"'The True Psalmody' is a book that is calculated, we firmly believe, to convince any mind that is open to conviction, that the Psalms alone are to be employed in the service of God, and that the use of hymns is wholly unwarrantable."—REFORMED PRESBYTERIAN MAGAZINE.

"All that can be said in favour of using the Book of Psalms, and none other, in the worship of the sanctuary."—EDINBURGH COURANT.

"All who believe that nothing should be sung in the worship of God but Psalms will find in it a repertory of argument on the subject, ably and popularly put."—THE WITNESS.

"Those who deny the right or the propriety of Christian people to sing uninspired compositions in the services of the Church .... will find the arguments in favour of their opinion set forth in this volume with all the lucidity and force that can be given them."—NORTH BRITISH DAILY MAIL.

The Kittlegairy Vacancy; or, a New Way
of Getting Rid of Old Ministers. By JOHN PLENDER-LEITH. 143 pp., crown 8vo, sewed, price 1/6.

"This is an excellent satire on the democratic spirit which manifests itself too often in the heartless treatment of ancient ministers, who deserve well of their Church and people."—PRESBYTERIAN CHURCHMAN.

"A very clever story of the difficulties which beset certain ministers—especially of the old school—in the smaller towns of Scotland, and perhaps in England also........Many of the characters are well drawn, and the remarks of the ministers' clerical colleagues on their conduct and the harm they were doing to the 'cause' are clearly put."—THE BOOKSELLER.

"A story of ecclesiastical troubles, trenchantly exposing the scandals often associated with the selection and treatment of ministers......It will be read with interest."—LITERARY WORLD.

"One of the most racy contributions to ecclesiastical satire that has appeared for many years."—COURANT.

Pulpit Table-Talk; containing Remarks and
Anecdotes on Preachers and Preaching, by DEAN RAMSAY, Edinburgh. 18mo, sewed, (162 pp.) 1/6.

Two lectures of a popular and discursive character on styles of preaching, modes of preparing sermons, preachers of different eras, quaint texts, preachers of the Reformation and Puritan periods; French, Nonconformist, and American preachers, etc.

Our Children for Christ: a Plea for Infant
Church Membership, with a full Discussion on the Mode of Baptism. By the Rev. SAMUEL MACNAUGHTON, M.A., Preston. Cloth, price 9d. post free; or, for circulation, 12 copies post free for 6/.

"These arguments will no doubt be regarded as convincing by the numerous sections of the Christian Church who accept the doctrine."—SCOTSMAN.

"Free from all controversial bitterness."—DAILY REVIEW.

"The book is one of marked ability. In our opinion irresistible."—CHRISTIAN NEWS.

The Establishment Principle Defended; A

Reply to the Statement by the Committee of the United
Presbyterian Church on Disestablishment and Disen-
dowment. By the Rev. WILLIAM BALFOUR, *Holyrood*;
with Preface by Dr. BEGG. Crown 8vo, *sewed, 2nd edition, 1/6.*

"The book is very powerfully written; the discussion of the whole question in its Scriptural aspects is searching, logical, and exhaustive......Every
clergyman should procure the small volume."—BELFAST WEEKLY NEWS.

"One of the most fascinating works of the kind we ever read."—HUNTLY
EXPRESS.

"We most cordially recommend this very able work to all interested in the
subject."—WESTERN STANDARD.

"It has been perused by us with mingled admiration and satisfaction, and
most cordially do we thank the talented author for such a timely and powerful defence of the principle of Establishments, or of national obligation to
honour Christ by serving His Church."—Dr. MANSON, *Perth.*

—— × ——

Church Establishments; or, the Bible and

the Nation, with a Special Reference to the Church of
Scotland. By the Rev. DANIEL FRASER, A.M., *Helms-
dale.* Crown 8vo, *cl.* 3s. 6d.

"We recommend Mr. Fraser's book to the friends, but especially to the opponents, of National religion. In all cases he assigns a reason for what he
states, an example which we wish the Liberationists to follow." — PERTH-
SHIRE COURIER.

"An earnest and splendid plea for a National recognition of the Protestant
religion, and an exposure of the evils and follies of Voluntaryism......The
case of the Established Church of Scotland is admirably dealt with, and a
most fervid and powerful appeal is made in her behalf. The whole work
is carefully and thoughtfully composed."—THE PROTESTANT TIMES.

—— × ——

Statement of the Difference between the

Profession of the REFORMED CHURCH OF SCOT-
LAND, as adopted by the Seceders, and the Profession
contained in the New Testimony and other Acts lately
adopted by the GENERAL ASSOCIATE SYNOD: par-
ticularly on the POWER OF THE CIVIL MAGIS-
TRATE respecting Religion, National Reformation, etc.
By the late THOMAS M'CRIE, D.D., *Author of " Life of
John Knox,"* etc. With Preface by Prof. Smeaton,
D.D., Edinburgh. Crown 8vo, *cloth*, 499 pp., price 5/.

"It is a masterly defence of the principle of Establishments as a Scripture
truth; and the most complete vindication ever given to the whole of the
position occupied by the Reformed Church of Scotland on the whole subject
of National Religion, and of the magistrate's legitimate power in promoting
it."—Prof. SMEATON.

"A masterly and exhaustive treatise."—WATCHWORD.

"We heartily and earnestly recommend all who are in doubt and difficulty,
or who may wish instruction on the Voluntary controversy, and the principles that underlie it, to this reprint of Dr. M'Crie's Statement."—EDINBURGH
COURANT.

"Whoever wishes to study the important subject here treated of will do
well to have the little book beside him."—SCOTSMAN.

Principal Acts of Assembly (Handbook and

Index to the) of the Free Church of Scotland, 1843-1885.
By Rev. THOMAS COCHRANE, *Edinburgh. Second edition,*
brought up to date (1885). Cr. 8vo, 3/6.

"Students of ecclesiastical history belonging to other branches of the
Christian Church will not fail to bestow a benediction. ...... Masterpiece of
intelligent condensation. ...... Will stand years of wear and tear."—CHRIS-
TIAN LEADER.

"Admirable book, ... every kirk-session ought to possess."—DAILY
REVIEW.

"Most useful book."—SCOTSMAN.

"An ably constructed compend."—B. AND F. EVANGELICAL REVIEW.

Digest and Report of, and Handbook and

Index to, the Principal Cases Decided in the General.
Assembly of the Free Church, 1843-1886. By Rev.
THOMAS COCHRANE, *Edinburgh*, Cr. 8vo, 3/6.

"Evidently the result of great labour and infinite pains. .... indeed, an
indispensable hand-book . . . can heartily commend the clearness of method
and statement that marks the digest. An appendix containing the Acts of
Assembly which have a bearing on the cases reported completes a work which
must be of great use to those for whom it is intended."—SCOTSMAN.

Digest of Rules and Procedure in the In-

ferior Courts of the Free Church of Scotland. With an
Appendix, embracing a Ministerial Manual, and also containing Forms and Documents. By the late Rev. ROBERT
FORBES, M.A., *Minister of Woodside, and Joint-Clerk of
the Free Church Presbytery of Aberdeen. Fourth edition,*
revised and brought up to date (end of 1885). Cr. 8vo,
cl., price 3/6.

"The merits of Mr. Forbes' Manual have long been recognised, and its
indispensability as a Free Church ministers' and office-bearers' guide and
companion has been further increased by the conscientious and intelligent
labour put upon it by the Rev. Mr Cochrane."—DAILY REVIEW.

"It has long been acknowledged as an excellent and trustworthy guide to
the members of these courts, and as affording the best instruction for those
who wish information about their procedure."—SCOTSMAN.

"A capital manual for those who need some guidance in the subject which
it treats."—NORTH BRITISH DAILY MAIL.

"A clear and careful manual .... The Appendix includes a large amount
of varied and practically useful matter."—CHRISTIAN LEADER.

The Modern Scottish Pulpit : Sermons by

Eminent Presbyterian Ministers of various Denominations. 2 vols., demy 8vo, (577 pp.), 3/6 each, sold separately.

"There are weighty doctrinal discourses, scholarly expositions of Scripture,
ably maintained theses, pointed practical exhortations, and fervent evangelical appeals. The styles vary from the severely classic to the faultlessly
rhetoric. Variety and unity are apparent throughout. They are designed to
be useful rather than ornamental. They possess the best characteristics of
what has been known as distinctively Scottish preaching."—DAILY REVIEW.

"Here are discourses 'sound as a bell.'"—C. H. SPURGEON.

"The subjects treated are very varied, and the modes of treatment equally
so; but one and all of them, we believe, give forth a certain sound on the
great verities of the gospel."—O. S. MAGAZINE.

Perth — Ecclesiastical Annals of Perth to

the Period of the Reformation. By ROBERT SCOTT
FITTIS, 8vo, cl. 6s.

" One of the best local histories we have seen . . . . The scheme of arrangement is so simple and orderly that an index might have been dispensed with,
but Mr Fittis is too painstaking and thorough a workman to omit what is
generally regarded as an indispensable adjunct to a large historical book, and
his index is a satisfactory bit of workmanship."—DAILY REVIEW.
" Most attractive to those who have any leaning towards local antiquarian
studies. . . . . We can sincerely commend this book to all who desire to
deepen their acquaintance with the condition of Scotland prior to and at the
Reformation, and can only wish that every reader may derive the same pleasure from its perusal as it brought to us."—ORIGINAL SECESSION MAGAZINE.

Communion and other Sermons. By the Rev.

WILLIAM FORBES, A.M., late Minister of Tarbat, Easter
Ross. Partly Edited by the late Rev. JOHN KENNEDY,
D.D., Dingwall. Completed, with Life by Rev. M.
Macgregor, M.A., Ferintosh. Cr. 8vo, 3/6.

" We have here sermons of the good old evangelical type, rich in Scriptural
truth and unction."—Presbyterian Churchman.
" Sermons, all on important topics, all thoroughly evangelical, and they
all afford evidence of ability and scholarship of no mean order........This
volume will be prized by all who love and value pure Gospel truth."—Reformed Presbyterian Witness.
" The sermons speak with no uncertain sound of the great truths of
righteousness, temperance, and the judgment to come, and their voice is
always powerful, and often most eloquent."—Northern Chronicle.
" The sermons were partly edited by the Rev. Dr. Kennedy of Dingwall...
.... fifteen in number, are earnest and evangelical, and give evidence of
careful preparation."—Northern Ensign.
" They are evidently the production of a man of deep earnest piety, and
of considerable culture and accomplishments."—Original Secession Magazine.
" We commend the volume as furnishing a very admirable example of
preaching which was common in the days of the fathers in Ross-shire."—
FREE CHURCH MONTHLY.
" They form an excellent record of faithful work done."—JOHN O' GROAT
JOURNAL.

A Method of Prayer, with Scripture Ex-

pressions proper to be used under each Head. By the
Rev. MATTHEW HENRY. 16mo, cloth, (288 pp.) 1/.

OUR MOTHER : A LIFE PICTURE ; being a Life of Mrs.

Krummacher, wife of Author of " The Suffering Saviour,"
etc. Translated from the German by a well-known
Author. Fcap. 8vo, cloth, price 1/6.

" Possesses all the pathos, sweet simplicity, and lofty teaching which
characterises the best German story writers."—IRISH BAPTIST MAGAZINE.
" Will be perused with profit and delight."—ALLOA CIRCULAR.
" Of more than ordinary interest."—EVENING TELEGRAPH.
" The book is a very attractive one."—CHRISTIAN BANNER.
" An unusually attractive biography."—CHRISTIAN TREASURY.

Demy 16mo, in Ornamental Cloth Covers.

BIOGRAPHIES OF SCOTTISH REFORMERS, MARTYRS, PREACHERS, etc.

BY JEAN L. WATSON.

LIFE OF RICHARD CAMERON. 70 pp., with View of Monument at Airsmoss, and of Falkland Palace, price 6d.

"A brief and appreciative biography of Cameron."—*Edinburgh Courant.*

LIFE OF HUGH MILLER. 132 pp., with View of Bass Rock on Cover, price 9d.

"A well-condensed biographical notice."—*Daily Review.*

LIFE OF RALPH ERSKINE. 99 pp., with Portrait, price 9d.

"This lady wields the pen of a ready writer."—*Northern Ensign.*

LIFE OF EBENEZER ERSKINE. 104 pp., with Portrait, price 9d.

"Few religious biographies are more instructive."—*Leith Burghs Pilot.*

LIFE OF THOMAS GUTHRIE, D.D. 106 pp., with Portrait and Illustration on Cover, price 9d.

"A short, well-written sketch of the great preacher's life and work."—*Rock.*

LIFE OF DONALD CARGILL. 60 pp., with Views of Glasgow Cathedral, and Martyrs' Monument, Edinburgh, price 6d.

"The reader will lay down exclaiming, 'Grand old Donald Cargill!'"—*Kirkcudbright Advertiser.*

LIFE OF ROBERT MURRAY M'CHEYNE. With View of his Church in Dundee, price 9d.

"Could not have a briefer or better."—*Aberdeen Journal.*

LIFE OF THOMAS CHALMERS, D.D., LL.D. With View of Kilmany Church, 134 pp., price 9d.

"Essentially just and true, as it certainly is attractive."—*Daily Review.*

LIFE OF NORMAN MACLEOD, D.D. With Portrait and View of Barony Church on cover, price 9d.

"Well written . . . . the leading events pass rapidly before us."—*Reformed Presbyterian Witness.*

BY ROBERT MACGREGOR.

LIFE OF JOHN MACDONALD, D.D., "The Apostle of the North." 96 pp., price 9d.

"In the ninety-six pages of this book there is not one without interest."— HUNTLY EXPRESS.

THE JESUITS: a Sketch of the Origin and Progress of the Society of Jesus. 110 pp., price 9d.

"Contains pages of thrilling interest."—DUMFRIES ADVERTISER.

MEMORIALS OF THE BASS ROCK. 136 pp., price 9d.

"A very interesting account of the Rock."—KELSO CHRONICLE.

BY JOHN KER, D.D.

THE ERSKINES: EBENEZER AND RALPH. With Engraving of Gairney Bridge, price 6d.

"These biographies are well written. The leading events in each life pass rapidly before us, and the story is so well told that the reader will find it difficult to lay down any of the 'Lives' until he has finished it."—REFORMED PRESBYTERIAN WITNESS.

BY ANNIE C. MACLEOD.

GIROLAMO SAVONAROLA (LIFE AND TIMES OF). Demy 16mo, cloth, 132 pp., with Portrait, price 9d.

"The author is a daughter of the late Dr. Norman Macleod. She has done her work extremely well."—SCOTSMAN.

"To those who have little time to read, desire to read profitably, and for the young who must necessarily begin their studies of great subjects with short books. this life of Savonarola can be most confidently recommended as a slight sketch of Florence in the fifteenth and sixteenth centuries, and also of that time."—EDINBURGH COURANT.

BY JEAN L. WATSON.

THE WATER-CRESS BOY. Demy 16mo, cloth, with Frontispiece, price 6d.

"This is a fresh pretty little story."—COURANT.

WILLIE'S BRINGING UP. Demy 16mo, limp cloth, with Frontispiece, price 6d.

"Forms a wonderfully true picture of Scottish peasant life. Must have been drawn from nature."—FIFESHIRE ADVERTISER.

"The story is well told."—CHRISTIAN TREASURY.

"This is a nice story very becomingly told in simple language. ...... It is true to the life, as few readers will fail to see."—HAWICK EXPRESS.

U 2

BY JOHN KER, D.D., AND J. L. WATSON.

THE ERSKINES: EBENEZER AND RALPH. Cr. 8vo, cloth, with Two Portraits and Engraving of Gairney Bridge. Price 1/6.

"This is the joint production of a distinguished U.P. divine and a well-known Free Church authoress. They have succeeded between them in making a very readable book. ...... It is written in an agreeable and attractive style, which is certain to ensure its popularity."—EDINBURGH COURANT.

BY JEAN L. WATSON.

Life of Dr Andrew Thomson, Minister of St. George's Church, *Edinburgh. Price* 1/6
" Her biography will be prized by many admirers of its subject."—SCOTSMAN.
"Has done her work with conscientious care."—ABERDEEN FREE PRESS.
"Interesting, ... will do much to supply a long-felt want."—DAILY REVIEW.

PRINCIPAL CANDLISH.

LIFE OF ROBERT SMITH CANDLISH, D.D., Minister of Free St. George's Church, and Principal of the New College, Edinburgh. By JEAN L. WATSON. Crown 8vo, cloth, with *portrait*, price 2/.

"In selection, arrangement, and graphic description, the little volume is all that could be desired."—EDINBURGH COURANT.

THOMAS BOSTON (LIFE AND TIMES OF), Pastor of Ettrick. Crown 8vo, cloth, price 2/.

"That the autobiography is so little known is much to be regretted: it is a picture of one of the most momentous periods in the religious history of Scotland; it is, moreover, the mirror of a life spent in high communion with God, and gifted with a vision penetrating far into the kingdom. Miss Watson's 'Life' is based upon this larger work, and abundant extracts are given from it. She has selected her materials wisely, and the result is a book which cannot fail to interest."—BRITISH MESSENGER.

Disruption Memories : being the Personal Narrative of a Lay Voluntary. With Remarks on the Present Condition of the Church. Fcap. 8vo, 1/.
"Of the many books about the Disruption this is one of the most readable."—COURANT.

The School of Christ: a Song to Christ the Lord. A Metrical Rhyme. Crown 8vo, *post free* 1/.
" The spirit breathed is one saturated with Scripture, and one of glowing admiration of Christ, His truth and ways."—O. S. MAGAZINE.
" The spirit breathed is admirable."—REF. PRESB. MAGAZINE.

Just published, cr. 8vo, cloth, (341 pp.), price 5/.

REAL RELIGION AND REAL LIFE.

BY THE

Rev. SAMUEL MACNAUGHTON, M.A.,

AUTHOR OF "OUR CHILDREN FOR CHRIST," "DOCTRINE AND DOUBT," ETC. ETC.

"'Real Religion and Real Life' is clear in style, practical in aim, direct in appeal, and the discourses are models of what popular preaching should be. They deserve the study of all who desire to cultivate a mode of speaking which shall interest and impress alike the educated and the uneducated."—*The Literary World.*

"A volume of rare excellence."—*Christian Commonwealth.*

"A strong, healthy book, admirably suited to present times. Many striking thoughts will be found in its pages. . . . . The author is widely known by his other works."—*The Christian.*

"The conspicuous typographical clearness of this collection of discourses is a fair measure of its inner beauty. . . . 'The Reality of God,' 'The Reality of Sin,' 'Christian Toleration,' are ensamples of the deep things discussed by this chastened preacher to men. . . . . For those content with solid thoughtfulness nothing could be better than the book before us."—*The Methodist Recorder.*

"A clear, vigorous, and able exposition of the duty of Christian men to carry their Christianity into daily life. In every sense of the word it is a well-timed book. . . . . Take it as a whole it is one of the most readable and freshest religious books that has appeared for a long time, and it well deserves and will receive general acceptance."—*Dundee Advertiser.*

"By the publication of this volume the author will add to his reputation as a learned theologian and able preacher. . . . . His pages are eminently readable, pervaded as they are all through with earnest thought, often new, and always unhackneyed and lucidly expressed."—*Dumfries Standard.*

"Some of these discourses are of high excellence."—*Glasgow Herald.*

"Marked by much intelligence and earnestness."—*Scottish Leader.*

"These sermons are fitted to be widely useful, and they cannot be too extensively circulated."—*Liverpool Mercury.*

"Mr. MacNaughton's sermons are quite worthy of a place beside some of the best of his land. They are fresh in treatment, original in idea, tolerant in spirit, and quite in touch with the most recent thought. They breathe the spirit of devout thoughtfulness. No one can read them without having that true delight of a thoughtful reader,—viz., the mind stirred and led unconsciously into new tracts of meditation. . . . . The book as a whole will prove suggestive to many preachers, and helpful to many believers."—*Christian Advocate.*

Treatise on the Lord's Supper; Its Nature,

Uses, Ends, and Perpetual Obligation.   Exposure of
Romanist and Ritualistic Perversions.   With Practical
Directions for its Observance.   By PROF. THOMAS
HOUSTON, D.D., R. P. Church of Ireland, *Knockbracken*,
Belfast.   Crown 8vo, (350 pp.), *price* 5/.

"This work, undertaken by Dr. Houston partly at the suggestion of friends
who knew his competency, is really a treatise on the Lord's Supper. The
author is well acquainted with the history and literature of the subject, and
has succeeded in his aim, which was to present a comprehensive exhibition
of the doctrine of the Lord's Supper as it appeared in its primitive institu-
tion and apostolic practice, and as it is held forth in the symbolic books of
the purest Protestant Churches. The questions, ancient and modern, that
have arisen round this sacrament are more or less touched upon—the 'un-
fermented wine' question, and also simultaneous communion, being referred
to. . . . . However the shaking theology of the present day may receive the
work, it is full of the 'old wine' of Scriptural and Puritan teaching, such as
would have delighted the communicants of other days, and will still be re-
lished by those who prefer the old to the new, for the old is better. . . . .
This volume is a compact treatise, elegantly got up and full of excellent
matter."—*Presbyterian Monthly.*
"The volume is the result of extensive reading and much thought. The
list of books upon the subjects which appear in the Appendix is taken from
all sections of the Church of Christ, and will give the reader some idea of
the literature of the question. . . . . The book will repay an attentive perusal, and is well fitted to impress on devout readers the spiritual advantages
to be derived from the frequent observance of the ordinance."—*Scottish Congregational Magazine.*
"Full of excellent matter."—*Presbyterian Monthly.*
"A most valuable treatise on the Lord's Supper."—IRISH BAPTIST MAGA-
ZINE.
"The result of extensive reading and much thought."—SCOTTISH CONGRE-
GATIONAL MAGAZINE.

The Dominion and Glory of the Redeemer,

The Support and Confidence of the Church, and the Joy
of the Saints.   By PROF. THOMAS HOUSTON, D.D., R.
P. Church of Ireland, *Knockbracken, Belfast.*   Crown
8vo, *cl.*, *with port.*, (480 pp.), *price* 5/.

"We have here twenty-three sermons selected by Dr. Houston from 'the
numerous manuscripts that have been accumulating during a lengthened
ministry of more than fifty-two years.' . . . . 'The chief aim in delivering
these discourses was to display the Saviour in the transcendent glory of His
Person, Character, and Work, ... while some of the subjects are more
directly connected with the subjective condition of believers—their labours,
trials, conflicts, and deliverances in life and death' . . . . The sermons are
Scriptural, sound, earnest, and mingle the doctrinal and practical elements
as these should ever be mingled in the preaching of the Word. There are no
modern vagaries or aberrations."—*Witness.*
"From the author's familiar acquaintance with the original languages, he
often . . . . throws what will be to the unlearned reader new or clearer
light on a word or phrase. . . . . None more suitable could be found for
family reading on the evening of the Sabbath."—*The Covenanter.*

The Scots Worthies.   By JOHN HOWIE, of

Lochgoin.   New edition, with Notes, 464 pp., 32mo, 6d,
or in *cloth* 1/.

Dissertations on the Philosophy of the Crea-

tion and the First Ten Chapters of Genesis allegorized in Mythology : containing Expositions of the Ancient Cosmogonies, the Invention of Hieroglyphics and of the Ancient Hebrew Language and Alphabet. By WILLIAM GALLOWAY, M.A., Ph.D., M.D., Licentiate of the Royal College of Physicians, *Edinburgh*, and of the Royal College of Surgeons, *Edinburgh*. Demy 8vo, (660 pp.,) *price* 14/

"The style is a pleasing one and free from obscurity, and the book through" out is a monument of careful thought and laborious research."—*Dundee Courier and Argus*.

"A monument of patient industry and devotion, ... a welcome introduction to lives of thought and research, ... will prove a useful repertory of out-of-the-way information."—*Aberdeen Journal*.

"Curious and interesting."—*Christian World Pulpit*.

"Immense labour has been evidently spent in preparing this work, which contains many curious facts."—*The Bookseller*.

"One of the ablest, noblest, and most instructive works which have in recent years been written on the scientific, and the Biblical aspects of the creation, ... a most brilliant contribution towards current controversies, and sure to take a first position. .... Ministers, divinity students, teachers, and thoughtful Christians generally ought to lose no time in securing this invaluable, charming, and stimulating work."—*Oldham Chronicle*.

"Crammed with learning."—*North British Mail*.

"This work is both learned and luminous. .... He is most familiar with the literature of his great theme, and hence his volume, which is well got up, is quite a storehouse of interesting and important fact and arguments, ... deserves a wide circulation."—*Sword and Trowel*.

The Future as Revealed in Divine Predic-

tion. By the Rev. JOHN STORIE, LATE MINISTER OF ST. ANDREW'S, HOBART ; AUTHOR OF "THE SACRAMENTS ;" "THE PAGANISM OF ROME ;" etc. Cr. 8vo, *cl., price* 5/

"Proceeds on strictly literal lines of interpretation, ... contains many valuable hints on passages taken from both the Old and New Testaments, ... the book will yield interest to students of prophecy ; bears the impress of earnest thought and honest purpose."—THE CHRISTIAN.

"I look upon your book as one of, if not, the very best books on the Revelation of our beloved Lord. .... I have read it with the intensest pleasure."—MAJOR-GEN. HOGGAN, C.B.

In the Press.

The Heroic Days of the Church : being

Sketches in the Struggle for Religious Liberty. By Rev. DAVID MERSON, M.A., B.D., Presbyterian Church of England, *Stamfordham*. Crown 8vo, *cl., price* 2/6.

In the Press.

South African Traits. By the Rev. JAMES

MACKINNON, *Edinburgh*. Cr. 8vo, *cl., price* 7/6.

U 3

The Pastor's Diary and Daily Record.

Non-Denominational.   Prepared by Rev. LEWIS H.
JORDAN, B.D., Erskine Church, Montreal.   Handsomely bound in flexible covers, of convenient size for
pocket.   Price 2/.

"Decidedly the most comprehensive and cheapest yet produced. Every
minister should get it."—PRESBYTERIAN CHURCHMAN.
"We have used the Diary, and have found it all that could be desired."—
CONGREGATIONAL MAGAZINE.

Biblical Geography in a Nutshell, contain-

ing many of the most recent Identifications.   With
Specially Prepared Map.   By M. SHEKLETON.   Cr. 8vo,
cloth, price 3/.

"The Book will be found of real service in the systematic study of the
Scriptures."—SCOTSMAN.
"The study is made not only instructive but delightful."—THE LEAGUE
JOURNAL.

Wilson's Tales of the Borders and of Scot-

land. Vols. sold separately, each vol. complete in itself.
Recently issued, in 8 vols., *new edition*, 2/ per vol.

"Mr James Gemmell adds to the literature of this time of year in a very
pleasant way. He produces a new edition of Wilson's Tales of the Borders.
It is not, as we understand it, to be a complete work, but is to contain a
selection of some of the best stories. . . . . If the first two volumes which
we have received are to be taken as specimens of what the others will be,
then a distinct good is to be done to the reading public by their issue."—*The
Scotsman.*
"One of the neatest and cheapest we have seen, each volume being of cr.
8vo size, handsomely bound, with gilt top, and published at two shillings,
certainly a very moderate price for a book of 224 pages. . . . . All who wish,
in the words of Sir Walter Scott, to read of—'Lovers' sleights, of ladies'
charms, of witches' spells, of warriors' arms,' cannot do better than procure
these volumes, which contain quite a storehouse of material bearing upon the
hills, glens, and folk-lore of Scotland."—*Liverpool Mercury.*
"It is a great boon to ordinary readers to have these admirable tales
placed so handsomely and so cheaply before them. The series of eight
volumes furnishes as delightful a collection as any one could desire."—*The
Presbyterian Churchman.*
"This is one of the best collections of stories ever published."—*Bookseller.*
"There are, we imagine, few Scotchmen and Scotchwomen who are un-
acquainted with these charming stories. But there are also few, we are sure,
who will not welcome such an opportunity as these volumes present of
renewing their acquaintance; and whoever sits down to read the stories
will soon be surprised into a feeling of regret that there are not so many,
but so few to read. Time flies quickly when one is listening to a Border
tale, even though it be to some extent familiar."—*Daily Review.*
"Seeing that on the average about a dozen complete stories appear in
each volume, nicely printed and neatly bound, for a florin, the opportunity
is afforded of adding a large amount of standard fiction to any library at a
moderate cost."—*Daily Chronicle.*

www.ingramcontent.com/pod-product-compliance
Lightning Source LLC
Chambersburg PA
CBHW020938030726
47496CB00005B/1250